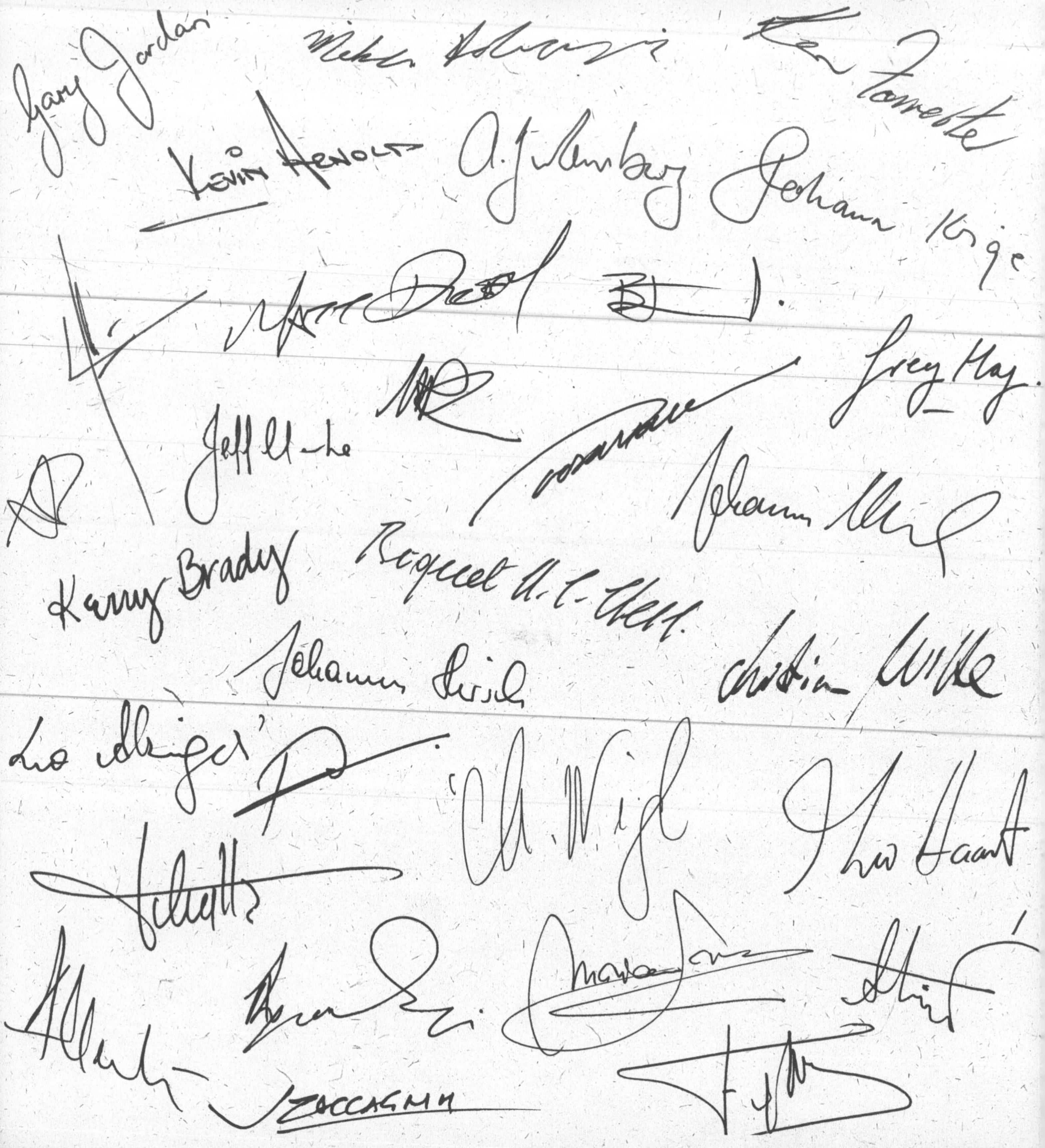
Gary Jordan
Kevin Arnold
Kerry Brady

WINDOWS ON THE WORLD
Complete Wine Course

Kevin Zraly

STERLING
New York / London
www.sterlingpublishing.com

PHOTO & ILLUSTRATION CREDITS

Vineyard near Beaune, Burgundy (pp. ii–iii)
© Charles O'Rear/Corbis

Insets p. ii: Wine tasting © Owen
Franken/Corbis; *Vineyard near Savigny-les-Beaune, Burgundy* © G. Bowater/Corbis;
Château Beycheville, Bordeaux © Adam
Woolfitt/Corbis

Grapes on the vine in Napa, California
(pp. xiv–1) © Morton Beebe/Corbis

Vineyards and fields in Chablis (pp. 20–21)
© Owen Franken/Corbis

Napa Valley vineyards (pp. 52–53)
© Charles O'Rear/Corbis

*Braune Kupp vineyard, Mosel-Saar-Ruwer,
Germany* (pp. 96–97) © Charles O'Rear/
Corbis

*Vineyard at Volnay, Côte de Beaune,
Burgundy* (pp. 120–121) © Charles O'Rear/
Corbis

Cellar at Château Mouton-Rothschild
(pp. 148–149) © Charles O'Rear/Corbis

Cabernet Sauvignon vineyard, Napa Valley
(pp. 172–173) © Jim Sugar/Corbis

Vineyards, Barolo, Piedmont (pp. 194–195)
© John Heseltine/Corbis

*Barrels of Port, Dow & Co. warehouse,
Oporto, Portugal* (pp. 224–225) © Charles
O'Rear/Corbis

Grapes, Avignonesi Winery, Tuscany
(p. 248–249) © Bob Krist/Corbis

Red wine and cheese at fireplace,
(pp. 286–287) © Ina Peters/istock

How Do We Smell? (p. 288), illustration
adapted by permission from Tim Jacob,
www.cf.ac.uk/biosi/staff/jacob

ACKNOWLEDGMENTS

This 2010 edition is dedicated to Robert Mondavi who not only led Napa Valley and California on the road to great wines but also had a tremendous influence on wine and winemaking throughout the world. Without his vision there probably would not have been a need for this kind of wine book. His energy, passion, commitment, and foresight, not only in winemaking but in combining wine with food, music, and art, paved the way for Americans to enjoy wine.

A special thanks to Robin Kelley O'Connor who traveled around the world with me in 2008 and 2009. His wine knowledge, tasting skills, and driving (car) stamina made this 25th anniversary book complete.

The signatures on the endpapers represent some of the owners of wineries, vineyardists, winemakers, and marketing and public relations professionals whose help was invaluable to me.

I welcome questions and comments. Please visit my Web site, www.kevinzraly.com, for updates and wine news.

LIBRARY OF CONGRESS CATALOGING-IN-PUBLICATION DATA AVAILABLE

10 9 8 7 6 5 4 3 2 1

Published by Sterling Publishing Co., Inc.
387 Park Avenue South, New York, NY 10016
© 2009 by Kevin Zraly
Distributed in Canada by Sterling Publishing
c/o Canadian Manda Group, 165 Dufferin Street
Toronto, Ontario, Canada M6K 3H6
Distributed in the United Kingdom by GMC Distribution Services
Castle Place, 166 High Street, Lewes, East Sussex, England BN7 1XU
Distributed in Australia by Capricorn Link (Australia) Pty. Ltd.
P.O. Box 704, Windsor, NSW 2756, Australia

Printed in China
All rights reserved

STERLING ISBN 978-1-4027-6767-8

For information about custom editions, special sales, premium and corporate purchases, please contact Sterling Special Sales Department at 800-805-5489 or specialsales@sterlingpublishing.com.

In 2010, I am celebrating my 34th anniversary teaching the Windows on the World Wine School. It all started in 1976 when Windows on the World, the restaurant on top of One World Trade Center, opened. We were a private lunch club, and I was asked to put together a six-week wine course as a club activity. We started off with only twenty people, and I taught the first class and the last class; the other four classes were taught by prominent wine writers. To this day, I have vivid memories of the great wines that we poured for that first class and the "happy" response of the students.

In fact, the club members were so happy with the wine school that they started asking if they could bring friends. By 1979 there were more friends than club members attending the class. The growing interest in wine was becoming obvious. In 1980 we opened our first classes for consumers. To date, more than nineteen thousand people have graduated from the Windows on the World Wine School. Many of my students have found their passion with wine—opening retail stores, restaurants, and wine bars. Some have started importing wine and a few have even started their own wineries.

Since my teenage years, wine has been my passion. In 1970, as a nineteen-year-old college student, I got a job as a waiter at a restaurant to pick up some "beer money." The restaurant received a four-star rating from *The New York Times* restaurant critic Craig Claiborne and the owner asked me to take over the bartending duties. (Luckily for me, back then the legal age to drink was eighteen in New York State.) I started studying about beer, distilled spirits, and wine, learning as much as I could. Within six months my interest in wine became an obsession. I quickly switched from Budweiser to Bordeaux. I read every book on wine I could find, and I visited all the wineries in New York. (I couldn't yet go to California—the drinking age there was twenty-one!)

A local college contacted the restaurant, suggesting a wine-and-cheese course for their adult-education program. So in 1971, at twenty years of age, I taught my first wine class. I continued to teach this class throughout college, and I was beginning to sense that wine appreciation was going to become a major area of interest in America.

I eventually graduated with an education degree and, combining that with my passion for wine, the Wine School for me has become the best of both worlds. After thirty-nine years of teaching about wine I am still fascinated by the subject, intrigued by its complexities, and "thirsty" to learn more with every new vintage. I would like to thank all of my graduates for supporting my passion.

This book is dedicated to everyone who has a passion for wine, from the grape growers to the winemakers, from the buyers and the sellers to, most important, the wine consumers.

May your glass always be more full than empty.

Contents

This picture was taken from the 107th floor of
One World Trade Center overlooking the East
River and the Brooklyn Bridge.

Introduction

THIS IS THE TWENTY-FIFTH anniversary of my book, and what a ride it has been! This book has been updated annually since its release in 1985 as I've strived to make this a "complete" wine course. I can honestly say, with this twenty-fifth edition, we have achieved just that. From the very beginning this book has been a work in progress and, just like a winery or a vineyard, every year I've introduced something new. This year I've added information on six new countries—Austria, Hungary, Canada, New Zealand, Greece, and South Africa—as well as updating all countries and elaborating on the material about Spain, Italy, Argentina, Chile, and American wine regions.

Even though the current book is much larger than the original edition, the core of the Windows on the Wine School, the eight main classes, have remained consistent in their simplicity. There is always a tendency to add more when writing a book, especially for it to be "complete." My friend Peter Sichel, himself a wine author, said it in the original foreword perfectly, "If I had more time I would have written a shorter book."

The origin of this book goes back to 1976, when the Windows on the World Restaurant opened on the 107th floor of One World Trade Center. I had just turned twenty-five and had accepted the position of cellar master, which meant that I was in charge of selecting, ordering, and selling all of the restaurant's wine. There I was, a kid in a candy store with carte blanche open-to-buy and only one mandate: Create the biggest and best wine list New York had ever seen. And so I did. Within five years of its opening, Windows on the World became the number one dollar-volume restaurant with the highest dollar wine sales of any restaurant in the world.

Windows on the World also hosted a private lunch club, and I was asked to put together a six-week wine course for members. I searched everywhere for a simple and straightforward wine guide to use as a textbook, but nothing I found was quite right. Every book I looked at was either too encyclopedic or too scientific.

That's why I began developing my own course material, which I kept simple, trying to give my students only the basic information they would need to understand and enjoy wine. I gave students photocopied labels, lists, and other information that could be used for home study and future reference. This proved so popular that, in 1981, five years after I had begun working at Windows on the World, I sat down to write this book. A lot of my teaching involved answering questions from the students in my classes, so the book quite naturally evolved with a question-and-answer format.

That format continues to work well for my students and readers. The layout of the book has also more or less stayed the same for twenty-five years. I have always loved memorizing statistics, so I added sidebars with anecdotes, facts and figures, personal commentary, and quotes to reinforce the text. To emphasize a specific point, I would add a boxed block of text to supplement the information in the chapter. I tried everything I could think of to make learning about and enjoying wine easier and more fun.

Full of naive enthusiasm, I researched publishers, looking for the best and the ones most likely to snap up the rights to my book. I quickly discovered that although I thought my idea for an easy-to-understand wine book was brilliant, finding a publisher who agreed with me was an entirely different matter. At least five of the largest publishers in the business turned down my book, telling me that a simple guide to wine would never sell. Rejection became all too familiar.

Eventually I was introduced to Sterling Publishing, a company I like to call the "little engine that could." Back then Sterling was a small, family-owned, "niche marketing" publisher known for its beautiful craft books. (Or, more accurately, unknown: Sterling was probably the most successful small publisher you'd never hear of!) About eight years ago, the "little" company was purchased by Barnes & Noble, and I am proud to say that today *Windows on the World Complete Wine Course,* with more than three million copies sold, is the best-selling wine book in the United States.

Annual supplements have really been what has kept this book new and fresh for me. Wine-Buying Strategies is a great section that I enjoy updating because I'm always trying to find a twenty-dollar bottle of wine that tastes like a fifty-dollar bottle. The Physiology of Tasting Wine was one of the most fascinating supplements to write. For the 2008 edition, we added the tasting notes for each class, which has added to the "course." To help you assess your own wine knowledge, tests were placed at the end of each chapter in 2009.

I've spent the last two years working on this twenty-fifth anniversary edition. In 2008 and 2009, I toured over eighty wine regions throughout the world in order to add new regions, as well as update all of the original wine regions covered in this book.

Over these last two year, traveling around the world tasting over 5,000 wines, I've realized that we truly are living in the golden age of winemaking. The quality and diversity of wine produced in the countries and regions I've updated has exploded over the last twenty-five years. Great wines are being made in every country featured in this book, and even their ordinary wines taste better than ever before. I study wine full-time and I can barely keep up with all of the new regions, wines, vintages, and mergers and acquisitions; it must be overwhelming for new students of wine. In keeping with my original philosophy, I've tried to make learning about this great world of wine as fun and as simple as possible.

Finally, I have come to the conclusion that with this new edition I can honestly say that *Windows on the World Complete Wine Course* is just that: complete. And the best work I have ever done. I hope you agree.

25 YEARS OF WINE CHANGES (1985–2010)

So much has changed since this book was first published; where to begin? But I'll try to give you the highlights of twenty-five years of astonishing and spectacular growth.

Wine is now grown, traded, and consumed in increasingly large quantities worldwide. Twenty-five years ago, I didn't include countries such as New Zealand and South Africa because their wines were not particularly remarkable and weren't widely available. Today, both countries produce delicious wines that can be purchased at many well-stocked stores throughout the world. In this edition I've included countries that I have never before written about, and I've expanded the information on many other countries and regions to keep up with the huge growth in quality and availability. Wine has become a truly global commodity.

Other significant wine industry developments are the growing and making of wine, the business of wine, and wine consumption.

Winemaking and Viticulture

Overall wine quality has improved significantly over the last two and a half decades. Vast strides have been made in the science and technology of winemaking, growers have readapted back-to-the-earth farming techniques, and there has been widespread planting of international grapes. These three reasons alone are responsible for much of the improvement in quality, which has led to its rise in popularity.

Here are some of the specific changes in winemaking and viticulture over the last twenty-five years:

- More attention is paid to the individual vineyards, clonal selection, and trellis systems

- More care is taken to match grape varieties with specific sites

- There is far less filtering of wine, leading to a fuller, more complex, and natural taste

- Oak is used far more judiciously

- Wine alcohol levels have reached historic highs

- Sustainability has become the international buzz word in viticulture: Wine growers are becoming more organic and are using fewer herbicides and pesticides. While there are still very few producers of biodynamic wines, elite wineries such as Benziger, Chapoutier, Domaine Leflaive, Zind Humbrecht, Domaine Leroy, and Araujo are practicing biodynamic techniques.

- The number of vines planted per acre (vine density) has increased dramatically. This has allowed the viticulturalist more freedom to produce better grapes.

- Screw-caps are gradually replacing corks on more than just inexpensive wines: screw-caps seal 75 percent of Australian and 93 percent of New Zealand wines

- Global warming may be real: Between 1960 and 1969, grape harvesting in Burgundy, France, on average began September 27. From 2000 to 2004, grape harvesting began closer to the first week of September. To help offset the effects of a shorter growing season, some viticulturists have begun planting grapes vertically rather than horizontally to avoid excess sun.

- Chaptalization is now rarely used

- Winemakers increasingly are using natural rather than laboratory yeasts

- The European Union has standardized basic wine labeling rules for member nations, and countries exporting to the EU (and worldwide) are following their regulations. For example, one new law states that if a grape is on the label, the wine must contain a minimum of 85% of that grape.

The Business of Wine

Besides the tremendous growth in wine quality, the business of wine has also benefited greatly from the global planting of *Vitis vinifera* grapes. Cabernet Sauvignon, Merlot, Pinot Noir, Chardonnay, Riesling, Sauvignon Blanc, and other familiar grapes are now grown throughout the world, making it easier for consumers to buy unfamiliar wines with the expectation that they will be getting a wine that is familiar in style and of a fairly consistent quality.

Here are a few of the most significant advancements in the business of wine:

- In the year I first wrote this book (1985), Europe was by far the number one producer of wine in the world, with 78 percent of the total. In 2009, Europe has dropped to 68 percent and the United States has increased from 16 percent to 18.5 percent of worldwide wine production.

- Wine has enjoyed the largest growth rate of all alcoholic beverages since 2001

- The United States has become the largest wine market in the world, with retail sales in excess of $30 billion

- American wine names are becoming more creative, for example: Red Truck, Pinot Evil, Killer Juice, Dog Juice, Fat Bastard, Marilyn Merlot, Kick Ass Red, and Mad Housewife

- In 2005, the U.S. Supreme Court approved the interstate shipping of wine directly to consumers, causing most states to rewrite their wine laws

- The quality of American wine lists has never been better, with some restaurants creating "monster" lists for promotional purposes (and intimidating "new" wine drinkers), while others list only the best wines in each category. You can now find wine lists in diners all across America!

- Costco sells annually over $750 million in wine, making it the largest retailer of wine in the United States

- Consolidation has reduced the number of U.S. wine wholesalers by 50 percent: two companies, Southern Wine & Spirits and the Charmer Sunbelt Group, control 38 percent of U.S. liquor and wine distribution

- Celebrity branding is big, from baseball stars (Tom Seaver) to racecar drivers (Jeff Gordon) to musicians (Bob Dylan). Celebrity wine sales exceeded $50 million in 2009.

- Thanks to Wine 2.0—wine blogs—now everyone can become a wine critic or ask the critics questions on eRobertParker.com, *Wine Spectator*'s Blog Index, winelibrary.com, or *Wine Enthusiast*'s unreserved, to name just a few

- Wine in a box is becoming more popular, especially among California jug wine producers, to reduce greenhouse emissions and lower carbon footprints

- Exports of American wine have gone from $27.6 million in 1985 to over $1 billion in 2009!

- 2008 marked the 75th anniversary of the end of prohibition and the year Gallo started making their wine

- Imported-wine statistics have not changed much: in 1985, 29 percent of wines consumed in the United States were imported; in 2008, it was 28 percent

Wine Consumers

Combining better quality, familiar varietals, and expert marketing has given consumers worldwide some of the best wines ever produced at some of the most reasonable prices. Consumers today have a better selection of wine at all price points than ever before. And it promises to get even better in the future!

Here are my picks for the wine consumer highlights of the last twenty-five years:

- Consumers are reaching for reds more often than whites

- Americans are drinking more and better wine than ever before. Wine consumption in the United States reached a record 745 million gallons—an increase of over 165 million gallons since 1985. In 2007, the United States overtook Italy to become the number two consumer of wine. Next stop, France! Within the next five years, the United States will be the world's biggest wine consumer.

- 2008 was the sixteenth consecutive year of growth in U.S. wine consumption, with total wine sales reaching over 300 million cases

- The millennial generation (ages 21–30) has shown the largest percentage increase in wine consumption over generation X (ages 31–42) and the baby boomers (ages 43–61)

- U.S. wine events proliferate, and almost all donate some proceeds to charity. In 2008, Auction Napa Valley raised $10.35 million, and in 2008, the Naples, Florida, wine festival raised $14 million.

- Wine lovers turn increasingly to auctions: worldwide auction sales totaled $276 million in 2008, compared to $33 million in 1994. 2008 U.S. auction sales were over $164 million, and Internet auction sales exceeded $32 million.

- Fraudulent wines have become more prevalent

- The best chateaux of Bordeaux have been priced out of reach for the average consumer. Some 2005 Bordeaux sell at over $5,000 a bottle!

- French wine consumption has dropped more than 50 percent since 1985

- Rose wines are back in fashion

- American wine critic Robert Parker has become an international icon with his 100-point scoring method

- ***Super Wines***
  - California superpremium wines, such as Opus One and Harlan Estate, are born

  - "Super Tuscans," such as Sassicaia and Ornellaia, have become collector's items

  - "Super Everywhere" wines priced over $100 are now available from Australia, Chile, Argentina, and South Africa

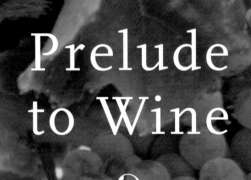

Prelude
to Wine

THE BASICS • ON TASTING WINE • THE 60-SECOND WINE EXPERT •

WHITE GRAPES OF THE WORLD • RED GRAPES OF THE WORLD

The Basics

Y OU'RE IN A WINE SHOP looking for that "special" wine to serve at a dinner party. Before you walked in, you had at least an idea of what you wanted, but now, as you scan the shelves, you're overwhelmed. "There are so many wines," you think, "and so many prices." You take a deep breath, boldly pick up a bottle that looks impressive, and buy it. Then you hope your guests will like your selection.

Does this sound a little farfetched? For some of you, yes. Yet the truth is, this is a very common occurrence for the wine beginner, and even someone with intermediate wine knowledge, but it doesn't have to be that way. Wine should be an enjoyable experience. By the time you finish this book, you'll be able to buy with confidence from a retailer or even look in the eyes of a wine steward and ask with no hesitation for the selection of your choice. But first let's start with the basics—the foundation of your wine knowledge. Read carefully, because you'll find this section invaluable as you relate it to the chapters that follow. You may even want to refer back to it occasionally to reinforce what you learn.

For the purpose of this book, wine is the fermented juice of grapes.

What's fermentation?

Fermentation is the process by which the grape juice turns into wine. The simple formula for fermentation is:

$$\text{Sugar} + \text{Yeast} = \text{Alcohol} + \text{Carbon Dioxide (CO}_2\text{)}$$

The fermentation process begins when the grapes are crushed and ends when all of the sugar has been converted to alcohol or the alcohol level has reached around 15 percent, the point at which the alcohol kills off the yeast. Sugar is naturally present in the ripe grape through photosynthesis. Yeast also occurs naturally as the white bloom on the grape skin. However, this natural yeast is not always used in today's winemaking. Laboratory strains of pure yeast have been isolated and may be used in many situations, each strain contributing something unique to the style of the wine. The carbon dioxide dissipates into the air, except in Champagne and other sparkling wines, in which this gas is retained through a special process which we will discuss in Class Eight.

What are the three major types of wine?

Table wine: approximately 8 to 15 percent alcohol

Sparkling wine: approximately 8 to 12 percent alcohol + CO_2

Fortified wine: 17 to 22 percent alcohol

All wine fits into at least one of these categories.

Why do the world's fine wines come only from certain areas?

A combination of factors is at work. The areas with a reputation for fine wines have the right soil and favorable weather conditions, of course. In addition, these areas look at winemaking as an important part of their history and culture.

Is all wine made from the same kind of grape?

No. The major wine grapes come from the species *Vitis vinifera*. In fact, European, North American, Australian, and South American winemakers use the *Vitis vinifera*, which includes many different varieties of grapes—both red and white. However, there are other grapes used for winemaking. The most important native grape species in America is *Vitis labrusca*, which is grown widely in New York State as well as other East Coast and Midwest states. Hybrids, which are also used in modern winemaking, are a cross between *Vitis vinifera* and native American grape species, such as *Vitis labrusca*.

Does it matter where grapes are planted?

Yes, it does. Grapes are agricultural products that require specific growing conditions. Just as you wouldn't try to grow oranges in Maine, you wouldn't try to grow grapes at the North Pole. There are limitations on where vines can be grown. Some of these limitations are: the growing season, the number of days of sunlight, angle of the sun, average temperature, and rainfall. Soil is of primary concern, and adequate drainage is a requisite. The right amount of sun ripens the grapes properly to give them the sugar/acid balance that makes the difference between fair, good, and great wine.

KEVIN ZRALY'S FAVORITE WINE REGIONS

Napa
Sonoma
Bordeaux
Burgundy
Champagne
Rhône Valley
Tuscany
Piedmont
Mosel
Rhine
Rioja
Douro (Port)
Mendoza
Maipo Valley
South Australia
Stellenbosch

PLANTING OF vineyards for winemaking began more than 8,000 years ago.

A SAMPLING OF THE MAJOR GRAPES

Vitis vinifera
Chardonnay
Cabernet Sauvignon

Vitis labrusca
Concord
Catawba

Hybrids
Seyval Blanc
Baco Noir

VITIS is Latin for vine.
VINUM is Latin for wine.

THE TOP five countries in wine grape acreage worldwide:
1. Spain
2. France
3. Italy
4. Turkey
5. United States

WINEMAKERS SAY that winemaking begins in the vineyard with the growing of the grapes.

THE MOST important factors in winemaking:
Geographic location
Soil
Weather
Grapes
Vinification (the actual winemaking process)

VINES ARE planted during their dormant periods, usually in the months of April or May. Most vines will continue to produce good-quality grapes for forty years or more.

DON'T FORGET that the seasons in the Southern Hemisphere—which includes Australia, New Zealand, Chile, Argentina, and South Africa—are reversed.

A VINE doesn't usually produce grapes suitable for winemaking until the third year.

"BRIX" IS the winemaker's measure of sugar in grapes.

AS SUGAR levels increase, acidity decreases.

IT TAKES an average of 100 days between a vine's flowering and the harvest.

Where are the best locations to plant grapes?

Traditionally, many grape varieties produce better wines when planted in certain locations. For example, most red grapes need a longer growing season than do white grapes, so red grapes are usually planted in warmer locations. In colder northern regions—in Germany and northern France, for instance—most vineyards are planted with white grapes. In the warmer regions of Italy, Spain, and Portugal, and in California's Napa Valley, the red grape thrives.

When is the harvest?

Grapes are picked when they reach the proper sugar/acid ratio for the style of wine the vintner wants to produce. Go to a vineyard in June and taste one of the small green grapes. Your mouth will pucker because the grape is so tart and acidic. Return to the same vineyard—even to that same vine—in September or October, and the grapes will taste sweet. All those months of sun have given sugar to the grape as a result of photosynthesis.

June
3% acid
0 Brix

July
2.3% acid
10 Brix

August
1.7% acid
15 Brix

Harvest
September
0.9% acid
22 Brix

What effect does weather have on the grapes?

Weather can interfere with the quality of the harvest, as well as its quantity. In the spring, as vines emerge from dormancy, a sudden frost may stop the flowering, thereby reducing the yields. Even a strong windstorm can affect the grapes adversely at this crucial time. Not enough rain, too much rain, or rain at the wrong time can also wreak havoc.

Rain just before the harvest will swell the grapes with water, diluting the juice and making thin, watery wines. Lack of rain will affect the wines' balance by creating a more powerful and concentrated wine, but will result in a smaller crop. A severe drop in temperature may affect the vines even outside the growing season. Case in point: In New York State the winter of 2003–04 was one of the coldest in fifty years. The result was a major decrease in wine production, with some vineyards losing more than 50 percent of their crop for the 2004 vintage.

What can the vineyard owner do in the case of adverse weather?

A number of countermeasures are available to the grower. Some of these measures are used while the grapes are on the vine; others are part of the winemaking process.

PROBLEM	RESULTS IN	SOME SOLUTIONS
Frost	Reduced yield	Various frost protection methods: wind machines, sprinkler systems, and flaming heaters
Not enough sun	Underripe, green herbal, vegetal character, high acid, low sugar	Chaptalization (the addition of sugar to the must—fresh grape juice—during fermentation)
Too much sun	Overripe, high-alcohol, prune character	Amelioration (addition of water)
Too much rain	Thin, watery wines	Move vineyard to a drier climate
Mildew	Rot	Spray with copper sulfate
Drought	Scorched grapes	Irrigate or pray for rain
High alcohol	Change in the balance of the components	De-alcoholize
High acidity	Sour, tart wine	De-acidify
Phylloxera	Dead vines	Graft vines onto resistant rootstock

STORM STORIES

- In 2009, major fires hit the Yarra Valley in Australia during the start of the harvest.
- In 2008, a spring frost affected the vineyards all over the state of California. It was the worst frost since the early seventies.
- In 2008, Australia got hit with everything—the worst drought ever and scorching heat in South Australia and record-breaking rain and major flooding in the Hunter Valley.
- In Alsace, France, a hailstorm in June 2007 destroyed entire vineyards.
- In 2007, hailstorms in Mendoza, Argentina, from December to February dramatically reduced yields.
- In 2004, Burgundy suffered major hailstorms in July and August that damaged or destroyed at least 40% of the grapes.
- The historic 2003 heat wave in Europe changed the balance of the traditional style of wines produced in most regions.
- A spring frost damaged 80% of the 2002 vintage Champagne grapes.
- Poor weather conditions for the 2002 vintage in Tuscany resulted in no production of Chianti Classico Reserva.
- In 2002, the Piedmont region of Italy (Barolo, Barbaresco) was hit with a September hailstorm that destroyed some of the best vineyards in the region.
- A rainy September made the 2001 Champagne harvest the wettest since 1873.
- From 1989 to 1999 in Bordeaux, France, it rained during the harvest of eight out of ten vintages, which affected picking dates, yields, and the quality of the wine.
- An April frost in Bordeaux destroyed more than 50% of 1991's grape harvest.

What is phylloxera?

Phylloxera, a grape louse, is one of the grapevine's worst enemies, because it eventually kills the entire plant. An epidemic infestation in the 1870s came close to destroying all the vineyards of Europe. Luckily, the roots of native American vines are immune to this louse. After this was discovered, all the European vines were pulled up and grafted onto phylloxera-resistant American rootstocks.

Can white wine be made from red grapes?

Yes. The color of wine comes entirely from the grape skins. By removing the skins immediately after picking, no color is imparted to the wine, and it will be white. In the Champagne region of France, a large percentage of the grapes grown are red, yet most of the resulting wine is white. California's White Zinfandel is made from red Zinfandel grapes.

What is tannin, and is it desirable in wine?

Tannin is a natural preservative and is one of the many components that give wine its longevity. It comes from skins, pits, and stems of the grapes. Another source of tannin is wood, such as the French oak barrels in which some wines are aged or fermented. Generally, red wines have a higher level of tannin than whites because red grapes are usually left to ferment with their skins.

A word used to describe the sensation of tannins is "astringent." Especially in young wines, tannin can be very astringent and make the wine taste bitter. Tannin is not a taste, however—it's a tactile sensation.

Tannin is also found in strong tea. And what can you add to tea to make is less astringent? Milk—the fat and the proteins in milk soften the tannin. And so it is with a highly tannic wine. If you take another milk by-product, such as cheese, and have it with wine, it softens the tannin and makes the wine more appealing. Enjoy a beef entrée or one served with a cream sauce and a good bottle of red wine to experience it for yourself.

Is acidity desirable in wine?

All wine will have a certain amount of acidity. Generally, white wines have more perceived acidity than reds, though winemakers try to have a balance of fruit and acid. An overly acidic wine is also described as tart or sour. Acidity is a very important component in the aging of wines.

What is meant by "vintage"? Why is one year considered better than another?

A vintage indicates the year the grapes were harvested, so every year is a vintage year. A vintage chart reflects the weather conditions for various years. Better weather usually results in a better rating for the vintage, and therefore a higher likelihood that the wine will age well.

Are all wines meant to be aged?

No. It's a common misconception that all wines improve with age. In fact, more than 90 percent of all the wines made in the world should be consumed within one year, and less than 1 percent of the world's wines should be aged for more than five years. Wines change with age. Some get better, but most do not. The good news is that the 1 percent represents more than 350 million bottles of wine every vintage.

What makes a wine last more than five years?

The color and the grape: Red wines, because of their tannin content, will generally age longer than whites. And certain red grapes, such as Cabernet Sauvignon, tend to have more tannin than, say, Pinot Noir.

The vintage: The better the weather conditions in one year, the more likely the wines from that vintage will have a better balance of fruits, acids, and tannins, and therefore have the potential to age longer.

Where the wine comes from: Certain vineyards have optimum conditions for growing grapes, including such factors as soil, weather, drainage, and slope of the land. All of this contributes to producing a great wine that will need time to age.

THE FIRST known reference to a specific vintage was made by Roman scientist Pliny the Elder, who rated the wines of 121 B.C. "of the highest excellence."

2005 WAS a great vintage year in every major wine region on earth!

THREE MAJOR wine collectibles that will age more than ten years:
1. Great châteaux of Bordeaux
2. Best producers of California Cabernet Sauvignon
3. Finest producers of vintage Port

"*The truth of wine aging is that it is unknown, unstudied, poorly understood, and poorly predicted!*"
    —ZELMA LONG, *California winemaker*

A BOTTLE of wine contains 600–800 grapes (2.4 lbs.).

5 bottles of wine produced annually from one grapevine
240 bottles of wine in a barrel
720 bottles of wine from a ton of grapes
5,500 bottles of wine produced annually from an acre of grapevines

Source: Napa Valley Vintners

THERE ARE more than seventy wine-producing countries in the world.

ACCORDING TO *Wines & Vines*, the value of wine sold worldwide is now more than $100 billion.

"There are no standards of taste in wine, cigars, poetry, prose, etc. Each man's own taste is the standard, and a majority vote cannot decide for him or in any slightest degree affect the supremacy of his own standard."

—MARK TWAIN, 1895

How the wine was made (vinification): The longer the wine remains in contact with its skins during fermentation (maceration), and if it is fermented and/or aged in oak, the more of the natural preservative tannin it will have, which can help it age longer. These are just two examples of how winemaking can affect the aging of wine.

Wine storage conditions: Even the best-made wines in the world will not age well if they are improperly stored.

How is wine production regulated worldwide?

Each major wine-producing country has government-sponsored control agencies and laws that regulate all aspects of wine production and set certain minimum standards that must be observed. Here are some examples:

France: Appellation d'Origine Contrôlée (AOC)

Italy: Denominazione di Origine Controllata (DOC)

United States: Alcohol and Tobacco Tax and Trade Bureau

Germany: Ministry of Agriculture

Spain: Denominación de Origen (DO)

ON TASTING WINE

You can read all the books (and there are plenty) written on wine to become more knowledgeable on the subject, but the best way to truly enhance your understanding of wine is to taste as many wines as possible. Reading covers the more academic side of wine, while tasting is more enjoyable and practical. A little of each will do you the most good.

The following are the necessary steps for tasting wine. You may wish to follow them with a glass of wine in hand.

Wine tasting can be broken down into five basic steps: Color, Swirl, Smell, Taste, and Savor.

Color

The best way to get an idea of a wine's color is to get a white background—a napkin or tablecloth—and hold the glass of wine on an angle in front of it. The range of colors that you may see depends, of course, on whether you're tasting a white or red wine. Here are the colors for both, beginning with the youngest wine and moving to an older wine:

IF YOU can see through a red wine, it's generally ready to drink!

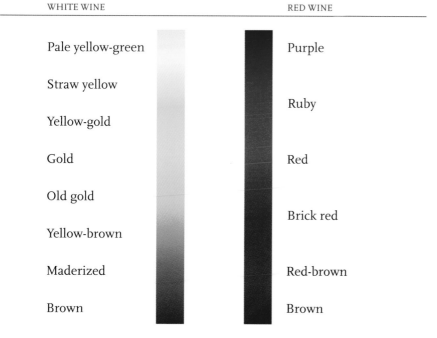

WHITE WINE	RED WINE
Pale yellow-green	Purple
Straw yellow	
Yellow-gold	Ruby
Gold	Red
Old gold	
Yellow-brown	Brick red
Maderized	Red-brown
Brown	Brown

AS WHITE wines age, they gain color. Red wines, on the other hand, lose color as they age.

Color tells you a lot about the wine. Since we start with the white wines, let's consider three reasons why a white wine may have more color:

1. It's older.
2. Different grape varieties give different color. (For example, Chardonnay usually gives off a deeper color than does Sauvignon Blanc.)
3. The wine was aged in wood.

In class, I always begin by asking my students what color the wine is. It's not unusual to hear that some believe that the wine is pale yellow-green, while others say it's gold. Everyone begins with the same wine, but color perceptions vary. There are no right or wrong answers, because perception is subjective. So you can imagine what happens when we actually taste the wine!

TYPES OF TASTINGS

HORIZONTAL	Tasting wines from the same vintage
VERTICAL	Comparing wines from different vintages
BLIND	The taster does not have any information about the wines
SEMI-BLIND	The taster knows only the style of wine (grape) or where it comes from

I LIKE TO have my students put their hands over the glass of wine when they swirl to create a more powerful bouquet and aroma.

BOUQUET IS the total smell of the wine. Aroma is the smell of the grapes. "Nose" is a word that wine tasters use to describe the bouquet and aroma of the wine.

THIS JUST IN: It is now known that each nostril can detect different smells.

THE OLDEST part of the human brain is the olfactory region.

THE 2004 Nobel prize for medicine was awarded to two scientists for their research on the olfactory system and the discovery that there are more than 10,000 different smells!

ONE OF THE most difficult challenges in life is to match a smell or a taste with a word that describes it.

SOME CLASSIC DESCRIPTORS

Zinfandel	spiciness, blackberry
Cabernet Sauvignon	chocolate, cassis
Old Bordeaux	wet fallen leaves
Old Burgundy	gamey, mushrooms
Rhône	black pepper
Pouilly-Fumé or Sancerre	gunflint
Chablis	mineral
White Burgundy	chalky
Chardonnay	buttery, apple
Sauvignon Blanc	grapefruit
Riesling	green apple
Pinot Noir	red cherry
Gewürztraminer	lychee

Swirl

Why do we swirl wine? To allow oxygen to get into the wine. Swirling releases the esters, ethers, and aldehydes that combine with oxygen to yield a wine's bouquet. In other words, swirling aerates the wine and releases more of the bouquet and aroma.

Smell

This is the most important part of wine tasting. You can perceive just four tastes—sweet, sour, bitter, and salty—but the average person can identify more than two thousand different scents, and wine has more than two hundred of its own. Now that you've swirled the wine and released the bouquet, I want you to smell the wine at least three times. You may find that the third smell will give you more information than the first smell did. What does the wine smell like? What type of nose does it have? Smell is the most important step in the tasting process and most people simply don't spend enough time on it.

Pinpointing the nose of the wine helps you to identify certain characteristics. The problem here is that many people in class want me to tell them what the wine smells like. Since I prefer not to use subjective words, I may say that the wine smells like a French white Burgundy. Still, I find that this doesn't satisfy the majority of the class. They want to know more. I ask these people to describe what steak and onions smell like. They answer, "Like steak and onions." See what I mean?

The best way to learn what your own preferences are for styles of wine is to "memorize" the smell of the individual grape varieties. For white, just try to memorize the three major grape varieties: Chardonnay, Sauvignon Blanc, and Riesling. Keep smelling them, and smelling them, and smelling them until you can identify the differences, one from the other. For the reds it's a little more difficult, but you still can take three major grape varieties: Pinot Noir, Merlot, and Cabernet Sauvignon. Try to memorize those smells without using flowery words, and you'll understand what I'm talking about.

For those in the Wine School who remain unconvinced, I hand out a list of five hundred different words commonly used to describe wine. Here is a small excerpt:

acetic	character	legs	seductive
aftertaste	corky	light	short
aroma	delicate	maderized	soft
astringent	developed	mature	stalky
austere	earthy	metallic	sulfury
baked-burnt	finish	moldy	tart
balanced	flat	nose	thin
big-full-heavy	fresh	nutty	tired
bitter	grapey	off	vanilla
body	green	oxidized	woody
bouquet	hard	pétillant	yeasty
bright	hot	rich	young

You're also more likely to recognize some of the defects of a wine through your sense of smell.

Following is a list of some of the negative smells in wine:

SMELL	WHY
Vinegar	Too much acetic acid in wine
Sherry*	Oxidation
Dank, wet, moldy, cellar smell	Wine absorbs the taste of a defective cork (referred to as "corked wine")
Sulfur (burnt matches)	Too much sulfur dioxide

* Authentic Sherry, from Spain, is intentionally made through controlled oxidation.

All wines contain some sulfur dioxide since it is a by-product of fermentation. Sulfur dioxide is also used in many ways in winemaking. It kills bacteria in wine, prevents unwanted fermentation, and acts as a preservative. It sometimes causes a burning and itching sensation in your nose.

Taste

To many people, tasting wine means taking a sip and swallowing immediately. To me, this isn't tasting. Tasting is something you do with your taste buds. You have taste buds all over your mouth—on both sides of the tongue, underneath, on the tip, and extending to the back of your throat. If you do what

WHAT KIND of wine do I like? I like my wine bright, rich, mature, developed, seductive, and with nice legs!

NEED MORE WORDS?

A new book, *WineSpeak*, by Bernard Klem, includes 36,975 wine-tasting descriptions. Who knew?

OXYGEN CAN be the best friend of a wine, but it can also be its worst enemy. A little oxygen helps release the smell of the wine (as with swirling), but prolonged exposure can be harmful, especially to older wines.

EVERY WINE contains a certain amount of sulfites. They are a natural by-product of fermentation.

EACH PERSON has a different threshold for sulfur dioxide, and although most people do not have an adverse reaction, it can be a problem for individuals with asthma. To protect those who are prone to bad reactions to sulfites, federal law requires winemakers to label their wines with the warning that the wine contains sulfites.

THE AVERAGE person has 5,000 taste buds. (That means that some of you have 10,000 and some of you have none!!)

TASTING WINE is confirming what the color and smell are telling you.

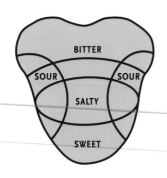

THERE IS now evidence that people may perceive five tastes: sweet, sour, bitter, salty, and possibly umami.

OTHER SENSATIONS associated with wine include numbing, tingling, drying, cooling, warming, and coating.

BITTER: Think endive or arugula.
TANNIN: Think gritty.

"One not only drinks wine, one smells it, observes it, tastes it, sips it, and—one talks about it."

—KING EDWARD VII OF ENGLAND

many people do, you take a gulp of wine and bypass all of those important taste buds. When I taste wine I leave it in my mouth for three to five seconds before swallowing. The wine warms up, sending signals about the bouquet and aroma up through the nasal passage then on to the olfactory bulb, and then to the limbic system of the brain. Remember, 90 percent of taste is smell.

What should you think about when tasting wine?

Be aware of the most important sensations of taste and your own personal thresholds of those tastes. Also, pay attention to where they occur on your tongue and in your mouth. As I mentioned earlier, you can perceive just four tastes: sweet, sour, bitter, and salty (but there's no salt in wine, so we're down to three). Bitterness in wine is usually created by high alcohol and high tannin. Sweetness occurs only in wines that have some residual sugar left over after fermentation. Sour (sometimes called "tart") indicates the acidity in wine.

Sweetness: The highest threshold is on the tip of the tongue. If there's any sweetness in a wine whatsoever, you'll get it right away.

Acidity: Found at the sides of the tongue, the cheek area, and the back of the throat. White wines and some lighter-style red wines usually contain a higher degree of acidity.

Bitterness: Tasted on the back of the tongue.

Tannin: The sensation of tannin begins in the middle of the tongue. Tannin frequently exists in red wines or white wines aged in wood. When the wines are too young, tannin dries the palate to excess. If there's a lot of tannin in the wine, it can actually coat your whole mouth, blocking the fruit. Remember, tannin is not a taste: It is a tactile sensation.

Fruit and varietal characteristics: These are not tastes, but smells. The weight of the fruit (the "body") will be felt in the middle of the tongue.

Aftertaste: The overall taste and balance of the components of the wine that lingers in your mouth. How long does the balance last? Usually a sign of a high-quality wine is a long, pleasing aftertaste. The taste of many of the great wines lasts anywhere from one to three minutes, with all their components in harmony.

Savor

After you've had a chance to taste the wine, sit back for a few moments and savor it. Think about what you just experienced, and ask yourself the following questions to help focus your impressions.

- Was the wine light, medium, or full-bodied?

- For a white wine: How was the acidity? Very little, just right, or too much?

- For a red wine: Is the tannin in the wine too strong or astringent? Does it blend with the fruit or overpower it?

- What is the strongest component (residual sugar, fruit, acid, tannin)?

- How long did the balance of the components last (ten seconds, sixty seconds, etc.)?

- Is the wine ready to drink? Or does it need more time to age? Or is it past its prime?

- What kind of food would you enjoy with the wine?

- To your taste, is the wine worth the price?

- This brings us to the most important point. The first thing you should consider after you've tasted a wine is whether or not you like it. Is it your style?

You can compare tasting wine to browsing in an art gallery. You wander from room to room looking at the paintings. Your first impression tells whether or not you like something. Once you decide you like a piece of art, you want to know more: Who was the artist? What is the history behind the work? How was it done? And so it is with wine. Usually, once oenophiles (wine aficionados) discover a wine that they like, they want to learn everything about it: the winemaker; the grapes; exactly where the vines were planted; the blend, if any; and the history behind the wine.

How do you know if a wine is good or not?

The definition of a good wine is one that you enjoy. I cannot emphasize this enough. Trust your own palate and do not let others dictate taste to you!

When is a wine ready to drink?

This is one of the most frequently asked questions in my Wine School. The answer is very simple: when all components of the wine are in balance to your particular taste.

WINE TEXTURES:
Light: skim milk
Medium: whole milk
Full: heavy cream

"The key to great wine is balance, and it is the sum of the different parts that make a wine not only delicious but complete and fascinating as well as worthy of aging."
—FIONA MORRISON, M.W.

"A wine goes in my mouth, and I just see it. I see it in three dimensions. The textures. The flavors. The smells. They just jump out at me. I can taste with a hundred screaming kids in a room. When I put my nose in a glass, it's like tunnel vision. I move into another world, where everything around me is just gone, and every bit of mental energy is focused on that wine."
—ROBERT M. PARKER JR., author and wine critic, in The Atlantic Monthly

WHAT MAKES A GREAT WINE GREAT?

Varietal character
Balance of components
Complexity
Sense of place
Emotional response

"Great wine is about nuance, surprise, subtlety, expression, qualities that keep you coming back for another taste. Rejecting a wine because it is not big enough is like rejecting a book because it is not long enough, or a piece of music because it is not loud enough."
—KERMIT LYNCH, Adventures on the Wine Route

"Wine makes daily living easier, less hurried, with fewer tensions and more tolerance."
—BENJAMIN FRANKLIN

THE 60-SECOND WINE EXPERT

Over the last few years I have insisted that my students spend one minute in silence after they swallow the wine. I use a "60-second wine expert" tasting sheet in my classes for students to record their impressions. The minute is divided into four sections: 0 to 15 seconds, 15 to 30 seconds, 30 to 45 seconds, and the final 45 to 60 seconds. Try this with your next glass of wine.

Please note that the first taste of wine is a shock to your taste buds. This is due to the alcohol content, acidity, and sometimes the tannin in the wine. The higher the alcohol or acidity, the more of a shock. For the first wine in any tasting, it is probably best to take a sip and swirl it around in your mouth, but don't evaluate it. Wait another thirty seconds, try it again, and then begin the 60-second wine expert tasting.

0 to 15 seconds: If there is any residual sugar/sweetness in the wine, I will experience it now. If there is no sweetness in the wine, the acidity is usually at its strongest sensation in the first fifteen seconds. I am also looking for the fruit level of the wine and its balance with the acidity or sweetness.

15 to 30 seconds: After the sweetness or acidity, I am looking for great fruit sensation. After all, that is what I am paying for! By the time I reach thirty seconds, I am hoping for balance of all the components. By this time, I can identify the weight of the wine. Is it light, medium, or full-bodied? I am now starting to think about what kind of food I can pair with this wine (see page 295).

30 to 45 seconds: At this point I am beginning to formulate my opinion of the wine, whether I like it or not. Not all wines need sixty seconds of thought. Lighter-style wines, such as Rieslings, will usually show their best at this point. The fruit, acid, and sweetness of a great German Riesling should be in perfect harmony from this point on. For quality red and white wines, acidity—which is a very strong component, especially in the first thirty seconds—should now be in balance with the fruit of the wine.

45 to 60 seconds: Very often wine writers use the term "length" to describe how long the components, balance, and flavor continue in the mouth. I concentrate on the length of the wine in these last fifteen seconds. In big, full-bodied red wines from Bordeaux and the Rhône Valley, Cabernets from California, Barolos and Barbarescos from Italy, and even some full-bodied Chardonnays, I am concentrating on the level of tannin in the wine. Just as the acidity and fruit balance are my major concerns in the first thirty seconds, it is now the tannin and fruit balance I am looking for in the last thirty seconds. If the fruit, tannin, and acid are all in balance at sixty seconds, then I feel that the wine is probably ready to drink. Does the tannin overpower the fruit? If it does at the sixty-second mark, I will then begin to question whether I should drink the wine now or put it away for more aging.

It is extremely important to me that if you want to learn the true taste of the wine, you take at least one minute to concentrate on all of its components. In my classes it is amazing to see more than a hundred students silently taking one minute to analyze a wine. Some close their eyes, some bow their heads in deep thought, others write notes.

One final point: Sixty seconds, to me, is the minimum time to wait before making a decision about a wine. Many great wines continue to show balance well past 120 seconds. The best wine I ever tasted lasted more than three minutes—that's three minutes of perfect balance of all components!

"I like to think about the life of wine, how it is a living thing. I like to think about what was going on the year the grapes were growing. How the sun was shining, if it rained. I like to think about all the people who tended and picked the grapes. And if it's an old wine, how many of them must be dead by now. I like how wine continues to evolve, like if I opened a bottle of wine today it would taste different than if I'd opened it on any other day, because a bottle of wine is actually alive. And it's constantly evolving and gaining complexity, that is until it peaks, like your '61. And then it begins its steady inevitable decline."

—MAYA, *from the movie* Sideways *(2004)*

Part of the 60-second wine expert tasting sheet I gave out in my class:

TASTING WORKSHEET

60-Second Wine Expert:

Identify the major component in each time slot.

0–15 seconds _____

15–30 seconds _____

30–45 seconds _____

45–60 seconds _____

Color:

_____

Aroma/Bouquet:

_____

_____

_____

	Low	Medium	High
Residual Sugar			
Fruit			
Acid			
Tannin			

Light-Bodied _____ Medium-Bodied_____ Full-Bodied _____

Ageability: Ready to Drink? _____ Needs more time? _____ Past its prime? _____

Personal Rating/Comments _____

FOR FURTHER READING

I recommend Michael Broadbent's *Pocket Guide to Wine Tasting*; Jancis Robinson's *Vintage Timecharts*; and Alan Young's *Making Sense of Wine*.

White Grapes of the World

MORE THAN 50 major white-wine grape varieties are grown throughout the world.

OTHER WHITE grapes and regions you may wish to explore:

GRAPES	WHERE THEY GROW BEST
Albariño	Spain
Chenin Blanc	Loire Valley, France; California
Gewürztraminer, Pinot Blanc, Pinot Gris	Alsace, France
Pinot Grigio (aka Pinot Gris)	Italy; California; Oregon
Sémillon	Bordeaux (Sauternes); Australia
Viognier	Rhône Valley, France; California
Grüner Veltliner	Austria

NEW WORLD VS. OLD WORLD

Wines from the United States, Australia, Chile, Argentina, New Zealand, and South Africa usually list the grape variety on the label. French, Italian, and Spanish wines usually list the region, village, or vineyard where the wine was made—but not the grape.

NOW THAT YOU KNOW THE BASICS of how wine is made and how to taste it, you're almost ready to begin the first three classes on white wines.

Before you do, simplify your journey by letting me answer the question most frequently asked by my wine students on what will help them most in learning about wine. The main thing is to understand the major grape varieties and where they are grown in the world.

The purpose of this book is not to overwhelm you with information about every grape under the sun. My job as a wine educator is to try to narrow down this overabundance of data. So let's start off with the three major grapes you need to know to understand white wine. More than 90 percent of all quality white wine is made from these three grapes. They are listed here in order from the lightest style to the fullest:

Riesling   Sauvignon Blanc   Chardonnay

This is not to say that world-class white wine comes from only these grapes, but knowing these three is a good start.

One of the first things I show my students in Class One is a list indicating where these three grape varieties grow best. It looks something like this:

GRAPES	WHERE THEY GROW BEST
Riesling	Germany; Alsace, France; New York State; Washington State
Sauvignon Blanc	Bordeaux, France; Loire Valley, France; New Zealand; California (Fumé Blanc)
Chardonnay	Burgundy, France; Champagne, France; California; Australia

There are world-class Rieslings, Sauvignon Blancs, and Chardonnays made in other countries, but in general the above regions specialize in wines made from these grapes.

COMMON AROMAS

Riesling	**Sauvignon Blanc**	**Chardonnay**
Fruity	Grapefruit	Green apple, Butter, Citrus
Lychee nut	Grass, Herbs	Grapefruit, Melon, Oak
Sweet	Cat pee, Green olive	Pineapple, Toast, Vanilla

Red Grapes of the World

CLASSES FOUR THROUGH SEVEN will delve into the great red wines of the world. It is important that you review the major red grape varieties and where in the world they produce the best wines.

In Class Four, I start with a list of what I consider to be the major red-wine grapes, ranked from lightest to fullest-bodied style, along with the region or country in which the grape grows best. By looking at this chart, not only will you get an idea of the style of the wine, but also a feeling for gradations of weight, color, tannin, and ageability.

THERE ARE hundreds of different red-wine grapes planted throughout the world. California alone grows 31 different red-wine grape varieties.

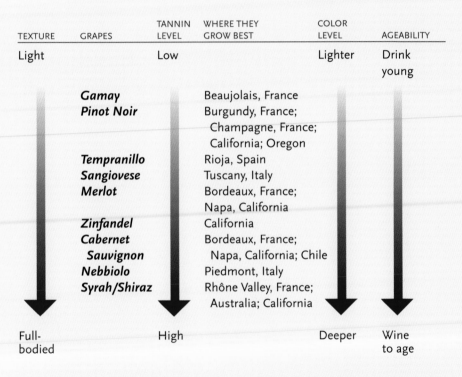

TEXTURE	GRAPES	TANNIN LEVEL	WHERE THEY GROW BEST	COLOR LEVEL	AGEABILITY
Light		Low		Lighter	Drink young
	Gamay		Beaujolais, France		
	Pinot Noir		Burgundy, France; Champagne, France; California; Oregon		
	Tempranillo		Rioja, Spain		
	Sangiovese		Tuscany, Italy		
	Merlot		Bordeaux, France; Napa, California		
	Zinfandel		California		
	Cabernet Sauvignon		Bordeaux, France; Napa, California; Chile		
	Nebbiolo		Piedmont, Italy		
	Syrah/Shiraz		Rhône Valley, France; Australia; California		
Full-bodied		High		Deeper	Wine to age

IN GENERAL, the lighter the color, the more perceived the acidity.

ONCE YOU have become acquainted with these major red-wine grapes, you may wish to explore the following:

GRAPES	WHERE THEY GROW BEST
Barbera	Italy
Dolcetto	Italy
Cabernet Franc	Loire Valley and Bordeaux, France
Grenache/ Garnacha	Rhône Valley, France Spain
Malbec	Bordeaux and Cahors, France; Argentina

To put this chart together is extremely challenging, given all the variables that go into making wine and the many different styles that can be produced. Remember, there are always exceptions to the rule, just as there are other countries and wine regions not listed here that produce world-class wine from some of the red grapes shown. You'll begin to see this for yourself if you do your homework and taste a lot of different wines. Good luck!

Questions for Prelude

	REFER TO PAGE
1. Which country produces the most amount of wine?	2
2. Sugar + _____ = _____ + Carbon Dioxide	2
3. What is the percentage range of alcohol in a table wine?	3
4. What is the percentage range of alcohol in a fortified wine?	3
5. What is the name of the species of grapes that is used to make the wines of Europe?	3
6. Which country has the most grape acreage in the world?	3
7. What does the term *Brix* refer to?	4
8. What is phylloxera?	6
9. Where does tannin come from?	6

CLASS ONE

The White Wines of France

❧

UNDERSTANDING FRENCH WINE • ALSACE • LOIRE VALLEY •

WHITE WINES OF BORDEAUX • GRAVES • SAUTERNES/BARSAC •

WHITE WINES OF BURGUNDY • CHABLIS • CÔTE DE BEAUNE •

CÔTE CHÂLONNAISE • MÂCONNAIS

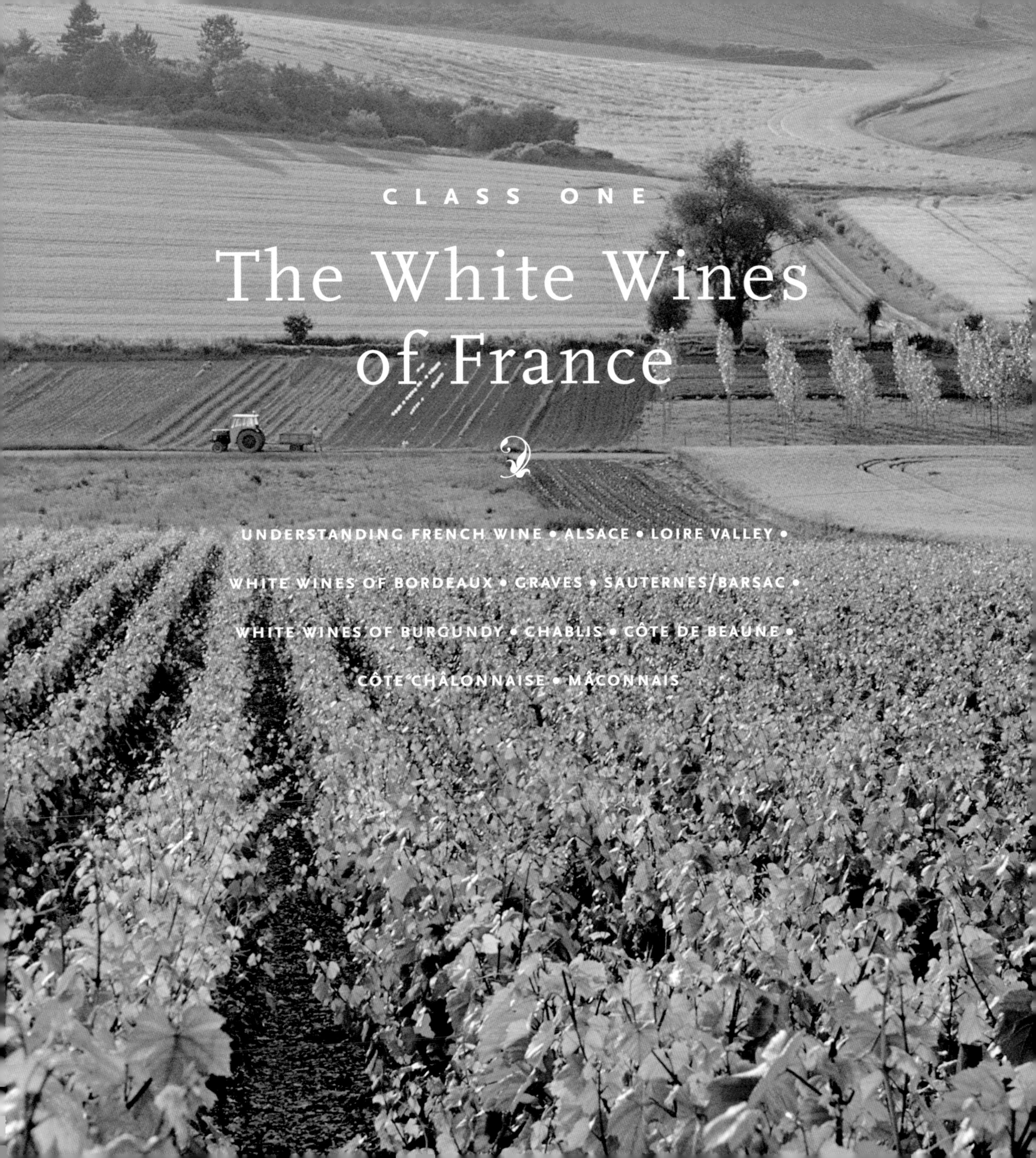

FRANCE

CHAMPAGNE

Paris ★

LOIRE VALLEY

ALSACE

BURGUNDY

Atlantic Ocean

BORDEAUX

CÔTES DU RHÔNE

LANGUEDOC-ROUSILLON

PROVENCE

o Miles   100   200

o Kilometers   200

Mediterranean Sea

Understanding French Wine

France is the #2 producer of wines in the world.

BEFORE WE BEGIN OUR FIRST CLASS, "The White Wines of France," I think you should know a few important points about all French wines. Take a look at a map of France to get familiar with the main wine-producing areas. As we progress, you'll understand why geography is so important.

Here's a quick rundown of which areas produce which styles of wine:

WINE REGIONS	STYLES	MAJOR GRAPES
Champagne	sparkling wine	Pinot Noir, Chardonnay
Loire Valley	mostly white	Sauvignon Blanc, Chenin Blanc, Cabernet Franc
Alsace	mostly white	Riesling, Gewürztraminer
Burgundy	red and white	Pinot Noir, Gamay, Chardonnay
Bordeaux	red and white	Sauvignon Blanc, Sémillon, Merlot, Cabernet Sauvignon, Cabernet Franc
Côtes du Rhône	mostly red	Syrah, Grenache
Languedoc-Roussillon	red and white	Carignan, Grenache, Syrah, Cinsault, Mourvèdre
Provence	red, white, and rosé	Grenache, Syrah

WHY WOULD Georges Duboeuf, Louis Latour, and many other famous wine-makers start wineries in Languedoc and Roussillon? For one thing, the land is much less expensive compared to regions such as Burgundy or Bordeaux, so the winemakers can produce moderately priced wines and still get a good return on their investment.

IN THE SOUTHERN French region of Provence, look for these producers:
Domaine Tempier
Château Routas

Anyone who is interested in wine is bound to encounter French wine at one time or another. Why? Because of thousands of years of history and wine-making tradition, because of the great diversity and variety of wines from the many different regions, and because French wines have the reputation for being among the best in the world. There's a reason for this, and it goes back to quality control.

French winemaking is regulated by strict government laws that are set up by the *Appellation d'Origine Contrôlée.* If you don't want to say "Appellation d'Origine Contrôlée" all the time, you can simply say "AOC." This is the first of many wine lingo abbreviations you'll learn in this book.

Vins de Pays: This is a category that's growing in importance. A 1979 French legal decision liberalized the rules for this category, permitting the use of nontraditional grapes in certain regions and even allowing vintners to label wines with the varietal rather than the regional name. For exporters to the American market, where consumers are becoming accustomed to buying wines by grape variety—Cabernet Sauvignon or Chardonnay, for example—this change makes their wines much easier to sell.

THE REGION most active in the production of Vin de Pays varietal wines is Languedoc-Roussillon, in southwest France. Called in the past the "wine lake" because of the vast quantities of anonymous wine made there, the Languedoc has more than 700,000 acres of vineyards, and produces more than 200 million cases a year, about a third of the total French crop.

TOP FRENCH WINE BRANDS

Georges Duboeuf: Beaujolais
Louis Jadot: Burgundy
Fat Bastard
B & G
Red Bicyclette

HECTARE—metric measure
1 hectare = 2.471 acres

HECTOLITER—metric measure
1 hectoliter = 26.42 U.S. gallons =
133 bottles (750ml)

FAMOUS NON-AOC French wines that are available in the United States include: Moreau, Boucheron, Chantefleur, and René Junot.

CHAMPAGNE IS another major white wine producer, but that's a chapter in itself.

FRENCH CONTROL LAWS

Established in the 1930s, the Appellation d'Origine Contrôlée (AOC) laws set minimum requirements for each wine-producing area in France. These laws also can help you decipher French wine labels, since the AOC controls the following:

	EXAMPLE	EXAMPLE
Geographic origin	*Chablis*	*Pommard*
Grape variety: Which grapes can be planted where	*Chardonnay*	*Pinot Noir*
Minimum alcohol content: This varies depending upon the particular area where the grapes are grown	*10%*	*10.5%*
Vine-growing practices: For example, a vintner can produce only so much wine per acre	*40 hectoliters/ hectare*	*35 hectoliters/ hectare*

Vins de Table: These are ordinary table wines and represent almost 35 percent of all wines produced in France.

Most French wine is meant to be consumed as a simple beverage. Many of the *vins de table* are marketed under proprietary names and are the French equivalent of California jug wines. Don't be surprised if you go into a grocery store in France to buy wine and find it in a plastic wine container with no label on it! You can see the color through the plastic—red, white, or rosé—but the only marking on the container is the alcohol content, ranging from 9 to 14 percent. You choose your wine depending on how sharp you need to be for the rest of the day!

When you buy wines, keep these distinctions in mind, because there's a difference not only in quality but also in price.

What are the four major white wine–producing regions of France?

ALSACE   **LOIRE VALLEY**   **BORDEAUX**   **BURGUNDY**

Let's start with Alsace and the Loire Valley, because these are the two French regions that specialize in white wines. As you can see from the map at the beginning of this chapter, Alsace, the Loire Valley, and Chablis (a white wine–producing region of Burgundy) have one thing in common: They're all located in the northern region of France. These areas produce white wines predominantly, because of the shorter growing season and cooler climate which are best suited for growing white grapes.

ALSACE

I often find that people are confused about the difference between wines from Alsace and those from Germany. Why do you suppose this is?

First of all, your confusion could be justified since both wines are sold in tall bottles with tapering necks. Just to confuse you further, Alsace and Germany grow the same grape varieties. But when you think of Riesling, what are your associations? You'll probably answer "Germany" and "sweetness." That's a very typical response, and that's because the German winemaker adds a small amount of naturally sweet unfermented grape juice back into the wine to create the distinctive German Riesling. The winemaker from Alsace ferments every bit of the sugar in the grapes, which is why 90 percent of all Alsace wines are totally dry.

Another fundamental difference between wine from Alsace and wine from Germany is the alcohol content. Wine from Alsace has 11 to 12 percent alcohol, while most German wine has a mere 8 to 9 percent.

What are the white grapes grown in Alsace?

The four grapes you should know are:

Riesling: accounts for 22 percent
Pinot Blanc: accounts for 21 percent
Gewürztraminer: accounts for 19 percent
Pinot Gris: accounts for 15 percent

FROM 1871 TO 1919, Alsace was part of Germany.

ALL WINES produced in Alsace are AOC-designated and represent nearly 20% of all AOC white wines in France.

ALSACE PRODUCES 8% of its red wines from the Pinot Noir grape. These generally are consumed in the region and are rarely exported.

WINE LABELING in Alsace is different from the other French regions administered by the AOC, because Alsace is the only region that labels its wine by varietal. All Alsace wines that include the name of the grape on the label must be made entirely from that grape.

GREAT SWEET (LATE HARVEST) WINES FROM ALSACE

Vendange Tardive
Sélection de Grains Nobles

IN THE LAST 10 years, there have been more Pinot Blanc and Riesling grapes planted in Alsace than any other variety.

What types of wine are produced in Alsace?

As mentioned earlier, virtually all the Alsace wines are dry. Riesling is the major grape planted in Alsace, and it is responsible for the highest-quality wines of the region. Alsace is also known for its Gewürztraminer, which is in a class by itself. Most people either love it or hate it, because Gewürztraminer has a very distinctive style. *Gewürz* is the German word for "spice," which aptly describes the wine.

Pinot Blanc and Pinot Gris are becoming increasingly popular among the growers of Alsace.

How should I select an Alsace wine?

Two factors are important in choosing a wine from Alsace: the grape variety and the reputation and style of the shipper. Some of the most reliable shippers are:

DOMAINE MARCEL DEISS	**F. E. TRIMBACH**
DOMAINE WEINBACH	**HUGEL & FILS**
DOMAINE ZIND-HUMBRECHT	**LÉON BEYER**
DOPFF "AU MOULIN"	

Why are the shippers so important?

The majority of the landholders in Alsace don't grow enough grapes to make it economically feasible to produce and market their own wine. Instead, they sell their grapes to a shipper who produces, bottles, and markets the wine under his own name. The art of making high-quality wine lies in the selection of grapes made by each shipper.

What are the different quality levels of Alsace wines?

Quality of Alsace wines is determined by the shipper's reputation rather than any labeling on the bottle. That said, the vast majority of any given Alsace wine is the shipper's varietal. A very small percentage is labeled with a specific vineyard's name, especially in the appellation "Alsace Grand Cru." Some wines are labeled "Réserve" or "Réserve Personelle," terms that are not legally defined.

Should I lay down my Alsace wines for long aging?

In general, most Alsace wines are made to be consumed young—that is, one to five years after they're bottled. As in any fine-wine geographic area, in

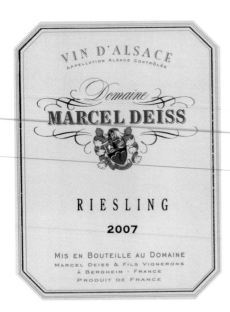

VIN D'ALSACE
APPELLATION ALSACE CONTRÔLÉE
Domaine
MARCEL DEISS

RIESLING
2007

MIS EN BOUTEILLE AU DOMAINE
MARCEL DEISS & FILS VIGNERONS
À BERGHEIM · FRANCE
PRODUIT DE FRANCE

THERE ARE 35,000 acres of grapes planted in Alsace, but the average plot of land for each grower is only 5 acres.

THE ALSACE region has little rainfall, especially during the grape harvest, and the town of Colmar—the Alsace wine center—is the second driest in France. That's why they say a "one-shirt harvest" will be a good vintage.

SOMETIMES YOU'LL SEE "Grand Cru" on an Alsace label. This wine can be made only from the best grape varieties of Alsace. There are more than 50 different vineyards entitled to the Grand Cru label.

Alsace there is a small percentage of great wines produced that may be aged for ten years or more.

How have Alsace wines changed in the past twenty-five years?

Twenty-five years later I am enjoying the same producers, such as Trimbach and Hugel, as I did then. A dry, crisp acidic Riesling is still one of my favorite wines to have at the beginning of a meal, especially with a fish appetizer. Pinot Blanc is a perfect summer picnic wine, or at a restaurant for wine by the glass, and the famous Gewürztraminer is one of the most unique and flavorful wines in the world.

The best part about Alsace wines is that they are still very affordable, of good quality, and available throughout the United States.

BEST BETS FOR RECENT VINTAGES FROM ALSACE

2001*   2002*   2003   2004   2005*   2006   2007*   2008

*Note: * signifies exceptional vintage*

FOR FURTHER READING

I recommend *Alsace* by S. F. Hallgarten and *Alsace* by Pamela Van Dyke Price.

WINE AND FOOD

During a visit to Alsace, I spoke with two of the region's best-known producers to find out which types of food they enjoy with Alsace wines. Here's what they prefer:

ÉTIENNE HUGEL: *"Alsace wines are not only suited to classic Alsace and other French dishes. For instance, I adore Riesling with such raw fish specialties as Japanese sushi and sashimi, while our Gewürztraminer is delicious with smoked salmon and brilliant with Chinese, Thai, and Indonesian food."*

Mr. Hugel describes Pinot Blanc as "round, soft, not aggressive . . . an all-purpose wine . . . can be used as an apéritif, with all kinds of pâté and charcuterie, and also with hamburgers. Perfect for brunch—not too sweet or flowery."

HUBERT TRIMBACH: *"Riesling with fish—blue trout with a light sauce."* He recommends Gewürztraminer as an apéritif, or with foie gras or any pâté at meal's end; with Muenster cheese, or a stronger cheese such as Roquefort.

ALSACE IS also known for its fruit brandies, or eaux-de-vie:
Fraise: strawberries
Framboise: raspberries
Kirsch: cherries
Mirabelle: yellow plums
Poire: pears

FOR THE TOURISTS

Visit the beautiful wine village of Riquewihr, whose buildings date from the 15th and 16th centuries.

FOR THE FOODIES

Alsace is not just about great wine. There are over 26 Michelin-rated restaurants, with three of them having three stars.

IN THE LOIRE Valley, 56% of the AOC wines produced are white, and 96% of those are dry.

THE LOIRE VALLEY is famous not only for its wines, but also as a summer retreat for royalty. Elegant and sometimes enormous châteaux embellish the countryside.

FOR RED wines look to Bourgueil, Chinon, and Saumur, all made from the Cabernet Franc grape.

THE DISTINCT nose, or bouquet, of Pouilly-Fumé comes from a combination of the Sauvignon Blanc grape and the soil of the Loire Valley.

MOST POUILLY-FUMÉ and Sancerre wines are not aged in wood.

THE LOIRE VALLEY is the largest white wine region in France and second largest in sparkling wine production.

OTHER SAUVIGNON BLANC wines from the Loire to look for: Menetou-Salon and Quincy. For Chenin Blanc try Savennières.

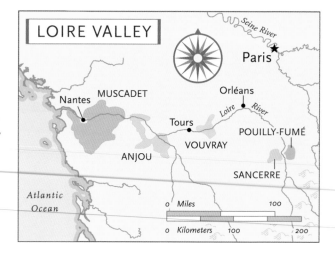

LOIRE VALLEY

Starting at the city of Nantes, a bit upriver from the Atlantic Ocean, the Loire Valley stretches inland for six hundred miles along the Loire River.

There are two white-grape varieties you should be familiar with:

SAUVIGNON BLANC   CHENIN BLANC

Rather than choosing by grape variety and shipper, as you would in Alsace, choose Loire Valley wines by style and vintage. Here are the main styles:

Pouilly-Fumé: A dry wine that has the most body and concentration of all the Loire Valley wines. It's made with 100 percent Sauvignon Blanc.

Muscadet: A light, dry wine, made from 100 percent Melon de Bourgogne grapes.

Sancerre: Striking a balance between full-bodied Pouilly-Fumé and light-bodied Muscadet, it's made with 100 percent Sauvignon Blanc.

Vouvray: The "chameleon" can be dry, semisweet, or sweet. It's made from 100 percent Chenin Blanc.

How did Pouilly-Fumé get its name, and what does *fumé* mean?

Many people ask me if Pouilly-Fumé is smoked, because they automatically associate the word *fumé* with smoke. Two of the many theories about the origin of the word come from the white morning mist that blankets the area. As the sun burns off the mist, it looks as if smoke is rising. Others say it is the "smokelike" bloom on Sauvignon Blanc grapes.

When are the wines ready to drink?

Generally, Loire Valley wines are meant to be consumed young. The exception is a sweet Vouvray, which can be laid down for a longer time.

Here are more specific guidelines:

Pouilly-Fumé: three to five years
Sancerre: two to three years
Muscadet: one to two years

What's the difference between Pouilly-Fumé and Pouilly-Fuissé?

My students often ask me this, expecting similarly named wines to be related. But Pouilly-Fumé is made from 100 percent Sauvignon Blanc and comes from the Loire Valley, while Pouilly-Fuissé is made from 100 percent Chardonnay and comes from the Mâconnais region of Burgundy.

Twenty-five years later in the Loire Valley

I am still enamored with the quality and diversity of the white wines of the Loire Valley. The wines have maintained their style and character representing great value for the consumer. Twenty-five years ago the most important Loire Valley wine was Pouilly-Fumé. Today Sancerre is the most popular Loire wine in the United States. Both wines are made from the same grape variety, 100 percent Sauvignon Blanc, both are medium-bodied with great acidity and fruit balance, and both are perfect food wines.

Twenty-five years later Muscadet continues to be a great value and Vouvray is still the best example of the quality that the grape Chenin Blanc can achieve.

BEST BETS FOR RECENT VINTAGES FROM THE LOIRE VALLEY

2004   2005*   2006   2007   2008

Note: * signifies exceptional vintage

KEVIN ZRALY'S FAVORITE PRODUCERS

Sancerre: Archambault, Roblin, Lucien Crochet, Jean Vacheron, Château de Sancerre, Domaine Fournier, Henri Bourgeois, Sauvion

Pouilly-Fumé: Guyot, Michel Redde, Château de Tracy, Dagueneau, Ladoucette, Colin, Jolivet, Jean-Paul Balland

Vouvray: Huët

Muscadet: Marquis de Goulaine, Sauvion, Métaireau

Savennières: Nicolas Joly

IF YOU see the phrase "sur lie" on a Muscadet wine label, it means that the wine was aged on its lees (sediment).

THE LOIRE VALLEY also produces the world-famous Anjou Rosé.

WINE AND FOOD

BARON PATRICK LADOUCETTE
suggests the following combinations:
Pouilly-Fumé: *"Smoked salmon; turbot with hollandaise; white meat chicken; veal with cream sauce."*
Sancerre: *"Shellfish, simple food of the sea, because Sancerre is drier than Pouilly-Fumé."*
Muscadet: *"All you have to do is look at the map to see where Muscadet is made: by the sea where the main fare is shellfish, clams, and oysters."*
Vouvray: *"A nice semidry wine to have with fruit and cheese."*

MARQUIS ROBERT DE GOULAINE
suggests these combinations:
Muscadet: *"Muscadet is good with a huge variety of excellent and fresh 'everyday' foods, including all the seafood from the Atlantic Ocean, the fish from the river— pike, for instance—game, poultry, and cheese (mainly goat cheese). Of course, there is a must in the region of Nantes: freshwater fish with the world-famous butter sauce, the beurre blanc, invented at the turn of the century by Clémence, who happened to be the chef at Goulaine. If you prefer, try Muscadet with a dash of crème de cassis (black currant); it is a wonderful way to welcome friends!"*

GRAND CRU CLASSÉ DE GRAVES

Château Olivier

PESSAC-LÉOGNAN
APPELLATION PESSAC-LÉOGNAN CONTROLÉE

GROUPEMENT FONCIER AGRICOLE DU CHATEAU OLIVIER
J.-J. DE BÉTHMANN - PROPRIÉTAIRE
LÉOGNAN - 33850 - GIRONDE - FRANCE

MIS EN BOUTEILLE AU CHATEAU
12,5% vol   PRODUCE OF FRANCE   75 cl

BORDEAUX PRODUCTION:
89% red
11% white

THE NAME "Graves" means
"gravel"—the type of soil
found in the region.

WHEN PEOPLE think of dry
white Bordeaux wines, they
normally think of the major
areas of Graves or Pessac-
Léognan, but some of the
best value/quality white
wines produced in Bordeaux
come from the Entre-Deux-
Mers area.

CLASSIFIED WHITE châteaux
wines make up only 3% of
the total production of white
Graves.

THE WHITE WINES OF BORDEAUX

Doesn't Bordeaux always mean red wine?

That's a misconception. Actually, two of the five major areas of Bordeaux—Graves and Sauternes—are known for their excellent white wines. Sauternes is world-famous for its sweet white wine.

The major white-grape varieties used in both areas are:

SAUVIGNON BLANC   SÉMILLON

GRAVES

How are the white Graves wines classified?

There are two levels of quality:

GRAVES   PESSAC-LÉOGNAN

The most basic Graves is simply called "Graves." The best wines are produced in Pessac-Léognan. Those labeled "Graves" are from the southern portion of the region surrounding Sauternes, while Pessac-Léognan is in the northern half of the region, next to the city of Bordeaux. The best wines are known by the name of a particular château, a special vineyard that produces the best-quality grapes. The grapes grown for these wines enjoy better soil and better growing conditions overall. The classified château wines and the regional wines of Graves are always dry.

How should I select a Graves wine?

My best recommendation would be to purchase a classified château wine.

BORDEAUX

Gironde River

Atlantic
Ocean

0 Miles   25   50

0 Kilometers   50   100

MÉDOC

POMEROL
ST-ÉMILION

Bordeaux

PESSAC-
LÉOGNAN   ENTRE-
DEUX-MERS

Dordogne River

GRAVES

Garonne River

SAUTERNES

The classified châteaux are:

CHÂTEAU HAUT-BRION
CHÂTEAU CARBONNIEUX*
CHÂTEAU COUHINS-LURTON
CHÂTEAU LA TOUR-MARTILLAC
CHÂTEAU MALARTIC-LAGRAVIÈRE
CHÂTEAU SMITH-HAUT-LAFITTE

CHÂTEAU BOUSCAUT*
DOMAINE DE CHEVALIER
CHÂTEAU LA LOUVIÈRE*
CHÂTEAU LAVILLE-HAUT-BRION
CHÂTEAU OLIVIER*

* The largest producers and the easiest to find.

Twenty-five years later in White Bordeaux

The dry white wines of Bordeaux were never considered equal to the great red Chateaux and sweet whites of Sauternes. That has all changed over the last twenty-five years. Millions of dollars has been spent on state-of-the-art wine-making equipment, and new vineyard management has created great white wine production, especially in the Pessac-Léognan.

There are very few regions in the world that blend Sauvignon Blanc and Sémillon and age them in oak. The winemakers have also been very careful to integrate the fruit and oak together to maintain the freshness and crispness of the wine. Recent vintages have been outstanding.

BEST BETS FOR RECENT VINTAGES OF WHITE GRAVES

2000*   2005*   2006   2007*   2008

Note: * signifies exceptional vintage

WINE AND FOOD

DENISE LURTON-MOULLE (*Château La Louvière, Château Bonnet*): With *Château La Louvière Blanc: grilled sea bass with a beurre blanc, shad roe, or goat cheese soufflé. With Château Bonnet Blanc: oysters on the half-shell, fresh crab salad, mussels, and clams.*

JEAN-JACQUES DE BETHMANN (*Château Olivier*): "*Oysters, lobster, Rouget du Bassin d'Arcachon.*"

ANTONY PERRIN (*Château Carbonnieux*): "*With a young Château Carbonnieux Blanc: chilled lobster consommé, or shellfish, such as oysters, scallops, or grilled shrimp. With an older Carbonnieux: a traditional sauced fish course or a goat cheese.*"

THE STYLE of classified white château wines varies according to the ratio of Sauvignon Blanc and Sémillon used. Château Olivier, for example, is made with 65% Sémillon, and Château Carbonnieux with 65% Sauvignon Blanc.

WHEN THE original edition came out in 1985, the appellation Pessac-Léognan had not yet been established. Since 1987, this "new" appellation is your guarantee of the finest dry white wines in Bordeaux.

WHEN BUYING regional Sauternes look for these reputable shippers: Baron Philippe de Rothschild and B&G.

THERE ARE more Sémillon grapes planted in Bordeaux than there are Sauvignon Blanc.

OTHER SWEET-WINE producers in Bordeaux: Ste-Croix-du-Mont and Loupiac.

SAUTERNES IS expensive to produce because several pickings must be completed before the crop is entirely harvested. The harvest can last into November.

NOT CLASSIFIED, but of outstanding quality: Château Fargues, Château Gilette, and Château Raymond Lafon.

WORLD RECORD

One bottle of Château d'Yquem 1847 sold for $71,675 at the Zachy's wine auction.

SAUTERNES IS a wine you can age. In fact, most classified château wines in good vintages can easily age for 10 to 30 years.

SAUTERNES/BARSAC

French Sauternes are always sweet, meaning that not all the grape sugar has turned into alcohol during fermentation. A dry French Sauternes doesn't exist. The Barsac district, adjacent to Sauternes, has the option of using Barsac or Sauternes as its appellation.

What are the two different quality levels in style?

1. Regional ($)
2. Classified château ($$$–$$$$)

Sauternes is still producing one of the best sweet wines in the world. With the great vintages of 2001, 2002, 2003, and 2005, you'll be able to find excellent regional Sauternes if you buy from the best shippers. These wines represent a good value for your money, considering the labor involved in production, but they won't have the same intensity of flavor as a classified château.

What are the main grape varieties in Sauternes?

SÉMILLON   SAUVIGNON BLANC

If the same grapes are used for both the dry Graves and the sweet Sauternes, how do you explain the extreme difference in styles?

First and most important, the best Sauternes is made primarily with the Sémillon grape. Second, to make Sauternes, the winemaker leaves the grapes on the vine longer. He waits for a mold called *Botrytis cinerea* ("noble rot") to form. When "noble rot" forms on the grapes, the water within them evaporates and they shrivel. Sugar becomes concentrated as the grapes "raisinate." Then, during the winemaking process, not all the sugar is allowed to ferment into alcohol: hence, the high residual sugar.

BEST BETS FOR VINTAGES OF SAUTERNES

1986*   1988*   1989*   1990*   1995   1996   1997*   1998
2000   2001*   2002   2003*   2005*   2006   2007*   2008

*Note: * signifies exceptional vintage*

How are Sauternes classified?

FIRST GREAT GROWTH—GRAND PREMIER CRU

Château d'Yquem*

FIRST GROWTH—PREMIERS

Château La Tour Blanche*   Château Lafaurie-Peyraguey*
Clos Haut-Peyraguey*   Château de Rayne-Vigneau*
Château Suduiraut*   Château Coutet* (Barsac)
Château Climens* (Barsac)   Château Guiraud*
Château Rieussec*   Château Rabaud-Promis
Château Sigalas-Rabaud*

DOESN'T CHÂTEAU d'Yquem make a dry white wine? Yes, it does, and it's simply called "Y." By law, dry wine made in Sauternes cannot be called Appellation Sauternes. It can only be called Appellation Bordeaux.

SECOND GROWTHS—DEUXIÈMES CRUS

Château Myrat (Barsac)   Château Doisy-Daëne (Barsac)
Château Doisy-Védrines* (Barsac)   Château Doisy-Dubroca (Barsac)
Château d'Arche   Château Filhot*
Château Broustet (Barsac)   Château Nairac* (Barsac)
Château Caillou (Barsac)   Château Suau (Barsac)
Château de Malle*   Château Romer du Hayot*
Château Lamothe   Château Lamothe-Guignard

* These are the châteaux most readily available in the United States.

CHÂTEAU RIEUSSEC is owned by the same family as Château Lafite-Rothschild.

JUST DESSERTS

My students always ask me, "What do you serve with Sauternes?" Here's a little lesson I learned when I first encountered the wines of Sauternes.

Many years ago, when I was visiting the Sauternes region, I was invited to one of the châteaux for dinner. Upon arrival, my group was offered appetizers of foie gras, and, to my surprise, Sauternes was served with it. All the books I had ever read said you should serve drier wines first and sweeter wines later. But since I was a guest, I thought it best not to question my host's selection.

When we sat down for the first dinner course (fish), we were once again served a Sauternes. This continued through the main course—which happened to be rack of lamb—when another Sauternes was served.

I thought for sure our host would serve a great old red Bordeaux with the cheese course, but I was wrong again. With the Roquefort cheese was served a very old Sauternes.

With dessert soon on its way, I got used to the idea of having a dinner with Sauternes, and waited with anticipation for the final choice. You can imagine my surprise when a dry red Bordeaux—Château Lafite-Rothschild—was served with dessert!

Their point was that Sauternes doesn't have to be served only with dessert. All the Sauternes went well with the courses, because all the sauces complemented the wine and food.

By the way, the only wine that didn't go well with dinner was the Château Lafite-Rothschild with dessert, but we drank it anyway!

Perhaps this anecdote will inspire you to serve Sauternes with everything. Personally, I prefer to enjoy Sauternes by itself; I'm not a believer in the "dessert wine" category. This dessert wine is dessert in itself.

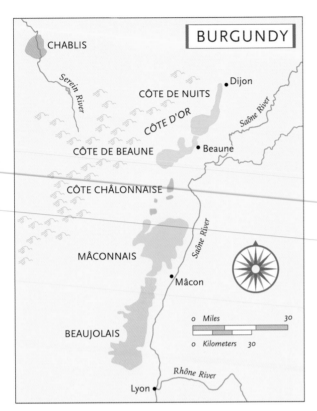

THE LARGEST city in Burgundy is known not for its wines but for another world-famous product. The city is Dijon, and the product is mustard.

THE WHITE WINES OF BURGUNDY

Where is Burgundy?

Burgundy is a region located in central eastern France. Its true fame is as one of the finest wine-producing areas in the world.

What is Burgundy?

Burgundy is one of the major wine-producing regions that hold an AOC designation in France. However, over the years, I have often found that people are confused about what a Burgundy really is, because the name has been borrowed so freely.

Burgundy is *not* a synonym for red wine, even though the color known as burgundy is obviously named after red wine. Many of the world's most renowned (and expensive) white wines come from Burgundy. Adding to the confusion (especially going back twenty-plus years) is that many red wines around the world were simply labeled "Burgundy" even though they were ordinary table wines. There are still some wineries, especially in the United States, that continue to label their wines as Burgundy, but these wines have no resemblance to the style of authentic French Burgundy wines.

What are the main regions within Burgundy?

CHABLIS   CÔTE D'OR}   CÔTE DE NUITS
                             CÔTE DE BEAUNE

CÔTE CHÂLONNAISE   MÂCONNAIS   BEAUJOLAIS

Before we explore Burgundy region by region, it's important to know the types of wine that are produced there. Take a look at the chart on the next page: It breaks down the types of wine and tells you the percentage of reds to whites.

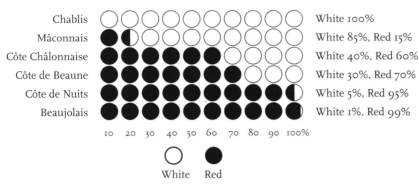

Chablis											White 100%
Mâconnais											White 85%, Red 15%
Côte Châlonnaise											White 40%, Red 60%
Côte de Beaune											White 30%, Red 70%
Côte de Nuits											White 5%, Red 95%
Beaujolais											White 1%, Red 99%

10 20 30 40 50 60 70 80 90 100%

○ White   ● Red

CÔTE D'OR PRODUCTION:
78% red
22% white

Burgundy is another region so famous for its red wines that people may forget that some of the finest white wines of France are also produced there. The three areas in Burgundy that produce world-famous white wines are:

CHABLIS   CÔTE DE BEAUNE   MÂCONNAIS

ALTHOUGH CHABLIS is part of the Burgundy region, it is a three-hour drive south from there to the Mâconnais area.

If it's any comfort to you, you need to know only one white-grape variety: Chardonnay. All the great white Burgundies are made from 100 percent Chardonnay.

Is there only one type of white Burgundy?

Although Chardonnay is used to make all the best French white Burgundy wines, the three areas produce many different styles. Much of this has to do with where the grapes are grown and the vinification procedures. For example, the northern climate of Chablis produces wines with more acidity than those in the southern region of Mâconnais.

With regard to vinification procedures, after the grapes are harvested in the Chablis and Mâconnais areas, most are fermented and aged in stainless-steel tanks. In the Côte de Beaune, after the grapes are harvested, a good percentage of the wines are fermented in small oak barrels and also aged in oak barrels. The wood adds complexity, depth, body, flavor, and longevity to the wines.

White Burgundies have one trait in common: They are dry.

DOMAINE LENOIR

MACON-VILLAGES
APPELLATION MACON-VILLAGES CONTROLEE
WHITE BURGUNDY WINE
MIS EN BOUTEILLE PAR
LES VINS GEORGES DUBŒUF
71570 ROMANÈCHE-THORINS FRANCE
PRODUCED AND BOTTLED IN FRANCE

ALC. 12.5% BY VOL.   750 ML
SELECTED AND BOTTLED FOR CALVERT WOODLEY
IMPORTED BY : W.J. DEUSTCH & SONS LTD., HARRISON, NY.

ANOTHER WHITE grape found in the Burgundy region is the Aligoté. It is a lesser grape variety and the grape name usually appears on the label.

ALSO LOOK for regional Burgundy wine, such as Bourgogne Blanc or Bourgogne Rouge.

MOST PREMIER Cru wines give you the name of the vineyard on the label, but others are simply called "Premier Cru," which is a blend of different cru vineyards.

THE AVERAGE yield for a Village wine in Burgundy is 360 gallons per acre. For the Grand Cru wines it is 290 gallons per acre, a noticeably higher concentration, which produces a more flavorful wine.

**OAK AND VINE CLASSIFICATIONS
(A GENERAL RULE)**

Village wine: 25% new oak
Premier Cru: 40–70% new oak
Grand Cru: 80–100% new oak

THE STORY OF KIR

The apéritif Kir has been popular from time to time. It is a mixture of white wine and crème de cassis (made from black currants). It was the favorite drink of the former mayor of Dijon, Canon Kir, who originally mixed in the sweet cassis to balance the high acidity of the local white wine made from the Aligoté grape.

How are the white wines of Burgundy classified?

The type of soil and the angle and direction of the slope are the primary factors determining quality. Here are the levels of quality:

Village Wine: Bears the name of a specific village. Cost: $.

Premier Cru: From a specific vineyard with special characteristics, within one of the named villages. Usually a Premier Cru wine will list on the label the village first and the vineyard second. Cost: $$.

Grand Cru: From a specific vineyard that possesses the best soil and slope in the area and meets or exceeds all other requirements. In most areas of Burgundy, the village doesn't appear on the label—only the Grand Cru vineyard name is used. Cost: $$$$.

A NOTE ON THE USE OF WOOD

Each wine region in the world has its own way of producing wines. Wine was always fermented and aged in wood—until the introduction of cement tanks, glass-lined tanks, and, most recently, stainless-steel tanks. Despite these technological improvements, many winemakers prefer to use the more traditional methods. For example, some of the wines from the firm of Louis Jadot are fermented in wood as follows:

> *One-third of the wine is fermented in new wood.*
> *One-third of the wine is fermented in year-old wood.*
> *One-third of the wine is fermented in older wood.*

Jadot's philosophy is that the better the vintage, the newer the wood: Younger wood imparts more flavor and tannin, which might overpower wines of lesser vintage. Thus, younger woods are generally reserved for aging the better vintages.

CHABLIS

Chablis is the northernmost area in Burgundy, and it produces only white wine.

ALL FRENCH Chablis is made of 100% Chardonnay grapes.

THERE ARE more than 250 grape growers in Chablis, but only a handful age their wine in wood.

Isn't Chablis just a general term for white wine?

The name "Chablis" suffers from the same misinterpretation and overuse as does the name "Burgundy." Because the French didn't take the necessary precautions to protect the use of the name, "Chablis" is now randomly applied to many ordinary bulk wines from other countries. Chablis has come to be associated with some very undistinguished wines, but this is not the case with French Chablis. In fact, the French take their Chablis very seriously. There are special classification and quality levels for Chablis.

What are the different quality levels of Chablis?

Petit Chablis: The most ordinary Chablis; rarely seen in the United States.

Chablis: A wine that comes from grapes grown anywhere in the Chablis district, also known as a village wine.

Chablis Premier Cru: A very good quality of Chablis that comes from specific high-quality vineyards.

Chablis Grand Cru: The highest classification of Chablis, and the most expensive because of its limited production. There are only seven vineyards in Chablis entitled to be called "Grand Cru."

OF THESE quality levels, the best value is a Chablis Premier Cru.

THERE ARE only 245 acres planted in Grand Cru vineyards.

CHABLIS VILLAGE $

CHABLIS PREMIER CRU $$

CHABLIS GRAND CRU $$$$

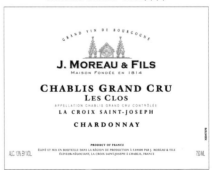

THE WINTER temperatures in some parts of Chablis can match those of Norway.

If you're interested in buying only the best Chablis, here are the seven Grands Crus and the most important Premiers Cru vineyards:

SOME OF THE GRAND CRU VINEYARDS OF CHABLIS

Blanchots	Preuses
Bougros	Valmur
Grenouilles	Vaudésir
Les Clos	

SOME OF THE TOP PREMIER CRU VINEYARDS OF CHABLIS

Côte de Vaulorent	Montmains
Fourchaume	Monts de Milieu
Lechet	Vaillon
Montée de Tonnerre	

How should I buy Chablis?

The two major aspects to look for in Chablis are the shipper and the vintage. Here is a list of the most important shippers of Chablis to the United States:

A. REGNARD & FILS	JOSEPH DROUHIN
ALBERT PIC & FILS	LA CHABLISIENNE
DOMAINE LAROCHE	LOUIS JADOT
FRANÇOIS RAVENEAU	LOUIS MICHEL
GUY ROBIN	RENÉ DAUVISSAT
J. MOREAU & FILS	ROBERT VOCORET
JEAN DAUVISSAT	WILLIAM FÈVRE

When should I drink my Chablis?

Chablis: within two years of the vintage
Premier Cru: between two and four years of the vintage
Grand Cru: between three and eight years of the vintage

BEST BETS FOR RECENT VINTAGES OF CHABLIS

2002*   2004   2005*   2006*   2007   2008

*Note: * signifies exceptional vintage*

CÔTE DE BEAUNE

This is one of the two major areas of the Côte d'Or. The wines produced here are some of the finest examples of dry white Chardonnay produced in the world and are considered a benchmark for winemakers everywhere.

The three most important white wine–producing villages of the Côte de Beaune are Meursault, Puligny-Montrachet, and Chassagne-Montrachet. All three produce their white wine from the same grape—100 percent Chardonnay.

CÔTE DE BEAUNE

Here is a list of my favorite white wine–producing villages and vineyards in the Côte de Beaune.

VILLAGE	PREMIER CRU VINEYARDS	GRAND CRU VINEYARDS
Aloxe-Corton		Corton-Charlemagne
		Charlemagne
Beaune	Clos des Mouches	None
Meursault	Les Perrières	None
	Les Genevrières	
	La Goutte d'Or	
	Les Charmes	
	Blagny	
	Poruzots	
Puligny-Montrachet	Les Combettes	Montrachet*
	Les Caillerets	Bâtard-Montrachet*
	Les Pucelles	Chevalier-Montrachet
	Les Folatières	Bienvenue-Bâtard-Montrachet
	Les Champs Gain	
	Clavoillons	
	Les Referts	
Chassagne-Montrachet	Les Ruchottes	Montrachet*
	Morgeot	Bâtard-Montrachet*
		Criots-Bâtard-Montrachet

* The vineyards of Montrachet and Bâtard-Montrachet overlap between the villages of Puligny-Montrachet and Chassagne-Montrachet.

THE LARGEST Grand Cru, in terms of production, is Corton-Charlemagne, which represents more than 50% of all white Grand Cru wines.

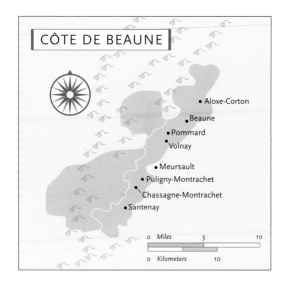

VILLAGE $	PREMIER CRU $$	GRAND CRU $$$
Puligny-Montrachet APPELLATION CONTROLÉE *Louis Latour* MIS EN BOUTEILLE PAR LOUIS LATOUR NÉGOCIANT A BEAUNE (COTE-D'OR)	*Puligny-Montrachet* LES REFERTS APPELLATION CONTROLÉE *Louis Latour* MIS EN BOUTEILLE PAR LOUIS LATOUR NÉGOCIANT A BEAUNE (COTE-D'OR), FRANCE	*Montrachet* APPELLATION CONTROLÉE MIS EN BOUTEILLE PAR LOUIS LATOUR, NÉGOCIANT A BEAUNE (CÔTE-D'OR), FRANCE

"The difference between the Village wine, Puligny-Montrachet, and the Grand Cru Montrachet is not in the type of wood used in aging or how long the wine is aged in wood. The primary difference is in the location of the vineyards, i.e., the soil and the slope of the land."

—ROBERT DROUHIN

What makes each Burgundy wine different?

In Burgundy, one of the most important factors in making a good wine is soil. The quality of the soil is the main reason why there are three levels and price points between a Village, a Premier Cru, and a Grand Cru wine. Another major factor that differentiates each wine is the vinification procedure the winemaker uses—the recipe. It's the same as if you were to compare the chefs at three gourmet restaurants: They may start out with the same ingredients, but it's what they do with those ingredients that matters.

BEST BETS FOR CÔTE DE BEAUNE WHITE

1996* 2000* 2002* 2004* 2005* 2006* 2007 2008

*Note: * signifies exceptional vintage*

CÔTE CHÂLONNAISE

The Côte Châlonnaise is the least known of the major wine districts of Burgundy. Although the Châlonnaise produces such red wines as Givry and Mercurey (see Class Four, "The Red Wines of Burgundy and the Rhône Valley"), it also produces some very good white wines that not many people are familiar with, which means value for you. I'm referring to the wines of Montagny and Rully. These wines are of the highest quality produced in the area, similar to the white wines of the Côte d'Or but less costly.

Look for the wines of Antonin Rodet, Faiveley, Louis Latour, Moillard, and Olivier Leflaive.

MÂCONNAIS

The southernmost white wine–producing area in Burgundy, the Mâconnais has a climate warmer than that of the Côte d'Or and Chablis. Mâcon wines are, in general, pleasant, light, uncomplicated, reliable, and a great value.

What are the different quality levels of Mâconnais wines?

From basic to best:

1. **Mâcon Blanc**

2. **Mâcon Supérieur**

3. **Mâcon-Villages**

4. **St-Véran**

5. **Pouilly-Vinzelles**

6. **Pouilly-Fuissé**

Of all Mâcon wines, Pouilly-Fuissé is unquestionably one of the most popular. It is among the highest-quality Mâconnais wines, fashionable to drink in the United States long before most Americans discovered the splendors of wine. As wine consumption increased in America, Pouilly-Fuissé and other famous areas such as Pommard, Nuits-St-Georges, and Chablis became synonymous with the best wines of France and could always be found on any restaurant's wine list.

In my opinion, Mâcon-Villages is the best value. Why pay more for Pouilly-Fuissé—sometimes three times as much—when a simple Mâcon will do just as nicely?

BEST BETS FOR RECENT VINTAGES OF MÂCON WHITE

2004*   2005*   2006*   2007   2008

Note: * signifies exceptional vintage

MORE THAN four-fifths of the wines from the Mâconnais are white.

THERE IS a village named Chardonnay in the Mâconnais area, where the grape's name is said to have originated.

IN AN average year, around 450,000 cases of Pouilly-Fuissé are produced—not nearly enough to supply all the restaurants and retail shops for worldwide consumption.

SINCE MÂCON wines are usually not aged in oak, they are ready to drink as soon as they are released.

If you're taking a client out on a limited expense account, a safe wine to order is Mâcon. If the sky's the limit, go for the Meursault!

OVERVIEW

Now that you're familiar with the many different white wines of Burgundy:

How do you choose the right one for you?

First look for the vintage year. With Burgundy, it's especially important to buy a good year. After that, your choice becomes a matter of taste and cost. If price is no object, aren't you lucky?

Also, after some trial and error, you may find that you prefer the wines of one shipper over another. Here are some of the shippers to look for when buying white Burgundy:

BOUCHARD PÈRE & FILS	**CHANSON**
JOSEPH DROUHIN	**LABOURÉ-ROI**
LOUIS JADOT	**LOUIS LATOUR**
OLIVIER LEFLAIVE FRÈRES	**ROPITEAU FRÈRES**
PROSPER MAUFOUX	

Although 80 percent of Burgundy wines are sold through shippers, some fine estate-bottled wines are available in limited quantities in the United States. The better ones include:

CHÂTEAU FUISSÉ (POUILLY-FUISSÉ)
DOMAINE BACHELET-RAMONET (CHASSAGNE-MONTRACHET)
DOMAINE BOILLOT (MEURSAULT)
DOMAINE BONNEAU DU MARTRAY (CORTON-CHARLEMAGNE)
DOMAINE COCHE-DURY (MEURSAULT, PULIGNY-MONTRACHET)
DOMAINE DES COMTES LAFON (MEURSAULT)
DOMAINE ÉTIENNE SAUZET (CHASSAGNE-MONTRACHET, PULIGNY-MONTRACHET)
DOMAINE LEFLAIVE (MEURSAULT, PULIGNY-MONTRACHET)
DOMAINE MATROT (MEURSAULT)
DOMAINE VINCENT GIRARDIN (CHASSAGNE-MONTRACHET, PULIGNY-MONTRACHET)

Twenty-five years later in white Burgundy

If you are looking for pure unoaked Chardonnay at its best, then the crisp flavorful Chablis region of France will satisfy your needs. Over the last twenty-

---

DOMAINE LEFLAIVE's wines are named for characters and places in a local medieval tale. The Chevalier of Puligny-Montrachet, lonely for his son who was off fighting in the Crusades, amused himself in the ravine-like vineyards (Les Combettes) with a local maiden (Pucelle), only to welcome the arrival of another son (Bâtard-Montrachet) nine months later.

ESTATE-BOTTLED wine: The wine is made, produced, and bottled by the owner of the vineyard.

five years these wines have only gotten better. After overcoming serious frosts in the late fifties through improved methods of frost protection, the region has increased its vineyard acreage from 4,000 acres to 12,000 acres without losing its quality. Great news for the consumer.

The white wines of the Mâconnais and Châlonnaise represent some of the great value wines made from 100 percent Chardonnay, yet most are usually priced under twenty dollars a bottle.

One of the big changes, especially in Mâcon, is the inclusion of the grape variety on the label. With increased competition from the new-world Chardonnay producers, the French government has finally realized that Americans and other countries buy wines by the grape variety.

The great white wines of the Côte d'Or have achieved greatness in the last twenty-five years. For me these are the best white wines in the world! With a new generation of winemakers who have studied around the world, there is more control in the vineyards and in the cellars, plantings of new clones, and picking lower yields. Chaptalization, the addition of sugar to the fermenting juice to increase the alcohol content which was prevalent in Burgundy, is rarely used today. The wines today have a better natural balance.

FOR FURTHER READING

I recommend *Burgundy* by Anthony Hanson; *Burgundy* by Robert M. Parker Jr.; *The Wines of Burgundy* and *Côtes d'Or* by Clive Coates, M.W.; and *Making Sense of Burgundy* by Matt Kramer.

WINE AND FOOD

When you choose a white Burgundy wine, you have a whole gamut of wonderful food possibilities. Let's say that you decide upon a wine from the Mâconnais area: Very reasonably priced, Mâconnais wines are suitable for picnics, as well as for more formal dinners. Or, you might select one of the fuller-bodied Côte de Beaune wines, or, if you prefer, an all-purpose Chablis that can even stand up to a hearty steak. Here are some tempting combinations offered by the winemakers.

ROBERT DROUHIN: *With a young Chablis or St-Véran, Mr. Drouhin enjoys shellfish. "Fine Côte d'Or wines match well with any fish or light white meat such as veal or sweetbreads. But please, no red meat."*

CHRISTIAN MOREAU: *"A basic Village Chablis is good as an apéritif and with hors d'oeuvres and salads. A great Premier Cru or Grand Cru Chablis needs something more special, such as lobster. It's an especially beautiful match if the wine has been aged a few years."*

PIERRE HENRY GAGEY *(Louis Jadot): "My favorite food combination with white Burgundy wine is, without doubt, homard grillé Breton (blue lobster). Only harmonious, powerful, and delicate wines are able to go with the subtle, thin flesh and very fine taste of the Breton lobster."*

Mr. Gagey says Chablis is a great match for oysters, snails, and shellfish, but a "Grand Cru Chablis should be had with trout."

On white wines of the Côte de Beaune,

Mr. Gagey gets a bit more specific: "With Village wines, which should be had at the beginning of the meal, try a light fish or quenelles (light dumplings). Premier Cru and Grand Cru wines can stand up to heavier fish and shellfish such as lobster—but with a wine such as Corton-Charlemagne, smoked Scottish salmon is a tasty choice."

Mr. Gagey's parting words on the subject: "Never with meat."

LOUIS LATOUR: *"With Corton-Charlemagne, filet of sole in a light Florentine sauce. Otherwise, the Chardonnays of Burgundy complement roast chicken, seafood, and light-flavored goat cheese particularly well." Mr. Latour believes that one should have Chablis with oysters and fish.*

CLASS ONE: THE WHITE WINES OF FRANCE

Wines for Class One

1. Alsace: Trimbach Riesling 2007
2. Loire Valley: Muscadet, Marquis de Goulaine 2007 **BEST VALUE**
3. Loire Valley: Pouilly Fumé, Jolivet 2007
4. Bordeaux: (Graves, Pessac-Léognan) Château Carbonnieux 2005
5. Burgundy: Mâcon-Villages, Louis Jadot 2007 **BEST VALUE**
6. Burgundy: Chablis Premier Cru, Vaillon, Christian Moreau 2006
7. Burgundy: Meursault, Chanson 2006
8. Burgundy: Puligny-Montrachet, Les Folatières, Olivier Leflaive 2006
9. Alsace: Gewürztraminer Hugel 2005
10. Bordeaux: Sauternes: Château Latour Blanche 1999

There are six parts to this tasting.

PART I: ALSACE (ONE WINE, TASTED ALONE)

Wine #1: Trimbach Riesling 2007

This is the first wine of the course and I have selected it to set the tone for the next eight classes. It is a first-impression wine from the Alsace region, which has produced wines for hundreds of years. Riesling is their best grape. The Trimbach winery, established in 1626, is in its twelfth generation of family ownership and has a long history and tradition of producing high-quality wine.

I pour Trimbach Riesling first because it is unoaked and light in style, with the great fruit taste typical of this varietal. Alsace Rieslings generally have higher acidity, which turbo charges everyone's palate.

Retail price $18
Ready to drink
Other recommended producers in Alsace are: Domaine Marcel Deiss, Domaine Weinbach, Domaine Zind-Humbrecht, Dopff "Au Moulin," Hugel & Fils, and Leon Beyer.

WITH THIS first wine we learn how to taste wine using the 60-second wine expert tasting instructions (p. 14). Pay attention to the balance of fruit and acid, and note that some high acid wines will taste better with food, especially shellfish.

Part II: Loire Valley
(two wines, tasted together)

We now move our tasting into the Loire Valley with two totally different styles of wines, a Muscadet from the west coast of France and a Pouilly Fumé from farther inland. Both are well-known French white wines. Neither wine is aged in wood so they are fruit friendly without any oak overtones.

Wine #2: Muscadet, Marquis de Goulaine 2007

The Muscadet is made with a grape variety called Melon de Bourgogne, a grape that originated in Burgundy, France, and was transported to the Loire Valley. It should be tasted before the Pouilly Fumé because all Muscadets are lighter in style than Pouilly Fumés. Muscadet is a favorite wine in Parisian bistros because it is easy, light in style, and has balanced fruit and acid. It is ready to drink when you buy it: the earlier the vintage, the better.

IF YOU can't find a Pouilly Fumé, use a Sancerre.

> Retail price $14 **BEST VALUE**
> Ready to drink
> Other recommended producers for Muscadet are: Sauvion or Metaireau.

Wine #3: Pouilly Fumé, Jolivet 2007

Pouilly Fumé is made from 100 percent Sauvignon Blanc grapes. It is medium-bodied with more depth, complexity, and fruit concentration than the Muscadet. It also has a pungent aroma and bouquet that is instantly recognizable; some say that cat pee is an apt descriptor.

> Retail price $20
> Ready to drink
> Other recommended producers for Pouilly Fumé are: Michel Redde, Château de Tracy, Ladoucette, or Colin.

Section II: Oaked Wines

The next two wines are from the Côte de Beaune region of Burgundy. They are from the most famous villages—Meursault and Puligny-Montrachet. They represent two different Burgundy quality levels. The Meursault is a village wine and the Puligny-Montrachet is a Premier Cru.

Wine #7: Meursault, Chanson 2006 (Côte de Beaune)

Depending upon the producer, a Meursault can range in style from medium to heavy. It is usually a fuller wine than Puligny-Montrachet and is one of the classic French wines usually included on French restaurant wine lists, and often on American Contemporary wine lists. Chanson, which has a history going back to 1750, has gone through a metamorphosis over the last few years and is once again producing the style of wines I remember from early in my career. This wine has all the characteristics of a Village wine: great fruit, acid, and oak balance, and it is accessible now.

> Retail price $63
> Ready to drink
> Other producers recommended are: Bouchard Père & Fils, Joseph Drouhin, Labouré-Roi, Louis Jadot, Louis Latour, or Olivier Leflaive Frères.

Wine #8: Puligny-Montrachet, Les Folatières, Olivier LeFlaive 2006 (Côte de Beaune)

One of my favorite wines, Puligny-Montrachet, is a perfect compilation of what the French call *terroir*. This Puligny has tremendous fruit concentration with a subtle backbone of acidity because it's from a great producer and a great vintage. It's a wine that you can drink alone or one that will enhance nearly any meal. Les Folatières is one of the great vineyards located in the village of Puligny-Montrachet, and Olivier LeFlaive always produces a stylistically correct and high quality Puligny-Montrachet.

> Retail price $75
> Ready to drink, but can age
> Other recommended producers are: Bouchard Père & Fils, Joseph Drouhin, Labouré-Roi, Louis Jadot, or Louis Latour.

PART V: ALSACE (ONE WINE, TASTED ALONE)

Wine #9: Gewürztraminer Hugel 2005

One of my favorite "unique" wines, "Gewürtz" means spicy and the wine has a distinctive aroma and dry, citric, flavorful taste. The Hugel Family has been making wine since 1639. The last two wines must be served after the White Burgundies since they would overpower the delicate flavor of the Chardonnay grape.

Retail price $28
Ready to drink
Other recommended producers for Alsace wines are: Domaine Marcel Deiss, Domaine Weinbach, Domaine Zind-Humbrecht, Dopff "Au Moulin," Hugel & Fils, and Leon Beyer.

PART VI: BORDEAUX, SAUTERNES (ONE WINE, TASTED ALONE)

Wine # 10: Château Latour Blanche 1999

Tasting this wine is truly a remarkable experience for anyone, and a great way to end the first class. The primary grape is Sémillon. The viscosity, the smell of *botrytis*, the natural sweetness, and the long sweet acid finish leave everyone wanting more.

Retail Price $55
Ready to Drink
Other recommended producers for Sauternes are: Château Suduirat, Château Climens, Château Rieussec, Château Lafaurie-Peyraguey, or Château Doisy-Vedrines.

Questions for Class One:
The White Wines of France

                                                                                       REFER TO PAGE

1. Match grape variety with wine region.   23

    a. Riesling   ___Champagne

    b. Sauvignon Blanc   ___Loire Valley

    c. Chardonnay   ___Alsace

    d. Sémillon   ___Burgundy

    e. Gewürztraminer   ___Bordeaux

    f. Grenache   ___Côtes du Rhône

    g. Pinot Noir

    h. Cabernet Sauvignon

    i. Chenin Blanc

    j. Syrah

    k. Merlot

2. When were the Appellation d'Origine Contrôlée (AOC) laws established?   23

3. How many acres are there in a hectare?   24

4. How many gallons are there in a hectoliter?   24

5. What is one difference in style between a Riesling from Alsace and a Riesling from Germany?   25

6. What is the most planted grape in Alsace?   25

7. Name two important shippers of Alsace wine.   26

8. What is the grape variety for the wines Sancerre and Pouilly Fumé?   28

9. What is the grape variety for the wine Vouvray?   28

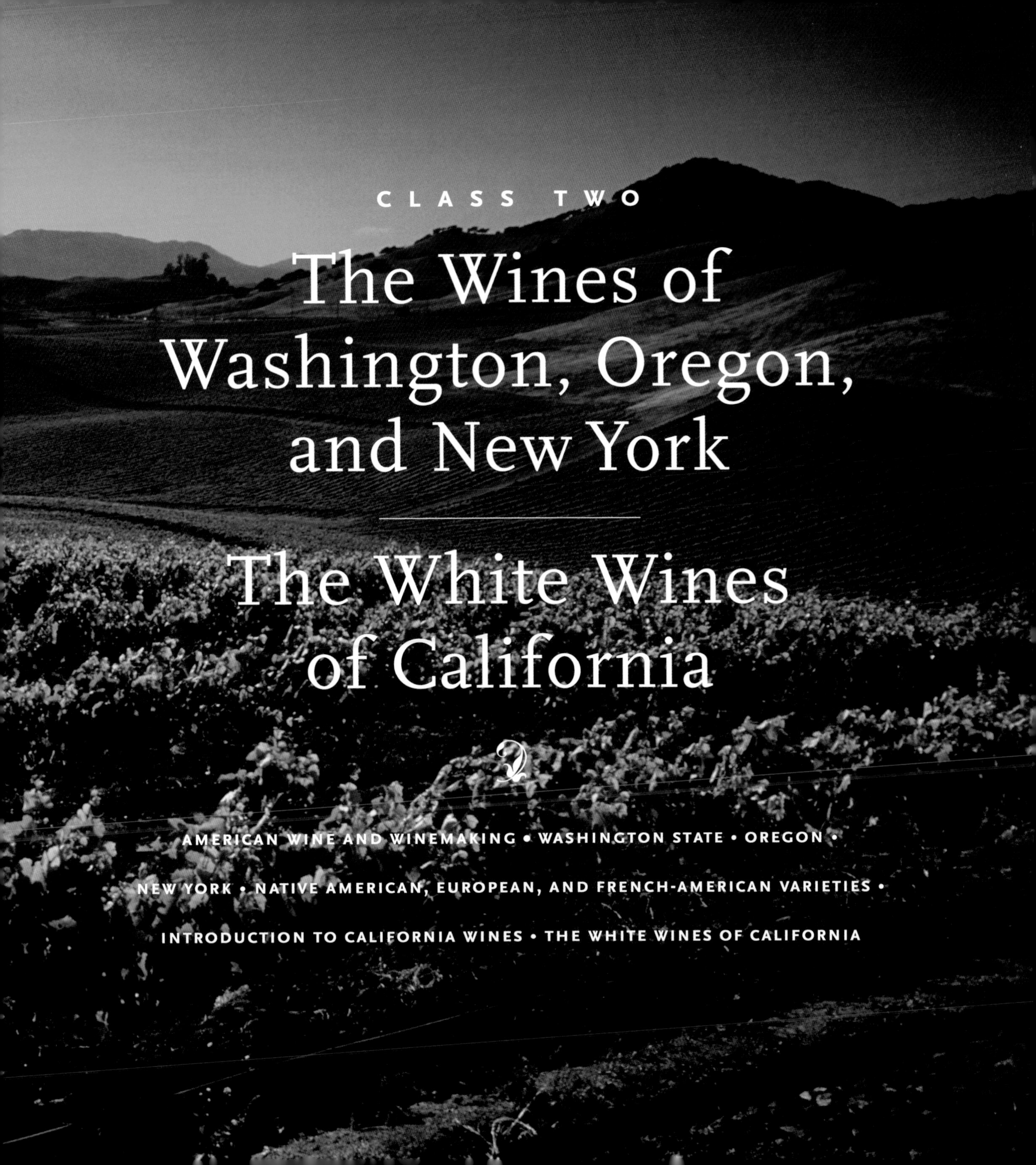

The Wines of Washington, Oregon, and New York

The White Wines of California

❧

AMERICAN WINE AND WINEMAKING • WASHINGTON STATE • OREGON •

NEW YORK • NATIVE AMERICAN, EUROPEAN, AND FRENCH-AMERICAN VARIETIES •

INTRODUCTION TO CALIFORNIA WINES • THE WHITE WINES OF CALIFORNIA

American Wine and Winemaking

AccORDING TO GALLUP, wine drinking has jumped by more than a third in the United States over the last twenty years, with about 30 percent of Americans drinking at least one glass of wine a week. Americans prefer domestic wines: more than three quarters of all wines consumed by Americans are produced in the United States. Meanwhile, the number of American wineries has doubled in the last two decades—to close to six thousand—and, for the first time in American history, all fifty states produce wine.

Because American wines are so dominant in the U.S. market, it makes sense to pause here and take a detailed look at winemaking in the United States. While we often think of the wine industry as "young" in America, in fact its roots go back some four hundred years.

What happened in the early days of winemaking in the United States?

A short time after arriving in America, the Pilgrims and early pioneers, accustomed to drinking wine with meals, were delighted to find grapevines growing wild. These thrifty, self-reliant colonists thought they had found in this species (*Vitis labrusca*, primarily) a means of producing their own wine, which would end their dependency on costly wine from Europe. They cultivated the existing local grapevines, harvested the grapes, and made their first American wine. The new vintage possessed an entirely different (and disappointing) flavor compared to wine made from European grapes. Cuttings were ordered from Europe of the *Vitis vinifera* vine, which had for centuries produced the finest wines in the world. Soon ships arrived bearing the tender cuttings, and the colonists, having paid scarce, hard-earned money for these new vines, planted and tended them with great care. They were eager to taste their first wine made from European grapes grown in American soil.

Despite their efforts, few of the European vines thrived. Many died, and those that survived produced few grapes, whose meager yield resulted in very poor quality wine. Early settlers blamed the cold climate, but today we know that their European vines lacked immunity to the New World's plant diseases and pests. For the next two hundred years every attempt at establishing varieties of vinifera—either intact or through crossbreeding with native vines—

LEIF ERIKSSON, upon discovering North America, named it Vineland. In fact, there are more species of native grapes in North America than on any other continent.

THE FRENCH Huguenots established colonies in Jacksonville, Florida, in 1562 and produced wine using the wild Scuppernong grape. Evidence indicates that there was a flourishing wine industry in 1609 at the site of the early Jamestown settlements. In 2004 an old wine cellar was discovered in Jamestown with an empty bottle dating back to the 17th century.

WILLIAM PENN planted the first vineyard in Pennsylvania in 1683.

EARLY GERMAN immigrants imported Riesling grapes and called their finished wine Hock; the French called their wine Burgundy or Bordeaux; and the Italians borrowed the name "Chianti" for theirs.

failed. Left with no choice, growers throughout the Northeast and Midwest returned to planting *Vitis labrusca*, North America's vine, and a small wine industry managed to survive.

European wine remained the preferred—though high-priced—choice. The failures of these early attempts to establish a wine industry in the United States, along with the high cost of imported wines, resulted in decreasing demand for wine. Gradually, American tastes changed and wine served at mealtime was reserved for special occasions; beer and whiskey had taken over wine's traditional place in American homes.

VITIS LABRUSCA, the "slip-skinned" grape, is native to both the Northeast and the Midwest and produces a unique flavor. It is used in making grape juice—the bottled kind you'll find on supermarket shelves. Wine produced from *labrusca* grapes tastes, well, more "grapey" (also described as "foxy") than that from European wines.

The major varieties of wine produced in the U.S. are made from these species:
American: *Vitis labrusca*, such as the Concord, Catawba, and Delaware; and *Vitis rotundifolia*, commonly called Scuppernong
European: *Vitis vinifera*, such as Riesling, Sauvignon Blanc, Chardonnay, Pinot Noir, Merlot, Cabernet Sauvignon, Zinfandel, and Syrah
Hybrids: A cross between *vinifera* and a native American species, such as Seyval Blanc, Vidal Blanc, Baco Noir, and Chancellor

---

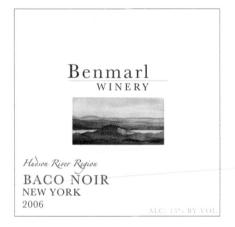

When I think of American wines I think of California. How and when did wine arrive in the West?

Wine production in the West began with the Spanish. As the Spanish settlers began pushing northward from Mexico, the Catholic Church followed, and a great era of mission building began. Early missions were more than just churches; they were entire communities conceived as self-sufficient fortifications protecting Spanish colonial interests throughout the Southwest and along the Pacific Coast. Besides growing their own food and making their own clothing, those early settlers also made their own wine, produced primarily for use in the Church. The demand for wine led Padre Junípero Serra to bring *Vitis vinifera* vines—brought to Mexico by the Spaniards—from Mexico to California in 1769. These vines took root, thriving in California due to its moderate climate. The first true California wine industry had been established, albeit on a small scale.

Two events occurred in the mid-1800s that resulted in an explosive growth of quality wine production. The first was the California Gold Rush in 1849, which brought immigrants from Europe and the East Coast along with

THE EARLY missionaries established wineries in the southern parts of California. The first commercial winery was established in what we know today as Los Angeles.

THE GRAPE variety the missionaries used to make their sacramental wine was actually called the Mission grape. Unfortunately, it did not have the potential to produce a great wine.

their winemaking traditions. They cultivated the vines and were soon producing good-quality commercial wine.

The second critical event occurred in 1861, when the governor of California, understanding the importance of viticulture to the state's growing economy, commissioned Count Agoston Haraszthy to select and import classic *Vitis vinifera* cuttings—such as Riesling, Zinfandel, Cabernet Sauvignon, and Chardonnay—from Europe. The count traveled to Europe, returning with more than one hundred thousand carefully selected vines. Not only did these grape varieties thrive in California's climate, they also produced good-quality wine! Serious California winemaking began in earnest.

So, the rest, as they say, is history?

Not at all. In 1863, while California wines were flourishing, European vineyards were in trouble. Phylloxera—an aphid pest native to the East Coast that is very destructive to grape crops—began attacking European vineyards. This infestation, which arrived in Europe on cuttings from native American vines exported for experimental purposes, proved devastating. Over the next two decades, the phylloxera blight destroyed thousands of acres of European vines, severely diminishing European wine production just as demand was rapidly growing.

Since California was now virtually the only area in the world producing wine made from European grapes, demand for its wines skyrocketed. This helped develop, almost overnight, two huge markets for California wine. The first market clamored for good, inexpensive, yet drinkable wine produced on a mass scale. The second market sought higher-quality wines. California growers responded to both demands, and by 1876 California was producing more than 2.3 million gallons of wine per year, some of remarkable quality. California was, for the moment, the new center of global winemaking.

Unfortunately, in that same year, phylloxera arrived in California and began attacking its vineyards. Once it got there, it spread as rapidly as it had in Europe. With thousands of vines dying, the California wine industry faced financial ruin. To this day, the phylloxera blight remains the most destructive crop epidemic of all time.

Luckily, other states had continued producing wine made from *labrusca* vines, and American wine production didn't grind to a complete halt. Meanwhile, after years of research, European winemakers finally found a defense against the pernicious phylloxera aphid. They were the first to successfully graft *Vitis vinifera* vines onto the rootstock of *labrusca* vines (which were immune to the phylloxera), rescuing their wine industry.

Americans followed, and the California wine industry not only recovered but began producing better-quality wines than ever before. By the late 1800s, California wines were winning medals in international competition, gaining the respect and admiration of the world. And it took only three hundred years!

FORTY DIFFERENT American wineries won medals at the 1900 Paris Exposition, including those from California, New Jersey, New York, Ohio, and Virginia.

Prohibition: Yet Another Setback

In 1920, the Eighteenth Amendment to the United States Constitution created yet another setback for the American wine industry. The National Prohibition Act, also known as the Volstead Act, prohibited the manufacture, sale, transportation, importation, exportation, delivery, or possession of intoxicating liquors for beverage purposes. Prohibition, which continued for thirteen years, nearly destroyed what had become a thriving and national industry.

IN 1920 there were more than 700 wineries in California. By the end of Prohibition there were 160.

One of the loopholes in the Volstead Act allowed for the manufacture and sale of sacramental wine, medicinal wines for sale by pharmacists with a doctor's prescription, and medicinal wine tonics (fortified wines) sold without prescription. Perhaps more important, Prohibition allowed anyone to produce up to two hundred gallons yearly of fruit juice or cider. The fruit juice, which was sometimes made into concentrate, was ideal for making wine. People would buy grape concentrate from California and have it shipped to the East Coast. The top of the container was stamped in big, bold letters: caution: do not add sugar or yeast or else fermentation will take place! Some of this yield found its way to bootleggers throughout America who did just that. But not for long, because the government stepped in and banned the sale of grape juice, preventing illegal wine production. Vineyards stopped being planted, and the American wine industry came to a halt.

"Once, during Prohibition, I was forced to live for days on nothing but food and water."
—W. C. FIELDS

Fortified wine, or medicinal wine tonic—containing about 20 percent alcohol, which makes it more like a distilled spirit than regular wine—was still available and became America's number-one wine. American wine was soon popular more for its effect than its taste; in fact, the word *wino* came into use during the Depression from the name given to those unfortunate souls who turned to fortified wine to forget their troubles.

Prohibition came to an end in 1933, but its impact would be felt for decades. By its end, Americans had lost interest in quality wine. During

SOME OF THE dilemmas facing winemakers after Prohibition:

Locate on the East Coast or the West Coast?

Make sweet wine or dry wine?

Make high-alcohol wine or low-alcohol wine?

Make inexpensive bulk wine or premium wine?

BEST-SELLING wineries, from 1933 to 1968, were Almaden, Gallo, and Paul Masson.

IN 1933, more than 60% of wine sold in the United States contained more than 20% alcohol.

SOME EXAMPLES of fortified wine may be familiar to consumers today. The list includes Thunderbird and Wild Irish Rose.

THE BEST-KNOWN wineries of California in the 1960s and 1970s:

Almaden	Korbel
Beaulieu	Krug
Beringer	Martini
Concannon	Paul Masson
Inglenook	Wente

Prohibition, thousands of acres of valuable grapes around the country had been plowed under. Wineries nationwide shut down and the winemaking industry dwindled to a handful of survivors, mostly in California and New York. Many growers on the East Coast returned to producing grape juice—the ideal use for the American *labrusca* grape. From 1933 to 1968, grape growers and winemakers had little more than personal incentive to produce any wine of quality. Jug wines, which got their name from the containers in which they were bottled, were inexpensive, nondescript, and mass produced. A few wineries, notably in California, were producing some good wines, but the majority of American wines produced during this period were ordinary.

Although Prohibition was devastating to the majority of American wine producers, some endured by making sacramental wines. Beringer, Beaulieu, and the Christian Brothers are a few of the wineries that managed to survive this dry time. Since these wineries didn't have to interrupt production during Prohibition, they had a jump on those that had to start all over.

The federal government, in repealing Prohibition, empowered states to legislate the sale and transportation of alcohol. Some states handed control to counties and, occasionally, even municipalities—a tradition that continues today, varying from state to state and often from county to county.

The Renaissance of American Wine

I can't say when, exactly, the American wine renaissance began, but let's start in 1968, when, for the first time since Prohibition, table wines—wines with alcohol content between 7 and 14 percent—outsold fortified wines. Although American wines were improving, consumers still believed the best wines were made in Europe, especially France.

In the midsixties and early seventies, a small group of dedicated California winemakers began concentrating on making high-quality wine to equal Europe's best. Their early wines demonstrated potential and began attracting the attention of astute wine writers and wine enthusiasts around the country.

As they continued to improve their product, these same winemakers began to realize that they had to find a way to differentiate their quality wines from California's mass-produced wines—which had such generic names as Burgundy, Chablis, or Chianti—and to ally their wines, at least in the minds of wine buyers and consumers, with European wines. Their solution was brilliant: They chose to label their best wines by varietal.

Varietal designation calls the wine by the name of the predominant grape used to produce it: Chardonnay, Cabernet Sauvignon, Pinot Noir, etc. The savvy consumer learned that a wine labeled Chardonnay would have the general characteristics of any wine made from that grape. This made wine buying easier for both wine buyers and sellers.

Varietal labeling quickly spread throughout the industry and became so successful that, in the eighties, varietal designation became an American industry standard, forcing the federal government to revise its labeling regulations.

Today, varietal labeling is the norm for the highest-quality American wines, has been adopted by many other countries, and has helped bring worldwide attention to California wine. While California still produces 90 percent of American wine, its success has inspired winemakers in other areas of the United States to refocus on producing high-quality wines.

Where exactly do they make these quality American wines?

To buy American wines intelligently means having knowledge about and familiarity with each state whose wine you're interested in buying, as well as the regions within the state. Some states—or even regions within a state—may specialize in white wine, others in red; and there are even regions that specialize in wine made from a specific grape variety. Therefore, it is helpful to know the defined grape-growing areas within each state or region, the American Viticultural Areas (AVAs).

An AVA, or American Viticultural Area, is a specific grape-growing area within a state or a region recognized by and registered with the federal government. AVA designation began in the 1980s and is a system styled after the European regional system. In France, Bordeaux and Burgundy are strictly enforced regional appellations (marked *Appellation d'Origine Contrôlée*, or AOC); in Italy, Tuscany and Piedmont are recognized as zones (marked *Denominazione di Origine Controllata,* or DOC).

The Napa Valley, for example, is a defined viticultural area in the state of California. Columbia Valley is an AVA located in Washington State; both Oregon's Willamette Valley and New York's Finger Lakes district are similarly identified.

Vintners are discovering, as their European counterparts did years ago, which grapes grow best in which particular soils and climatic conditions.

IN THE early 1970s, Chenin Blanc was the best-selling white wine and Zinfandel the best-selling red.

THREE MAJOR grapes consumed by Americans are:
1. Chardonnay
2. Cabernet Sauvignon
3. Merlot

THERE ARE more than two hundred viticultural areas in the United States, 108 of which are located in California.

THE UNITED STATES

511/9 Washington

321/16 Oregon

36/1 Idaho

9 Montana

7 North Dakota

15 South Dakota

2 Wyoming

3 Nevada

3 Utah

80/1 Colorado

2219/108 California

37/1 Arizona

35/3 New Mexico

26 Nebraska

17 Kansas

49/1 Oklahoma

150/8 Texas

33/1 Minnesota

47/1 Wisconsin

67 Iowa

90/4 Missouri

9/3 Arkansas

5/1 Louisiana

28/1 Mississippi

9 Alabama

100/4 Michigan

84/1 Illinois

40/1 Indiana

106/6 Ohio

20/3 W.V.

40/1 Kentucky

33/1 Tennessee

25 Georgia

10 South Carolina

86/1 North Carolina

152/6 Virginia

127/5 Pennsylvania

232/9 New York

15 Maine

Vermont 15

New Hampshire 16

Mass. 23/2

R.I. 7/1

Conn. 29/2

New Jersey 40/3

Delaware 2

Maryland 37/3

Florida 42

Hawaii 5   Alaska 5

67 Number of bonded wineries in state

4 Number of AVAs in state

Pacific Ocean

CANADA

MEXICO

Gulf of Mexico

Atlantic Ocean

o Miles 250 500

o Kilometers 500

THE TOP TEN STATES IN NUMBER OF WINERIES

1. California (2,219)
2. Washington (511)
3. Oregon (321)
4. New York (232)
5. Virginia (152)
6. Texas (150)
7. Pennsylvania (127)
8. Ohio (106)
9. Michigan (100)
10. Missouri (90)

Source: Wine Business Monthly

I believe the AVA concept is important to wine buying and will continue to be so as individual AVAs become known for certain grape varieties or wine styles. If an AVA is listed on the label, at least 85 percent of the grapes must come from that region.

For example, let's look at the Napa Valley, which is probably the best-known AVA in the United States, renowned for its Cabernet Sauvignon. Within Napa, there is a smaller inner district called Carneros, which has a cooler climate. Since Chardonnay and Pinot Noir need a cooler growing season to mature properly, these grape varieties are especially suited to that AVA. In New York, the Finger Lakes region is noted for Riesling. And those of you who have seen the movie *Sideways* know that Santa Barbara is a great place for Pinot Noir.

Although not necessarily a guarantee of quality, an AVA designation identifies a specific area well known and established for its wine. It is a point of reference for winemakers and consumers. A wine can be better understood by its provenance, or where it came from. The more knowledge you have about a wine's origin by region and grape, the easier it is to buy even unknown brands with confidence. As you learn more about the characteristics of major grapes and styles of wine—and which you prefer—you'll be able to identify the AVAs that produce wines you're most likely to enjoy.

Is that all I need to know?

There is more: An even higher quality of wine is now given a "proprietary" name.

The most recent worldwide trend is to ignore all existing standards by giving the highest-quality wines a proprietary name. A proprietary name helps high-end wineries differentiate their best wines from other wines from the same AVA, from similar varietals, and even from their own other offerings. In the United States, many of these proprietary wines fall under the category called Meritage (see page 180). Some examples of American proprietary wines are Dominus, Opus One, and Rubicon.

Federal laws governing standards and labels are another reason select wineries are increasingly using proprietary names. Federal law mandates, for example, that if a label lists a varietal, at least 75 percent of the grapes used to make the wine must be of that varietal.

Imagine a talented, innovative winemaker in the Columbia Valley region of Washington State. This winemaker is determined to produce an outstanding, full-bodied Bordeaux-style wine consisting of 60 percent Cabernet Sauvignon blended with several other grapes. Our ambitious winemaker has invested considerable time and labor to produce a really great wine: a wine suitable for aging that will be ready to drink in five years—but will be even better in ten.

After five years, our winemaker tastes the fruits of his labor and voilà! It is delicious, with all the promise of a truly outstanding wine. But how does he distinguish this wine; how can he attract buyers willing to pay a premium price for an unknown wine? He can't label it Cabernet Sauvignon, because less than 75 percent of the grapes used are of that type. For this reason, many producers of fine wine are beginning to use proprietary names. It's indicative of the healthy state of the American wine industry as well. More and more winemakers are turning out better and better wines, and the very best is yet to come!

IN 2008, there were more 5,900 wineries in the United States, up from 580 in 1975. Ninety-nine percent are small and family owned.

THE MAJORITY (57%) of American wineries are located in states other than California.

TOP FIVE STATES IN WINE PRODUCTION (2008)

1. California (3.4 million tons of grapes crushed for wine)
2. Washington (145,000 tons)
3. New York (45,000 tons)
4. Oregon (40,000 tons)
5. Pennsylvania (13,200 tons)

WINERIES IN the United States are opening at the rate of 300 per year.

OPUS ONE

THE TOP SEVEN STATES IN WINE CONSUMPTION

1. California
2. New York
3. Florida
4. Texas
5. Illinois
6. New Jersey
7. Pennsylvania

The "Big Four" of U.S. Winemaking

WASHINGTON

WASHINGTON
PUGET SOUND
•Seattle
COLUMBIA VALLEY
Spokane•
•Tacoma
Olympia
WAHLUKE SLOPE
RATTLESNAKE HILLS
Yakima•
RED MOUNTAIN
YAKIMA VALLEY
Richland
HORSE HEAVEN HILLS
Vancouver•
WALLA WALLA VALLEY
COLUMBIA GORGE

0 Miles 100
0 Kilometers 200

Pacific Ocean

WASHINGTON IS the second-largest wine-producing state.

THE PACIFIC NORTHWEST winegrowing region includes Washington, Oregon, and Idaho in the United States and British Columbia in Canada.

BEFORE WE TACKLE the exciting world of California wines, I'd like to talk about three other major winemaking regions in the United States: Washington State, Oregon, and New York State.

THE WINES OF WASHINGTON STATE

I began teaching about the vineyards and wines of Washington State in the early 1970s, just as I was starting out as a wine educator and only a few years after Washington had begun producing its first quality wine. Forty years later, Washington's wine industry has matured considerably and within the state there are some of the best wine regions of the world.

It has taken Americans a while to understand and appreciate the wines of Washington State for many reasons, not the least of which is weather. Ask the average American wine drinker about winemaking in this northwestern U.S. region and one of the most common responses you'll get is, "How do you make great wine in a rainy climate like Seattle's?"

Of course, Washington State is also split into two regions—the east and the west—by the Cascade Mountains, which include two active volcanoes, Mount Rainier and Mount St. Helens. On the eastern side of this mountain range, geologic cataclysms—dramatic lava flows from fifteen million years ago and monstrous floods that took place during the last Ice Age—created soil conditions ideal for growing superior grapes and making high-quality wine. There is an enormous difference between Washington's west-coast maritime climate and its eastern continental climate: sixty inches of annual rainfall along the Pacific coast versus eight inches in eastern Washington where wine grapes thrive in its arid, hot summers. The eastern wine-growing region also has an ideal irrigation system that is partly sourced from the Columbia River, which helps produce perfectly ripe grapes.

Unlike California, Washington's winemaking history is all about the present and future, not about the past, and the recent changes have not been *bam*, but *boom*! Some say, "A new winery opens in Washington every week."

After only ten wineries in 1970, there are more than five hundred today. It was wheat to grapes, orchards to vineyards, and Rieslings to reds (think Cabernet Sauvignon, Merlot, and Syrah). Still, Washington State remains the number-one American producer of Riesling, and its Chardonnays, with their balance, great fruit, and lively acidity, are some of the best in the country.

What are the major grapes grown in Washington State?

The major white grapes are:

Chardonnay (6,000 acres)   *Sauvignon Blanc* (990 acres)

Riesling (4,400 acres)   *Gewürztraminer* (630 acres)

The major red grapes are:

Cabernet Sauvignon (6,000 acres)   *Syrah* (2,800 acres)

Merlot (5,800 acres)

What are the wine regions of Washington State?

AVA (Date AVA established)	
Yakima Valley (1983)	*Red Mountain* (2001)
Walla Walla Valley (1984)	*Columbia Gorge* (2004)
Columbia Valley* (1984)	*Horse Heaven Hills* (2005)
Puget Sound (1995)	*Wahluke Slope* (2006)
	Rattlesnake Hills (2006)

*Largest viticultural area, responsible for 95 percent of wine production.

BEST BETS FOR WASHINGTON WINES

2001*   2002*   2003   2004*   2005*   2006*   2007*   2008

Note: * signifies exceptional vintage

FOR FURTHER READING

Washington Wines & Wineries, The Essential Guide by Paul Gregutt.

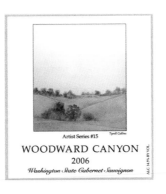

WASHINGTON STATE's wine production is 56% white versus 44% red.

CHATEAU STE. MICHELLE is the world's largest Riesling producer and has recently formed a winemaking partnership with the famous German wine producer Dr. Loosen to produce a new Riesling wine called Eroica.

California	Washington
470,000 acres	31,000+ acres
2,219 wineries	511 wineries
Oregon	**New York**
17,400 acres	30,000 acres
321 wineries	232 wineries

KEVIN ZRALY'S FAVORITE WASHINGTON STATE PRODUCERS

Andrew Hill	Hogue Cellars
Betz	L'Ecole No. 41
Canoe Ridge	Leonetti Cellars
Cayuse	McCrea Cellars
Chateau	Pepper Bridge
Ste. Michelle	Quilceda Creek
Columbia Crest	Seven Hills
Columbia Winery	Woodward Canyon
DiStefano	Winery

THE WINES OF OREGON

The Burgundy of the United States

Although grapes were planted and wine was made as early as 1847, Oregon's modern viticultural era began roughly forty years ago with a handful of intrepid wine pioneers including David Lett (Erie winery), Dick Erath (Erath winery), and Dick Ponzi (Ponzi winery). This new breed of grape growers and winemakers were convinced that the cool-climate varietals such as Pinot Noir, Chardonnay, and Pinot Gris would not only grow in Oregon, but would produce world-class wines as well—and they have! What separated Oregon winemaking from its neighbors in California and Washington was their importation of French clones from Burgundy and Alsace.

Most of the Oregon wineries are small, family-owned, artisanal producers. Their proximity to the city of Portland and Oregon's beautiful coastline make this a "must visit" wine region.

Past and Present
1970
5 wineries and 35 acres
2008
321 wineries and 17,400 acres

COLUMBIA VALLEY and Walla Walla Valley are AVAs whose boundaries encompass parts of Oregon as well as Washington state.

MORE THAN 70% of Oregon wineries are located in the Willamette Valley.

BOTH THE Willamette Valley and Burgundy, France, are located at 45 degrees north latitude.

What are the major grapes grown in Oregon?

> **Pinot Noir** (9,858 acres)
> **Pinot Gris** (2,588 acres)
> **Chardonnay** (972 acres)

What are the major wine regions in Oregon?

Oregon has sixteen AVAs. Here are the ones you are most likely to find in wine stores:

AVA (Date AVA established)

Willamette Valley (1984)
Umpqua Valley (2004)
Rogue Valley (2004)
Applegate Valley (2004)

Kevin Zraly's Favorite Oregon Wineries

ARCHERY SUMMIT
ARGYLE
ADELSHEIM
BEAUX FRÈRES
BERGSTRÖM
BETHEL HEIGHTS
CRISTOM
DOMAINE DROUHIN
DOMAINE SERENE
ERATH

EYRIE
KEN WRIGHT
KING ESTATE
PONZI
REX HILL
SHEA
SOKOL BLOSSER
SOTER
ST. INNOCENT
TUALATIN

BEST BETS FOR WINES FROM OREGON

2002*   2004*   2005*   2006*   2007   2008

Note: * signifies exceptional vintage

FOR FURTHER READING

I recommend *The Oxford Companion to the Wines of North America* by Bruce Cass and Jancis Robinson; *The Wines of the Pacific Northwest* by Lisa Shara Hall; and *The Northwest Wine Guide* by Andy Perdue.

OVER HALF of Oregon's vineyards are planted with Pinot Noir.

OREGON STATE law requires that a wine labeled Pinot Noir must contain 100% Pinot Noir.

BEFORE SIDEWAYS: IN SEARCH OF THE BEST PINOT NOIR

One of the great wine festivals in the United States is the International Pinot Noir Celebration, which has been held in Oregon since 1987.

THE KING Estate in Oregon is the largest producer of Pinot Gris in the United States.

NEW YORK's Hudson Valley is one of America's oldest winegrowing regions. French Huguenots planted the grapevines in the 1600s. The Hudson Valley also boasts the oldest active winery in the United States—Brotherhood, which recorded its first vintage in 1839.

THE FIRST winery on Long Island was started in 1973 by Alex and Louisa Hargrave.

THE WINES OF NEW YORK STATE

New York is the third largest wine-producing state in the United States, with nine AVAs. The three premium wine regions in New York are:

Finger Lakes: with the largest wine production east of California
Hudson Valley: concentrating on premium farm wineries
Long Island: New York's red wine region

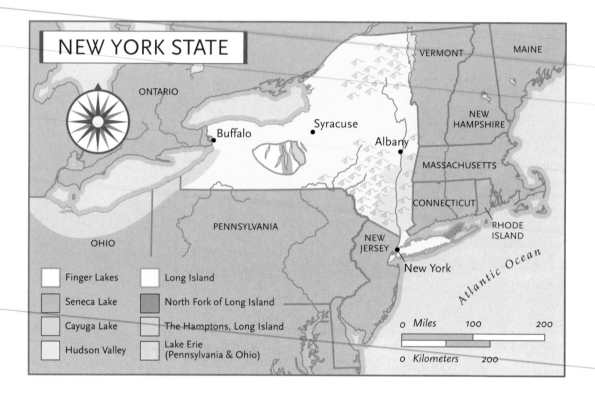

THE THREE AVAs on Long Island are the North Fork, the Hamptons, and Long Island.

Which grapes grow in New York State?

There are three main categories:

Native American: *Vitis labrusca*
European: *Vitis vinifera*
French-American: hybrids

NATIVE AMERICAN VARIETIES

The *Vitis labrusca* vines are very popular among grape growers in New York because they are hardy grapes that can withstand cold winters. Among the most familiar grapes of the *Vitis labrusca* family are Concord, Catawba, and Delaware. Until the last decade, these were the grapes that were used to make most New York wines. In describing these wines, words such as "foxy," "grapey," "Welch's," and "Manischewitz" are often used. These words are a sure sign of *Vitis labrusca*.

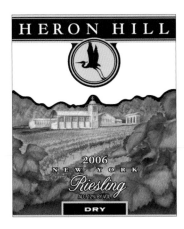
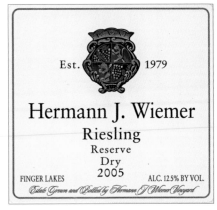

EUROPEAN VARIETIES

Forty years ago, some New York wineries began to experiment with the traditional European (*Vitis vinifera*) grapes. Dr. Konstantin Frank, a Russian viticulturist skilled in cold-climate grape growing, came to the United States and catalyzed efforts to grow *Vitis vinifera* in New York. This was unheard of—and laughed at—back then. Other vintners predicted that he'd fail, that it was impossible to grow *vinifera* in New York's cold and capricious climate.

"What do you mean?" Dr. Frank replied. "I'm from Russia—it's even colder there."

Most people were still skeptical, but Charles Fournier of Gold Seal Vineyards was intrigued enough to give Konstantin Frank a chance to prove his theory. Sure enough, Dr. Frank was successful with the *vinifera* and has produced some world-class wines, especially his Riesling and Chardonnay. So have many other New York wineries, thanks to the vision and courage of Dr. Frank and Charles Fournier.

THE CLIMATE on Long Island has more than 200 days of sunshine and a longer growing season, making it perfect for Merlot- and Bordeaux-style wines.

EXAMPLES OF *Vitis vinifera* grapes are Pinot Grigio, Riesling, Sauvignon Blanc, Chardonnay, Pinot Noir, Merlot, Cabernet Sauvignon, and Syrah.

THERE ARE more than 200 wineries in New York State, up from just 19 in 1975. In the three major regions, the Finger Lakes region has 73, the Hudson Valley has 28, and Long Island has 33.

WINERIES TO LOOK
FOR IN NEW YORK STATE

The Finger Lakes
Dr. Konstantin Frank
Glenora
Hermann Wiemer
Heron Hill
Wagner
Fox Run
Standing Stone
Château Lafayette-Reneau
Red Newt

The Hudson Valley
Benmarl
Brotherhood
Millbrook
Rivendell
Clinton Vineyards

Long Island
Lenz
Castello di Borghese (Hargrave)
Pindar
Palmer
Raphael
Schneider
Shinn Estate
Galluccio Estates
Pellegrini
Bedell
Wölffer
Paumanok
Channing Daughters
Osprey's Dominion
Peconic Bay

THE FINGER LAKES wineries produce 85% of New York's wine.

2007 IS the best vintage in New York State since 1995.

FRENCH-AMERICAN VARIETIES

Some New York and East Coast winemakers have planted French-American hybrid varieties, which combine European taste characteristics with American vine hardiness to withstand the cold winters in the Northeast. French viticulturists originally developed these varieties in the nineteenth century. Seyval Blanc and Vidal are the most prominent white wine varieties; Baco Noir and Chancellor are the most common reds.

Twenty-five years later in New York

The most significant developments are taking place on Long Island and in the Finger Lakes region. Both have experienced tremendous growth of new vineyards. Over the last twenty-five years on Long Island, grape-growing acreage has increased from one hundred acres to more than three thousand acres, with more expansion expected in the future.

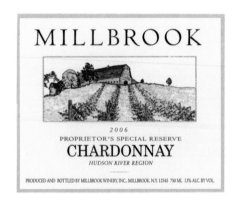

The predominant use of *Vitis vinifera* varieties allows Long Island wineries to compete more effectively in the world market, and Long Island's longer growing season offers greater potential for red grapes.

The Millbrook Winery in the Hudson Valley has shown that this region can produce world-class wines—not only white, but red too, from such grapes as Pinot Noir and Cabernet Franc.

The wines of the Finger Lakes region continue to get better as the winemakers work with grapes that thrive in the cooler climate, including European varieties such as Riesling, Chardonnay, and Pinot Noir.

THE WINES OF CALIFORNIA

CALIFORNIA WINES dominate American wine consumption, equaling 65% of all sales in the United States.

THERE ARE more than 60,000 wine labels registered in California.

No winegrowing area in the world has come so far so quickly as California. It seems ironic, because Americans historically have not been very interested in wine. But from the moment Americans first became "wine conscious," wine-makers in California rose to the challenge. Thirty years ago we were asking if California wines were entitled to be compared to European wines. Now California wines are available worldwide—exports have increased dramatically in recent years to countries such as Japan, Germany, and England. California produces more than 90 percent of U.S. wine. If the state were a nation, it would be the third leading wine producer in the world!

AN INTRODUCTION TO CALIFORNIA WINES

What are the main viticultural areas of California?

The map on this page should help familiarize you with the wine-making regions. It's easier to remember them if you divide them into four groups:

> **North Coast:** Napa County, Sonoma County, Mendocino County, Lake County (*Best wines: Cabernet Sauvignon, Zinfandel, Sauvignon Blanc, Chardonnay, Merlot*)
> **North Central Coast:** Monterey County, Santa Clara County, Livermore County (*Best wines: Chardonnay, Syrah, Grenache, Viognier, Marsanne, Roussane*)
> **South Central Coast:** San Luis Obispo County, Santa Barbara County (*Best wines: Sauvignon Blanc, Chardonnay, Pinot Noir, Syrah*)
> **San Joaquin Valley:** Known for jug wines, see page 72

Although you may be most familiar with the names Napa and Sonoma, less than 10 percent of all California wine comes from these two regions combined. Even so, Napa alone accounts for over 30 percent of dollar sales of California wines. In fact, the bulk

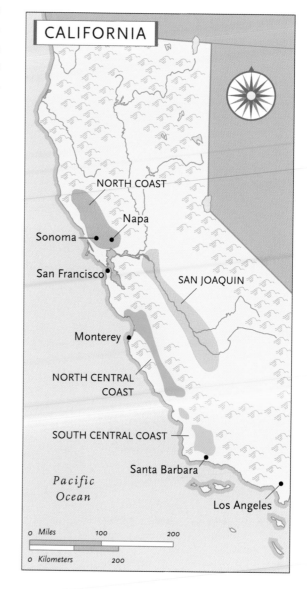

NORTH COAST, CALIFORNIA

0 Miles 20 40

0 Kilometers 40

MENDOCINO COUNTY

LAKE COUNTY

- Benmore Valley
- Clear Lake
- Guenoc Valley

Pacific Ocean

Ukiah •

LAKE COUNTY

Lakeport •

YOLO

MENDOCINO COUNTY

- Alexander Valley
- Cole Ranch
- McDowell Valley
- Mendocino Ridge
- Potter Valley
- Redwood Valley
- Yorkville Highlands

SONOMA COUNTY

NAPA COUNTY

Napa •

Sonoma •

SOLANO

MARIN

San Francisco •

THERE ARE more than 470,000 acres of vineyards in California.

ACRES OF wine grapes planted in Napa: 43,259

NUMBER OF wineries in Napa: 391

TOP GRAPES PLANTED IN NAPA

1. Cabernet Sauvignon (18,045 acres)
2. Merlot (7,281 acres)
3. Chardonnay (6,989 acres)

1838: First wine grapes planted in Napa.

of California wine is from the San Joaquin Valley, where mostly jug wines are produced. This region accounts for 58 percent of the wine grapes planted. Maybe that doesn't seem too exciting—that the production of jug wine dominates California winemaking history—but Americans are not atypical in their preferences for this type of wine. In France, for example, AOC wines account for only 35 percent of all French wines, while the rest are everyday table wines.

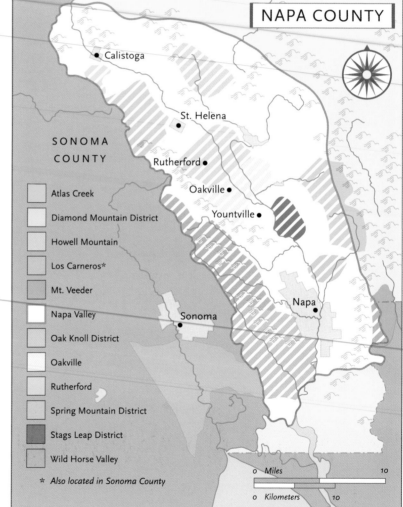

NAPA COUNTY

Calistoga •

St. Helena •

SONOMA COUNTY

Rutherford •

- Atlas Creek
- Diamond Mountain District
- Howell Mountain
- Los Carneros*
- Mt. Veeder
- Napa Valley
- Oak Knoll District
- Oakville
- Rutherford
- Spring Mountain District
- Stags Leap District
- Wild Horse Valley

Oakville •

Yountville •

Napa •

Sonoma •

* Also located in Sonoma County

0 Miles 10

0 Kilometers 10

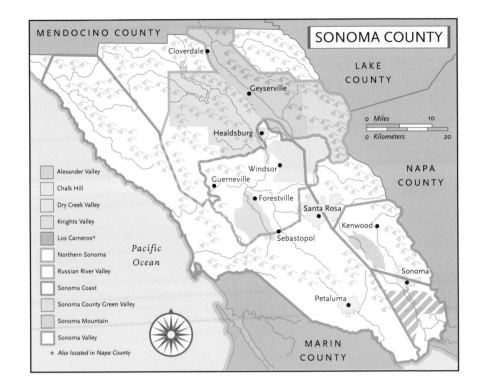

MENDOCINO COUNTY

SONOMA COUNTY

LAKE COUNTY

Cloverdale

Geyserville

0 Miles 10
0 Kilometers 20

Healdsburg

NAPA COUNTY

Windsor
Guerneville

Forestville

Santa Rosa

Kenwood

*Pacific
Ocean*

Sebastopol

Sonoma

Petaluma

MARIN COUNTY

Alexander Valley
Chalk Hill
Dry Creek Valley
Knights Valley
Los Carneros*
Northern Sonoma
Russian River Valley
Sonoma Coast
Sonoma County Green Valley
Sonoma Mountain
Sonoma Valley
★ Also located in Napa County

ACRES OF wine grapes planted in Sonoma: 60,000

NUMBER OF wineries in Sonoma: 260

TOP GRAPES PLANTED IN SONOMA

1. Chardonnay (16,000 acres)
2. Cabernet Sauvignon (12,600 acres)
3. Pinot Noir (11,000 acres)

LAST YEAR, more than 20 million people visited California winegrowing areas. Vineyards and wineries are the second-most popular California tourist destinations after Disneyland!

When did California begin to make better-quality wines?

As early as the 1940s, Frank Schoonmaker, an importer and writer and one of the first American wine experts, convinced some California winery owners to market their best wines using varietal labels.

Robert Mondavi may be one of the best examples of a winemaker who concentrated solely on varietal wine production. In 1966, Mondavi left his family's Charles Krug Winery and started the Robert Mondavi Winery. His role was important to the evolution of varietal labeling of California wines. He was among the first major winemakers to make the total switch that led to higher-quality winemaking.

BIGGER THAN HOLLYWOOD

Wine is California's most valuable finished agricultural product, with a $52 billion economic impact. The film industry: $30 billion.

HOLLYWOOD AND VINE

Many movie actors, directors, and producers have invested in vineyards and wineries throughout California, including Francis Ford Coppola.

ROBERT MONDAVI was a great promoter for the California wine industry. "He was able to prove to the public what the people within the industry already knew—that California could produce world-class wines," said Eric Wente.

A NOTE ON JUG WINES

The phrase jug wine *refers to simple, uncomplicated, everyday drinking wine. You're probably familiar with these types of wine: They're sometimes labeled with a generic name, such as Chablis or Burgundy. Inexpensive and well made, these wines were originally bottled in jugs, rather than in conventional wine bottles, hence the name "jug wine." They are very popular and account for the largest volume of California wine sold in the United States.*

Ernest and Julio Gallo, who began their winery in 1933, are the major producers of jug wines in California. In fact, many people credit the Gallo brothers with converting American drinking habits from spirits to wine. Several other wineries also produce jug wines, among them Almaden, Paul Masson, and Taylor California Cellars.

In my opinion, the best-made jug wines in the world are from California. They maintain both consistency and quality from year to year.

How did California become a world-class producer in just forty years?

There are many reasons for California's winemaking success, including:

Location: Napa and Sonoma counties, two of the major quality-wine regions, are both less than a two-hour drive from San Francisco. The proximity of these regions to the city encourages both residents and tourists to visit the wineries in the two counties, most of which offer wine tastings and sell their wines in their own shops.

Weather: Abundant sunshine, warm daytime temperatures, cool evenings, and a long growing season all add up to good conditions for growing many grape varieties. California is certainly subject to sudden changes in weather, but a fickle climate is not a major worry.

The University of California at Davis and Fresno State University: Both schools have been the training grounds for many young California winemakers, and their curricula concentrate on the scientific study of wine, viticulture, and, most important, technology. Their research, focused on soil, different strains of yeast, hybridization, temperature-controlled fermentation, and other viticultural techniques, has revolutionized the wine industry worldwide.

EARLY PIONEERS

Some of the pioneers of the back-to-the-land movement:

"FARMER"	WINERY	ORIGINAL PROFESSION
Robert Travers	Mayacamas	Investment banker
David Stare	Dry Creek	Civil engineer
Tom Jordan	Jordan	Geologist
James Barrett	Chateau Montelena	Attorney
Tom Burgess	Burgess	Air Force pilot
Jess Jackson	Kendall-Jackson	Attorney
Warren Winiarski	Stag's Leap	College professor
Brooks Firestone	Firestone	Take a guess!

Money and Marketing Strategy: This cannot be overemphasized. Marketing may not make the wine, but it certainly helps sell it. As more and more winemakers concentrated on making the best wine they could, American consumers responded with appreciation. They were willing to buy—and pay—more as quality improved. In order to keep up with consumer expectations, winemakers realized that they needed more research, development, and—most important—working capital. The wine industry turned to investors, both corporate and individual.

Since 1967, when the now defunct National Distillers bought Almaden, multinational corporations have recognized the profit potential of large-scale winemaking and have aggressively entered the wine business. They've brought huge financial resources and expertise in advertising and promotion that have helped promote American wines domestically and internationally. Other early corporate participants included Pillsbury and Coca-Cola.

On the other side of the investor scale are the individual investor/growers drawn to the business by their love of wine and their desire to live the winemaking "lifestyle." These individuals are more focused on producing quality wines.

Both corporate and individual investors had, by the 1990s, helped California fine-tune its wine industry, which today produces not only delicious and reliable wines in great quantity but also truly outstanding wines, many with investment potential.

SO YOU want to buy a vineyard in California? Today, one acre in the Napa Valley costs between $150,000 to $250,000 unplanted, and it takes an additional $20,000 per acre to plant. This per-acre investment sees no return for three to five years. To this, add the cost of building the winery, buying the equipment, and hiring the winemaker.

RECORD PRICE

In 2002, film director Francis Ford Coppola, owner of Niebaum-Coppola Wine Estate, paid a record price of $350,000 an acre for vineyard land in Napa.

IN 1970 the average price per acre in Napa was $5,000.

CREATIVE FINANCING

Overheard at a restaurant in Yountville, Napa Valley: "How do you make a small fortune in the wine business?" "Start with a large fortune and buy a winery."

IN CALIFORNIA many winemakers move around from one winery to another, just as good chefs move from one restaurant to the next. This is not uncommon. They may choose to carry and use the same "recipe" from place to place, if it is particularly successful, and sometimes they will experiment and create new styles.

I'VE MENTIONED stainless-steel fermentation tanks before, so I'll give a description, in case you need one. These tanks are temperature controlled, allowing winemakers to control the temperature at which the wine ferments. For example, a winemaker could ferment wines at a low temperature to retain fruitiness and delicacy, while preventing browning and oxidation.

"There is more potential for style variation in California than Europe because of the greater generosity of the fruit."
—WARREN WINIARSKI, *founder,*
Stag's Leap Wine Cellars, Napa Valley

AMBASSADOR ZELLERBACH, who created Hanzell Winery, was one of the first California winemakers to use small French oak aging barrels because he wanted to re-create a Burgundian style.

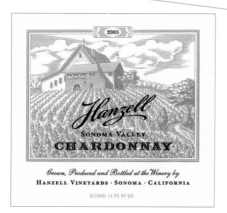

What's meant by *style*? How are different styles of California wine actually created?

Style refers to the characteristics of the grapes and wine. It is the trademark of the individual winemaker—an "artist" who tries different techniques to explore the fullest potential of the grapes.

Most winemakers will tell you that 95 percent of winemaking is in the quality of the grapes they begin with. The other 5 percent can be traced to the "personal touch" of the winemaker. Here are just a few of the hundreds of decisions a winemaker must make when developing his or her style of wine:

- When should the grapes be harvested?

- Should the juice be fermented in stainless-steel tanks or oak barrels? How long should it be fermented? At what temperature?

- Should the wine be aged at all? How long? If so, should it be aged in oak? What kind of oak—American, French?

- What varieties of grape should be blended, and in what proportion?

- How long should the wine be aged in the bottle before it is sold?

The list goes on. Because there are so many variables in winemaking, producers can create many styles of wine from the same grape variety—so you can choose the style that suits your taste. With the relative freedom of winemaking in the United States, the "style" of California wines continues to be "diversity."

Why is California wine so confusing?

The renaissance of the California wine industry began only about forty years ago. Within that short period of time, some 1,700 new wineries have been established in California. Today, there are more than 2,200 wineries in California, most of them making more than one wine, and the price differences are reflected in the styles (you can get a Cabernet Sauvignon wine in any price range from Two Buck Chuck at $1.99 to Harlan Estate at more than $500 a bottle—so how do you choose?). The constant changes in the wine industry through experimentation keep California winemaking in a state of flux.

American Wineries selected by *Wine Spectator* for the 2008 California Wine Experience

L'Angevin
A. P. Vin
Araujo
Archery Summit
Argyle
David Arthur
Au Bon Climat
L'Aventure
Bacio Divino Janzen
Barnett
Beaulieu
Bennett Lane
Bergstrom
Beringer
Betz Family
Big Basin
Black Kite
BOND
Bonny Doon
Bounty Hunter
Buccella
David Bruce
Buehler
Cadence
Calera
Carter
Caymus
Cayuse
Chalk Hill
Chalone
Chappellet
Chateau St. Jean
Chateau Ste. Michelle
Chehalem
Chimney Rock
Clos du Bois
Col Solare
Columbia Crest
Continuum
Cornerstone

Côte Bonneville
Robert Craig
Darioush
Dark Horse
Delectus
DeLille
Diamond Creek
Dolce
Domaine Alfred
Domaine Carneros
Domaine Chandon
Domain Drouhin Oregon
Domaine Serene
Dominus Estate
The Donum Estate
Duckhorn
DuMOL
Dunn
Merry Edwards
El Molino
Elk Cove
Emeritus
Eroica-Ste. Michelle/Dr.
      Loosen
Etude
Far Niente
Gary Farrell
Ferrari-Carano
Fisher
Flora Springs
Foley Estate
Robert Foley
Foursight
Foxen
Freestone
Gemstone
Girard
Gloria Ferrer
Goldeneye
Gorman

Grgich Hills Estate
Groth
HALL
Hanzell
Harlan
Heitz
Hess Collection
Hewitt
Hidden Ridge
Paul Hobbs
Honig
Iron Horse
J Vineyards & Winery
Jericho Canyon
John Anthony
Justin
Kamen Estate
Kapcsandy Family
Keller Estate
Kathryn Kennedy
TOR Kenward Family
Kistler
Kosta Browne
Kutch
Ladera
Lagier Meredith
Lail
Lang & Reed
Cliff Lede
Lewis
Londer
Long Shadows-Sequel
Loring
Luna
M by Michael Mondavi
MacRostie
Marston Family
Martinelli
McPrice Meyers
Merus
(continued)

A 40+-YEAR PERSPECTIVE

Number of Bonded Wineries in California

Year	Wineries
1965	232
1970	240
1975	330
1980	508
1983	641
1985	712
1990	807
1995	944
2000	1,450
2008	2,219

Source: The Wine Institute

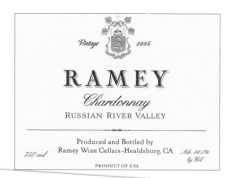

Peter Michael	Martin Ray	Sonoma-Loeb
Robert Mondavi	Realm	Souverain
Morgan	Revana	Spottswoode
Mount Eden	Ridge	Spring Valley
Mumm Napa	Rocca Family	Stag's Leap Wine Cellars
Neiman	Rochioli	Staglin Family
Neyers	Owen Roe	D.R. Stephens
Nickel & Nickel	Roederer Estate	Sterling
Northstar	Rosenblum	Rodney Strong
Novy Family	Stephen Ross	Orin Swift
Opus One	Rubicon Estate	Switchback Ridge
Outpost	Rutherford Hill	Tablas Creek
Pahlmeyer	St. Clement	Robert Talbott
Paloma	Sanford	Talley
Papapietro Perry	Sbragia Family	Testarossa
Paradigm	Schrader	Treana
Fess Parker	Schramsberg	Trefethen
Patz & Hall	Sebastiani	Truchard
Penner-Ash	Seghesio Family	Turnbull
Joseph Phelps	Selene	Versant
Pine Ridge	Shafer	Viader
PlumpJack	Shea	Vision
Pride Mountain	Siduri	Willakenzie
Provenance	Silver Oak	Robert Young Estate
Quintessa	W. H. Smith	Zepaltas
Ramey	Snowden	

What about the prices of California varietal wines?

You can't necessarily equate quality with price. Some excellent varietal wines that are produced in California are well within the budget of the average consumer. On the other hand, some varietals (primarily Chardonnay and Cabernet Sauvignon) may be quite expensive.

As in any market, it is mainly supply and demand that determines price. However, new wineries are affected by start-up costs, which sometimes are reflected in the price of the wine. Older, established wineries, which long ago amortized their investments, are able to keep their prices low when the supply/demand ratio calls for it. Remember, when you're buying California wine, price doesn't always reflect quality.

How do I choose a good California Wine?

One of the reasons California produces such a wide variety of wine is that it has so many different climates. Some are as cool as Burgundy, Champagne, and the Rhein, while others are as warm as the Rhône Valley, Portugal, and the southern regions of Italy and Spain. If that's not diverse enough, these wine-growing areas have inner districts with "microclimates," or climates within climates. One of the microclimates (which are among the designated AVAs) in Sonoma County, for example, is the Russian River Valley.

To better understand this concept, let's take a close look at the Rudd label.

State:
California
County:
Sonoma
Viticultural Area (AVA):
Russian River Valley
Vineyard:
Bacigalupi
Winery:
Rudd

California labels tell you everything you need to know about the wine—and more. Here are some quick tips you can use when you scan the shelves at your favorite retailer. The label shown above will serve as an example.

The most important piece of information on the label is the producer's name. In this case, the producer is Rudd.

If the grape variety is on the label, a minimum of 75 percent of the wine must be derived from that grape variety. This label shows that the wine is made from the Chardonnay grape.

If the wine bears a vintage date, 95 percent of the grapes must have been harvested that year.

If the wine is designated "California," then 100 percent of the grapes must have been grown in California.

If the label designates a certain federally recognized viticultural area (AVA), such as Russian River Valley (as on our sample label above), then at

CALIFORNIA WINE has no classification system that resembles the European equivalent.

THERE ARE 108 AVAs in California. Some of the best known are:

Napa Valley	Livermore Valley
Sonoma Valley	Paso Robles
Russian River Valley	Edna Valley
Alexander Valley	Fiddletown
Dry Creek Valley	Stag's Leap
Los Carneros	Chalk Hill
Anderson Valley	Howell Mountain
Santa Cruz Mountain	

FAMOUS INDIVIDUAL VINEYARDS OF CALIFORNIA

Bacigalupi
Bien Nacido
Dutton Ranch
Durell
Robert Young
Bancroft Ranch
Gravelly Meadow
Martha's Vineyard
McCrea
S.L.V.
To-Kalon
Beckstoffer
Monte Rosso

IF AN INDIVIDUAL vineyard is noted on the label, 95% of the grapes must be from the named vineyard, which must be located within an approved AVA.

I'M SURE you'll recognize the names of some of the early European winemakers:

Finland
Gustave Niebaum (Inglenook): 1879

France
Paul Masson: 1852
Étienne Thée and Charles LeFranc (Almaden): 1852
Pierre Mirassou: 1854
Georges de Latour (Beaulieu): 1900

Germany
Beringer Brothers: 1876
Carl Wente: 1883

Ireland
James Concannon: 1883

Italy
Giuseppe and Pietro Simi: 1876
John Foppiano: 1895
Samuele Sebastiani: 1904
Louis Martini: 1922
Adolph Parducci: 1932

"You are never going to stylize the California wines the same way that European wines have been stylized, because we have more freedom to experiment. I value my freedom to make the style of wine I want more than the security of the AOC laws. Laws discourage experimentation."
—LOUIS MARTINI

least 85 percent of the grapes used to make that wine must have been grown in that location.

The alcohol content is given in percentages. Usually, the higher the percentage of alcohol, the "fuller" the wine will be.

"Produced and bottled by" means that at least 75 percent of the wine was fermented by the winery named on the label.

Some wineries tell you the exact varietal content of the wine, and/or the sugar content of the grapes when they were picked, and/or the amount of residual sugar (to let you know how sweet or dry the wine is).

How is California winemaking different from the European technique?

Many students ask me this, and I can only tell them I'm glad I learned all about the wines of France, Italy, Germany, Spain, and the rest of Europe before I tackled California. European winemaking has established traditions that have remained essentially unchanged for hundreds of years. These practices involve the ways grapes are grown and harvested, and in some cases include winemaking and aging procedures.

In California, there are few traditions, and winemakers are able to take full advantage of modern technology. Furthermore, there is freedom to experiment and create new products. Some of the experimenting the California winemakers do, such as combining different grape varieties to make new styles of wine, is prohibited by some European wine-control laws. Californians thus have greater opportunity to try many new ideas.

Another way in which California winemaking is different from European is that many California wineries carry an entire line of wine. Many of the larger ones produce more than twenty different labels. In Bordeaux, most châteaux produce only one or two wines.

In addition to modern technology and experimentation, you can't ignore the fundamentals of winegrowing: California's rainfall, weather patterns, and soils are very different from those of Europe. The greater abundance of sunshine in California can result in wines with greater alcohol content, ranging on average from 13.5 percent to 14.5 percent, compared to 12 percent to 13 percent in Europe. This higher alcohol content changes the balance and taste of the wines.

EUROWINEMAKING IN CALIFORNIA

Many well-known and highly respected European winemakers have invested in California vineyards to make their own wine. There are more than forty-five California wineries owned by European, Canadian, or Japanese companies. For example:

- *One of the most influential joint ventures matched Baron Philippe de Rothschild, then the owner of Château Mouton-Rothschild in Bordeaux, and Robert Mondavi, of the Napa Valley, to produce a wine called Opus One.*
- *The owners of Château Pétrus in Bordeaux, the Moueix family, have vineyards in California. Their wine is a Bordeaux-style blend called Dominus.*
- *Moët & Chandon, which is part of Moët-Hennessy, owns Domaine Chandon in the Napa Valley.*

Other European wineries with operations in California:
- *Roederer has grapes planted in Mendocino County and produces Roederer Estate.*
- *Mumm produces a sparkling wine, called Mumm Cuvée Napa.*
- *Taittinger has its own sparkling wine called Domaine Carneros.*
- *The Spanish sparkling-wine house Codorniu owns a winery called Artesa; and Freixenet owns land in Sonoma County and produces a wine called Gloria Ferrer.*
- *The Torres family of Spain owns a winery called Marimar Torres Estate in Sonoma County.*
- *Frenchman Robert Skalli (Fortant de France) owns more than six thousand acres in the Napa Valley and the winery St. Supery.*
- *Tuscan wine producer Piero Antinori owns Atlas Peak winery in Napa.*

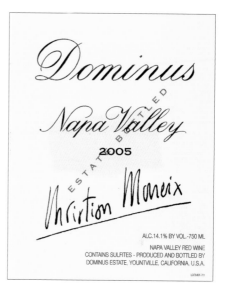

THE SPORTING LIFE

Athletes who have vineyards in California:
Tom Seaver (baseball)
Joe Montana (football)
John Madden (football)
Dick Vermeil (football)
Peggy Fleming (ice skating)
Arnold Palmer (golf)
Greg Norman (golf)
Mario Andretti (auto racing)
Randy Lewis (auto racing)
Jeff Gordon (auto racing)

What happened when phylloxera returned to the vineyards of California in the 1980s?

In the 1980s the plant louse phylloxera destroyed a good part of the vineyards of California, costing more than a billion dollars in new plantings. Now this may sound strange, but it proved that good can come from bad. So what's the good news?

This time, vineyard owners didn't have to wait to discover a solution; they already knew what they would have to do to replace the dead vines—by replanting with a different rootstock that they knew was resistant to phylloxera. So while the short-term effects were terribly expensive, the long-term effect should be better-quality wine. Why is this?

In the early days of California grape growing, little thought was given to where a specific grape would grow best. Many Chardonnays were planted in climates that were much too warm, and Cabernet Sauvignons were planted in climates that were much too cold.

With the onset of phylloxera, winery owners had a chance to rectify their errors; when replanting, they matched the climate and soil with the best grape variety. Grape growers also had the opportunity to plant different grape clones. But the biggest change was in the planting density of the vines themselves. Traditional spacing used by most wineries was somewhere between four hundred and five hundred vines per acre. Today with the new replanting, it is not uncommon to have more than a thousand vines per acre. Many vineyards have planted more than two thousand per acre.

The bottom line is that if you like California wines now, you'll love them more with time. The quality is already better and the costs are lower—making it a win-win situation for everyone.

THE WHITE WINES OF CALIFORNIA

What is the major white-grape variety grown in California?

The most important white-wine grape grown in California is Chardonnay. This green-skinned (*Vitis vinifera*) grape is considered by many the finest white-grape variety in the world. It is responsible for all the great French white Burgundies, such as Meursault, Chablis, and Puligny-Montrachet. In California, it has been the most successful white grape, yielding a wine of tremendous character and magnificent flavor. The wines are often aged in small oak barrels, increasing their complexity. In the vineyard, yields are fairly low and the grapes command high prices. Chardonnay is always dry, and benefits from aging more than any other American white wine. Superior examples can keep and develop well in the bottle for five years or longer.

Why do some Chardonnays cost more than other varietals?

In addition to everything we've mentioned before, the best wineries age these wines in wood—sometimes for more than a year. French oak barrels have doubled in price over the last five years, averaging eight hundred dollars per barrel. Add to this the cost of the grapes and the length of time before the wine is actually

THE TWO leading table wines produced in the United States in 2009:
1. Chardonnay
2. Sauvignon Blanc/Fumé Blanc

SOME 800 DIFFERENT California Chardonnays are available to the consumer.

CAIFORNIA HAS more Chardonnay planted than any other country in the world!

THERE ARE more than 24 different varieties of white wine grapes grown in California.

IN THE 2007 vintage, Kistler Vineyards produced six Chardonnays from six specific vineyards!

ONE-THIRD of all grapes grown in Sonoma are Chardonnay.

sold, and you can see why the best of the California Chardonnays cost more than twenty-five dollars.

What makes one Chardonnay different from another?

Put it this way: There are many brands of ice cream on the market. They use similar ingredients, but there is only one Ben & Jerry's. The same is true for wine. Among the many things to consider: Is a wine aged in wood or stainless steel? If wood, what type of oak? Was it barrel fermentation? Does the wine undergo a malolactic fermentation? How long does it remain in the barrel (part of the style of the winemaker)? Where do the grapes come from?

The major regions for California Chardonnay are Carneros, Napa, Santa Barbara, and Sonoma.

MALOLACTIC FERMENTATION is a second fermentation that lowers tart malic acids and increases the softer lactic acids, making for a richer style wine. The result is what many wine tasters refer to as a buttery bouquet.

Kevin Zraly's Favorite Chardonnays

ACACIA	LANDMARK
ARROWOOD	MARCASSIN
AU BON CLIMAT	MARTINELLI
BERINGER	PAUL HOBBS
CAKEBREAD	PETER MICHAEL
CHALK HILL	PHELPS
CHATEAU MONTELENA	RAMEY
CHATEAU ST. JEAN	ROBERT MONDAVI
DUTTON GOLDFIELD	RUDD ESTATE
FERRARI-CARANO	SBRAGIA FAMILY
GRGICH HILLS	SAINTSBURY
KISTLER	SILVERADO
KONGSGAARD	TALBOTT

THE 2005 HARVEST was the largest ever in California.

BEST BETS FOR CALIFORNIA CHARDONNAY

Carneros 2002* 2003 2004* 2006 2007* 2008
Napa 2002* 2004 2005 2006 2007* 2008
Sonoma 2002** 2003 2004** 2005** 2006 2007* 2008
Santa Barbara 2002* 2004 2005 2007* 2008

*Note: * signifies exceptional vintage*
**signifies extraordinary vintage

ROBERT MONDAVI WINERY

2007

FUMÉ BLANC

Napa Valley

What are the other major California white-wine grapes?

Sauvignon Blanc: Sometimes labeled Fumé Blanc. This is one of the grapes used in making the dry white wines of the Graves region of Bordeaux, and the white wines of Sancerre and Pouilly-Fumé in the Loire Valley of France, as well as New Zealand. California Sauvignon Blanc makes one of the best dry white wines in the world. It is sometimes aged in small oak barrels and occasionally blended with the Sémillon grape.

Chenin Blanc: This is one of the most widely planted grapes in the Loire Valley. In California, the grape yields a very attractive, soft, light-bodied wine. It is usually made very dry or semisweet; it is a perfect apéritif wine, simple and fruity.

Viognier: One of the major white grapes from the Rhône Valley in France, Viognier thrives in warmer and sunny climates, so it's a perfect grape for the weather conditions in certain areas of California. It has a distinct fragrant bouquet. Not as full-bodied as most Chardonnays, nor as light as most Sauvignon Blancs, it's an excellent food wine.

Kevin Zraly's Favorite Sauvignon Blancs

MANTANZAS CREEK	CAYMUS
ROBERT MONDAVI	MASON
SIMI	PHELPS
SILVERADO	CHALK HILL
FERRARI-CARANO	CHATEAU ST. JEAN
DRY CREEK	KENWOOD
MERRY EDWARDS	GREY STACK
BRANDER	

What have been the trends in wines of California over the last twenty-five years?

To best answer that question, we should go back even further to see where the trends have been going for the last forty years or so. The 1960s were a decade of expansion and development. The 1970s were a decade of growth, especially in terms of the number of wineries that were established in California and the corporations and individuals that became involved. The 1980s and 1990s were the decades of experimentation, in grape growing as well as in wine-making and marketing techniques.

Over the past ten years, I have seen the winemakers finally get a chance to step back and fine-tune their wine. Today, they are producing wines that have tremendous structure, finesse, and elegance that many lacked in the early years of the California winemaking renaissance. They are also making wines that can give pleasure when young, and also great wines that I hope I will be around to share with my grandchildren. The benchmark for quality has increased to such a level that the best wineries have gotten better, but more important to the consumer is that even the wines under twenty dollars are better than ever before.

There has been a trend toward wineries specializing in particular grape varieties. Twenty-five years ago, I would have talked about which wineries in California were the best. Today, I'm more likely to talk about which winery or AVA makes the best Chardonnay; which winery makes the best Sauvignon Blanc.

Chardonnay remains the major white-grape variety by far in California. Sauvignon Blancs/Fumé Blancs have greatly improved, and they're easier to consume young. Although they still don't have the cachet of a Chardonnay, I find them better matched with most foods. However, other white-grape varieties, such as Riesling and Chenin Blanc, aren't meeting with the same success, and they're harder to sell. Still, just to keep it interesting, some winemakers are planting more European varietals, including Viognier and Pinot Gris.

FOR FURTHER READING

I recommend *The Oxford Companion to the Wines of North America* by Bruce Cass and Jancis Robinson; *The Wine Atlas of California* by James Halliday; *Making Sense of California Wine* and *New California Wine* by Matt Kramer; *California Wine* by James Laube; *American Vintage: The Rise of American Wine* by Paul Lukacs; and *The Wine Atlas of California and the Pacific Northwest* by Bob Thompson. Lovers of gossip will have fun reading *The Far Side of Eden* and *Napa: The Story of an American Eden* by James Conaway. And, of course, *Kevin Zraly's American Wine Guide.*

1960s and 1970s: Jug wines (Chablis, Burgundy)
1980s: Varietal wines (Chardonnay, Cabernet Sauvignon)
1990s: Varietal location (Cabernet Sauvignon—Napa, Pinot Noir—Santa Barbara)
2000s: Specific vineyards for varietals

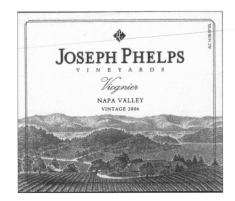

A WINERY BY ANY OTHER NAME

Here, listed by the parent company, is a selection of some well-known wineries and brands.

FOSTER'S GROUP (FOSTER'S WINE ESTATES)

Beringer Vineyards • Campanile • Cellar No. 8 • Château St. Jean • Etude • Meridian • Souverain • St. Clement • Stags' Leap • Talomas • Taz Vineyard

WJ DEUTSCH & SONS, LTD.

Atlas Peak • Buena Vista • Esser Vineyards • Gary Farrell • Geyser Peak Winery • Kunde

E&J GALLO

Andre • Ballatore • Barefoot Cellars • Carlo Rossi • Dancing Bull • Gallo Family Vineyards Twin Valley • Indigo Hills • Liberty Creek • Livingston Cellars • Peter Vella • Red Rock Winery • Redwood Creek • Tisdale Vineyards • Turning Leaf • Wild Vines • Wycliff Sparkling

DIAGEO

Beaulieu Vineyard • Blossom Hill • Sterling Vineyards

BROWN-FORMAN

Bel Arbor Wines • Bonterra Vineyards • Fetzer Wines • Five Rivers Wines • Jekel Vineyards • Sonoma-Cutrer Wines

CONSTELLATION WINES, U.S.

Franciscan Oakville Estate • Mount Veeder • Robert Mondavi • Simi • Estancia • Columbia Winery • Woodbridge by Robert Mondavi • Clos du Bois • Black Box • Robert Mondavi Private Selection • Ravenswood • Blackstone • Toasted Head • Alice White • Arbor Mist • Cook's • Talus • Vendange • Rex Goliath • RH Phillips • Turner Road

THE WINE GROUP

Franzia • Concannon • Corbett Canyon • Fish Eye • Foxhorn • Austin Vale • Glen Ellen • Mogen David • Tribuno • Almaden • Inglenook Winery • Paul Masson Winery • Pinot Evil • Herding Cats • Big House • Cardinal Zin • Tempra Tantrum

Three companies—Gallo, Constellation Brands, and the Wine Group—make up 60 percent of California wine sales.

Source: Wines & Vines

WINE AND FOOD

MARGRIT BIEVER AND ROBERT MONDAVI:
With Chardonnay: oysters, lobster, a more complex fish with sauce beurre blanc, pheasant salad with truffles. With Sauvignon Blanc: traditional white meat or fish course, sautéed or grilled fish (as long as it isn't an oily fish).

DAVID STARE *(Dry Creek): With Chardonnay: fresh boiled Dungeness crab cooked in Zatarain's crab boil, a New Orleans–style boil. Serve this with melted butter and a large loaf of sourdough French bread. With Sauvignon Blanc, "I like fresh salmon cooked in almost any manner. Personally, I like to take a whole fresh salmon or salmon steaks and cook them over the barbecue in an aluminum foil pocket. Place the salmon, onion slices, lemon slices, copious quantities of fresh dill, salt, and pepper on aluminum foil and make a pocket. Cook over the barbecue until barely done. Place the salmon in the oven to keep it warm while you take the juices from the aluminum pocket, reduce the juices, strain, and whisk in some plain yogurt. Enjoy!"*

WARREN WINIARSKI *(Stag's Leap Wine Cellars): With Chardonnay: seviche, shellfish, salmon with a light hollandaise sauce.*

JANET TREFETHEN: *With Chardonnay: barbecued whole salmon in a sorrel sauce. With White Riesling: sautéed bay scallops with julienne vegetables.*

RICHARD ARROWOOD: *With Chardonnay: Sonoma Coast Dungeness crab right from the crab pot, with fennel butter as a dipping sauce.*

BO BARRETT *(Chateau Montelena Winery): With Chardonnay: salmon, trout, or abalone, barbecued with olive oil and lemon leaf and slices.*

JACK CAKEBREAD: *"With my Cakebread Cellars Napa Valley Chardonnay: bruschetta with wild mushrooms, leek and mushroom–stuffed chicken breast, and halibut with caramelized endive and chanterelles."*

ED SBRAGIA *(Beringer Vineyards): With Chardonnay: lobster or salmon with lots of butter.*

U.S. WINE exports have increased from $98 million in 1989 to $1 billion in 2008. The top export markets are:
1. United Kingdom
2. Canada
3. Japan
4. Italy
5. Germany

THE CRYSTAL BALL

Over the next ten years, look for China, India, and Russia to become big importers of American wines.

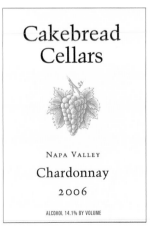

CLASS TWO: THE WHITE WINES OF CALIFORNIA

In the first class, we studied the white wines of France. In Class Two, we'll follow the same wine styles as with France, but this time we'll use American white wines.

Wines for Class Two

1. Dr. Konstantin Frank Riesling Dry 2007 (Finger Lakes, New York)
2. Dry Creek Fumé Blanc 2007 (Sonoma County)
3. Mason Sauvignon Blanc 2007 (Napa Valley)
4. Hawk Crest Chardonnay 2007 (California) **BEST VALUE**
5. Blind Tasting
6. Blind Tasting
7. Chateau St. Jean Chardonnay 2007 (Sonoma County) **BEST VALUE**
8. Au Bon Climat Chardonnay 2007 (Santa Barbara)
9. Talbott Sleepy Hollow Vineyard Chardonnay 2005 (Monterey)
10. Ramey Hudson Vineyard Chardonnay 2005 (Carneros)
11. Chateau Montelena 2001 (Napa Valley)

There are six parts to this tasting.

PART I: RIESLING (ONE WINE, TASTED ALONE)

Wine #1: Dr. Konstantin Frank Dry Riesling 2007 (Finger Lakes, New York)

In Class One, we started with a Riesling from Alsace. In this class we'll taste a Riesling from the Finger Lakes district of New York. Although this class is entitled White Wines of California, I believe the best American Rieslings are made in the Finger Lakes region of New York and also in Washington State.

I want my first wine to excite the palate and get the saliva going, and this Dr. Frank Riesling is the perfect wine to do just that. It is an unoaked Riesling with a touch of residual sugar (1.4 percent) which balances perfectly with the crisp acidity of the Riesling fruit. The low alcohol (12 percent) does not mask any of the other components of the wine and leaves the palate refreshingly light.

Retail price $20

Ready to drink

Other recommended producers of this style of Riesling are: Hermann Weimer, Fox Run (both New York), and Chateau Ste. Michelle Eroica (Washington).

PART II: SAUVIGNON BLANC (TWO WINES, TASTED TOGETHER)

In Class One we tried two wines from the same region: the Loire Valley. In Class Two we are tasting two Sauvignon Blancs together, one from Sonoma and the other from Napa, to highlight the stylistic differences of this varietal.

Sauvignon Blanc is second only to Chardonnay in quality white wine grapes grown in California. Most Sauvignon Blancs are unoaked, light in style, have a perceived higher acidity, and for my tastes are more food-friendly than most Chardonnays. In fact, when I dine out, I usually choose a Sauvignon Blanc over a Chardonnay for my first course not only because they're lighter in style but also because they're far less expensive.

The following two wines are from two different AVAs. One is from Sonoma County and the other from the Napa Valley; both are made with 100 percent Sauvignon Blanc. Both of them would be a perfect complement for any seafood appetizer.

Wine #2: Dry Creek Fumé Blanc 2007 (Sonoma County)

David Stare, the founder of Dry Creek Vineyards, was a pioneer in Sonoma, known especially for his work developing the Sauvignon Blanc grape. The AVA on this Dry Creek Sauvignon Blanc is Sonoma County, meaning that the grapes can come from anywhere within the county boundaries. The cooler climate of Sonoma County gives this wine lower alcohol content than our next wine. This wine has the distinctive Sauvignon Blanc bouquet with tangy grapefruit acidity.

Retail price $14

Ready to drink

Other recommended producers of this style Sonoma County Sauvignon Blancs are: Simi, Ferrari-Carano, Mantanzas Creek, Chalk Hill, and Chateau St. Jean.

Sonoma County
Fumé Blanc
Dry Sauvignon Blanc

PRODUCERS HAVE a choice when producing this varietal of either having the varietal name on the label or referring to it as Fumé Blanc. Dry Creek lists both on their label.

Wine #3: *Mason Sauvignon Blanc 2007 (Napa Valley)*

Because of its warmer climate, the Napa Valley is God's gift to wine lovers—mostly for the world-class red wine made from Cabernet Sauvignon and Merlot. It's not necessarily the region I look to for Sauvignon Blanc, which generally thrives in cooler climates. With that said, Randy Mason makes one of the best Sauvignon Blancs in California. Students will immediately taste the great balance of the fruit and acid with mineral flavors.

Retail price $18
Ready to drink
Other recommended producers of this style Napa Valley Sauvignon Blancs are: Robert Mondavi, Silverado, Phelps, and Caymus.

CHARDONNAY

So far we have tasted one Riesling and two Sauvignon Blancs. The next eight wines are made from the Chardonnay grape. Wine #4 is my French Mâconnais counterpart, an easy-drinking, light-style Chardonnay.

PART III: CHARDONNAY (ONE WINE, TASTED ALONE)

Wine #4: *Hawk Crest Chardonnay 2007 (California)*

Begin by looking at the label of this wine to find out where it comes from. The label states that the wine is from California, which means the grapes can come from any part of the state. The grapes for this Chardonnay are grown in the cool climate of Santa Lucia Highlands and are blended with grapes from Monterey County. This wine is styled after the Mâconnais region of France. Although the wine receives partial barrel fermentation, none of the oak overpowers the fruit. It is also aged *sur lie* and undergoes partial malolactic fermentation.

Retail price $12   **BEST VALUE**
Ready to drink
Other recommended producers for this style Chardonnay are: Benziger, Estancia, Meridian, Rutherford Ranch, and Napa Ridge.

ALTHOUGH AVAS are important to understand, I still recommend that you should first buy wines based on the reputation of the producer. In this case, Stag's Leap Wine Cellars has a history and reputation for the production of great wine.

Part IV: Chardonnay
(two wines, tasted together)

This is the first major blind tasting of the course (Wine #5 and Wine #6). I have always found in tasting wines that seeing a label is worth many years of experience. The only information I give the students is that both wines are made from 100 percent Chardonnay grapes. It's important to challenge yourself, as well as your guests, by testing your own abilities and thresholds of wine tasting. If you are conducting a tasting with friends, you should pour the wine first, without showing the label. Proceed with tasting by examining the color, smell, and taste of each wine, record your notes, and discuss the results with your friends.

Unfortunately, I can't tell you the exact wines I use since my students also get a copy of this book! Like any other blind tasting, this is a good exercise for anyone who wants to become better at wine judging. The wines should be served from lightest to heaviest.

The following are examples of some blind tastings that you can do at home:

> Example 1: Unoaked California Chardonnay vs. Heavily Oaked
>   California Chardonnay
> Example 2: Sonoma Valley Chardonnay vs. Napa Valley Chardonnay
> Example 3: White Burgundy vs. Napa or Sonoma Valley Chardonnay
> Example 4: New York Chardonnay vs. California Chardonnay
> Example 5: Australian Chardonnay vs. California Chardonnay

To be fair, both wines should be of the same quality, vintages within a year of each other, and in the same price range.

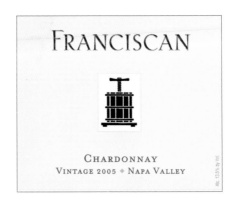

PART V: CHARDONNAY: EXPLORING FOUR DIFFERENT AVAS (FOUR WINES, TASTED TOGETHER)

The next four wines are Chardonnays produced in four different regions of California. Over the last thirty years, viticulturists have isolated the best soil and climatic conditions for growing the major grape varieties. For California Chardonnay, it is Sonoma, Monterey, Santa Barbara, and the Carneros region of Napa/Sonoma.

Just as in Class One with the white Burgundies, the four Chardonnays are poured out together. Once the wines are poured, stand up and look down at the colors of the wines. Before tasting anything, take the next five minutes to note the differences in color and smell among the four wines and decide which wines you think you will like the best.

Note on Wine #7 and Wine #8 that these wines should all be from the same vintage or within one year.

There are obvious differences in the style between the Chateau St. Jean and the Au Bon Climat Chardonnays. For years wine critics have said, "All California Chardonnays taste the same." By tasting these wines together, you'll understand that this criticism is not warranted.

Wine #7: Chateau St. Jean Chardonnay 2007 (Sonoma County)

The Chateau St. Jean winery is one of my favorite wineries of California. Since the early 1970s this producer has been making consistent top-quality wines at reasonable prices. In the early days it was mostly known for its production of white wines, and it continues to produce great Sauvignon Blancs and Chardonnays. It now produces Cinq Cépages, as well—one of the best red blends in California. This Chardonnay wine is barrel fermented with five months of *sur lie* aging and three quarters of the wine undergoes malolactic fermentation.

This wine is elegant, crowd-pleasing, and medium-bodied. It has perfect fruit oak balance and a lingering acidity. It is my number-one pick for best quality value Chardonnay in California. The winemaker, Margo Van Staaveren, has been at Chateau St. Jean since 1979 and she knows how to make exceptional wines at all price levels!

MALOLACTIC FERMENTATION means that a wine has undergone a two-step fermentation process. The secondary fermentation converts the stronger malic acid in wine into softer lactic acid. This adds complexity and lowers the acidity of wine. I always ask my students what the wine smells like. When it comes to Chardonnays, I often hear the word buttery (lactic). This is a sure sign that malolactic fermentation has taken place.

Retail price $14   **BEST VALUE**

Ready to drink

Other recommended producers of this style "value" Chardonnay are: Gallo of Sonoma, Buena Vista, Sonoma-Cutrer (Russian River Ranches), and Kendall Jackson Vintner's Reserve.

Wine #8: Au Bon Climat Chardonnay 2007 (Santa Barbara)

In 2007, Au Bon Climat celebrated its twenty-fifth anniversary, making owner and winemaker Jim Clendenen one of the pioneers of Santa Barbara County winemakers. He has always produced a personal, idiosyncratic style of wine, similar to a French Burgundy, by choosing the best Chardonnay from specific vineyards. This 2007 vintage Chardonnay comes from one of the top vineyard sites in California, the Bien Nacido Vineyard. This wine was fermented in small French Oak barrels, aged for another seven months *sur lie*, and bottled unfiltered after a year in barrel. The Au Bon Climat is a full-bodied, creamy, rich, and complex wine.

Retail price $25

Ready to drink, but will continue to age

Other recommended producers of this Santa Barbara–style Chardonnay are: Sanford and Babcock.

The next two Chardonnays are both from the 2005 vintage and are from specific vineyards.

Wine #9: Talbott Sleepy Hollow Vineyard Chardonnay 2005 (Monterey)

Talbott is one of the best wineries in Monterey County. They celebrated their twenty-fifth anniversary in 2007. Robert Talbott is one of the pioneers of high-quality winemaking in Monterey. The Sleepy Hollow Vineyard is located in the Santa Lucia Highlands AVA. All the grapes used in this Burgundian-style Chardonnay come from the oldest part of the Sleepy Hollow Vineyard. This is a ripe, rich, complex wine that has been 100 percent barrel fermented and barrel aged for one year *sur lie*. The toastiness of the oak blends in perfectly with the ripeness of the grapes. The biggest difference between the Chateau St. Jean, Au Bon Climat, and this Talbott Chardonnay is the alcohol content. It jumps to 14.7 percent, more than one degree higher than the others, creating much more density and weight in the wine.

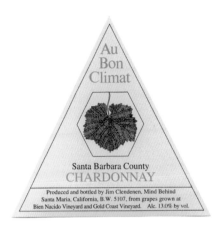

TALKING TO winemakers on the subject of "to filter or not to filter" always leads to great discussions and remains a controversial subject today. Filtration is the process by which solids in the wine are removed. By filtering a wine, you take out any impurities that can make the wine unstable. Many winemakers feel that filtering a wine will take away its varietal character and complexity. An unfiltered wine, especially after age, will "throw" sediment both in red or white wine.

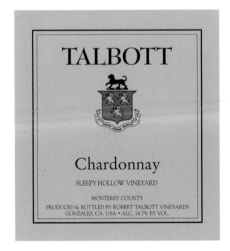

SUR LIE, a French term, is used when a wine is left aging with its sediment, such as dead yeast cells and grape skins and seeds.

Retail price $40
Continues to age
Other recommended producers of this Monterey-style Chardonnay are:
Mer Soleil, Chalone, Morgan, and Calera.

Wine #10: Ramey Hudson Vineyard Chardonnay 2005 (Carneros)

David Ramey has been one of the top winemakers in California for many years. I enjoyed tasting his earlier wines when he was a winemaker at the Chalk Hill and Dominus wineries. Two of the vineyards from Carneros that David has worked closely with over the years are the Hyde Vineyard and the Hudson Vineyard. They are both from the Carneros region, which has one of the coolest climatic conditions of the North Coast Counties, perfect for the Chardonnay grape.

This wine from the Hudson Vineyard produces a powerful full-bodied Chardonnay. The 2005 Hudson Vineyard grapes were whole-clustered pressed and fermented in small French Burgundian barrels (70 percent new barrels) using native yeast. At 14.8 percent alcohol content, this is a big style, in-your-face Chardonnay that will benefit from many more years of aging. Like the previous three Chardonnays, this wine was also aged *sur lie*, but for twenty-one months and bottled without filtration.

Retail price $55
Will benefit from further years of aging
Other recommended producers of this Carneros-style Chardonnay are:
Kistler Vineyards Hudson Vineyard, Kistler Vineyards Hyde Vineyard, and Williams Selyem Allen Vineyard.

PART VI: TASTING AN AGED CALIFORNIA CHARDONNAY (ONE WINE, TASTED ALONE)

One of the most common questions raised in my class is the ageability of wine. Our last Chardonnay is more than eight years old; it is extremely important that students understand what happens to a California Chardonnay as it gets older. This next wine well demonstrates the effects of age on wine.

Wine #11: Chateau Montelena 2001 (Napa Valley)

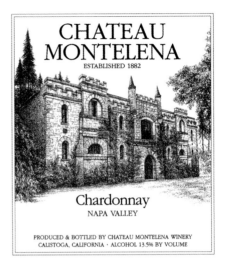

This winery was originally established in 1882 and was resurrected by the Barrett family in 1972, about the time I seriously began my wine career. We've grown up together, which is why it's always been one of my sentimental favorites. Chateau Montelena became one of the most famous wineries in California in 1976 when their 1973 Chardonnay took first place in a comparative tasting of California Chardonnays and French White Burgundies. This upset was so shocking, so revolutionary, that a book, *Judgment in Paris*, was written about the tasting, and it was recently made into a movie, *Bottle Shock*. The winemaker at that time was Mike Grgich, who now produces exceptional wines at his own winery, Grgich Hills.

This is a textbook-style Chardonnay conforming to every descriptive word critics write about great Chardonnays: great balanced fruit and a long, complex aftertaste with refreshing acidity. After nine years of age, the tannins have mellowed, the wine is softer, and fruit becomes the dominant factor, yet there is still enough acidity in this wine for it to age another five years.

The big difference between this Chardonnay versus the other Chardonnays you have just tasted is that the Chateau Montelena does not undergo malolactic fermentation. This is a Village-style Burgundian wine, elegant with perfectly integrated acid/fruit levels. It is also aged on its yeast and has spent eight months in oak.

Retail price $90+
Ready to drink, but will continue to age gracefully
Try finding a Chardonnay with some age, at least five years, in order to see how aging affects this type of wine.

Questions for Class Two: The Wines of Washington, Oregon, and New York; The White Wines of California

The White Wines of Germany

GRAPE VARIETIES · THE STYLE OF GERMAN WINES ·

PRÄDIKATSWEIN LEVELS · UNDERSTANDING GERMAN WINE LABELS · TRENDS

About German Wines

BEFORE WE BEGIN OUR STUDY of the white wines of Germany, tell me this: Have you memorized the 7 Grands Crus of Chablis, the 32 Grands Crus of the Côte d'Or, and the 391 different wineries of the Napa Valley? I hope you have, so you can begin to memorize the more than 1,400 wine villages and 2,600-plus vineyards of Germany. No problem, right? What's 4,000 simple little names?

Actually, if you were to have studied German wines before 1971, you would have had thirty thousand different names to remember. There used to be very small parcels of land owned by an assortment of different people; that's why so many names were involved.

THERE HAS been a 10% increase in German vineyards planted over the last 10 years.

FRANCE PRODUCES 10 times as much wine as Germany.

IN GERMANY, 100,000 grape growers cultivate nearly 270,000 acres of vines, meaning the average holding per grower is 2.7 acres.

In an effort to make German wines less confusing, the government stepped in and passed a law in 1971. The new ruling stated that a vineyard must encompass at least twelve and a half acres of land. This law cut the list of vineyard names considerably, but it increased the number of owners.

Germany produces only 2 or 3 percent of the world's wines. (Beer, remember, is the national beverage.) And what wines it does produce depends largely on the weather. Why is this? Well, look at where the wines are geographically. Germany is the northernmost country in which vines can grow. And 80 percent of the quality vineyards are located on hilly slopes. Germans can forget about mechanical harvesting.

The following chart should help give you a better idea of the hilly conditions vintners must contend with in order to grow grapes that produce the highest quality wines in Germany.

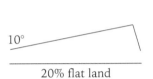

10°

20% flat land

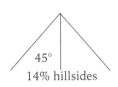

45°

14% hillsides

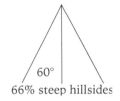

60°

66% steep hillsides

What are the most important grape varieties?

Riesling: This is the most widely planted and the best grape variety produced in Germany. If you don't see the name "Riesling" on the label, then there's probably very little, if any, Riesling grape in the wine. And remember, if the label gives the grape variety, then there must be at least 85 percent of that grape in the wine, according to German law. Of the grapes planted in Germany, 21 percent are Riesling.

Müller-Thurgau: A cross between two grapes (Riesling and Chasselas) and it accounts for 13.5 percent of Germany's wines.

Silvaner: This is another grape variety, and it accounts for 5 percent of Germany's wines.

HOW COLD IS IT?

If you were to look at a map of the world, put your finger on Germany, and then follow the 50-degree north latitude westward into North America, you'd be pointing to the island of Newfoundland, Canada.

ONE MECHANICAL harvester can do the work of 60 people.

GERMANY PRODUCES red wines, too, but only about 15%. Why? Red grapes simply don't grow as well as white ones in Germany's northerly climate.

WITH GERMAN WINES, 85 is the important number to remember:
• 85% of the wines Germany produces are white.
• If a wine label gives the grape variety—Riesling, for example—85% of the wine must be made from the Riesling grape.
• If a German wine shows a vintage on the label, 85% of the grapes used must be from that year. Top German wine producers use 100% of the varietal and the vintage on the label.

GRAPES IN GERMANY

Riesling: 21%
Müller-Thurgau: 13.5%
Silvaner: 5%

GERMANY IS RIESLING COUNTRY

Germany has more than 50,000 acres of Riesling and no other country comes close. Australia is next, with 10,000 acres, and France has 8,000.

Germany has been growing the Riesling grape since 1435.

THE "OTHER" NINE WINE REGIONS OF
GERMANY ARE:
Ahr
Baden
Franken
Hessische Bergstrasse
Mittelrhein
Nahe
Saale-Unstrut
Sachsen
Württemberg

OF MOSEL wines, 80% are made from the
Riesling grape, while 82% of Rheingau
wines are made from Riesling.

What are the main winemaking regions of Germany?

There are thirteen winemaking regions. Do you have to commit them all to memory like the hundreds of other names I've mentioned in the book so far? Absolutely not. Why should you worry about all thirteen when you only need to be familiar with four?

One of the reasons I emphasize these regions above the others is that in the United States you rarely see wine from the other German wine-growing regions. The other reason to look closely at these regions is that they produce the best German wines. They are:

RHEINHESSEN

RHEINGAU

MOSEL
(UNTIL 2007 KNOWN AS MOSEL-SAAR-RUWER)

PFALZ
(UNTIL 1992 KNOWN AS RHEINPFALZ)

What's the style of German wines?

Simply put, it's a balance of sweetness with acidity and low alcohol. Remember the equation:

$$\text{Sugar} + \text{Yeast} = \text{Alcohol} + \text{Carbon Dioxide (CO}_2\text{)}$$

Where does the sugar come from? The sun! If you have a good year, and your vines are on a southerly slope, you'll get a lot of sun, and therefore the right sugar content to produce a good wine. Many times, however, the winemakers aren't so fortunate and they don't have enough sun to ripen the grapes. The result: higher acidity and lower alcohol. To compensate for this, some winemakers add sugar to the must (the juice of the grape) before fermentation to increase the amount of alcohol. As mentioned before, this process is called chaptalization. (Note: Chaptalization is not permitted for higher-quality German wines.)

The three basic styles of German wine are:

GERMAN WINES tend to be 8% to 10% alcohol, compared to an average 11% to 13% for French wines.

Trocken: dry
Halbtrocken: medium-dry
Fruity: semidry to very sweet

What are the ripeness levels of German wine?

As a result of the German law of 1971, there are two main categories, Tafelwein and Qualitätswein.

Tafelwein: Literally, "table wine." The lowest designation given to a wine grown in Germany, it never carries the vineyard name. It is rarely seen in the United States.

Qualitätswein: Literally, "quality wine," of which there are two types.

1. *Qualitätswein bestimmter Anbaugebiete:* QbA indicates a quality wine that comes from one of the thirteen specified regions.

2. *Prädikatswein:* This is quality wine with distinction—the good stuff. These wines may not be chaptalized.

AS OF the 2007 vintage, Qualitätswein mit Prädikat has been replaced by Prädikatswein.

In ascending order of quality, price, and ripeness at harvest, here are the Prädikatswein levels:

Kabinett: Light, semidry wines made from normally ripened grapes. Cost: $15–$25.

Spätlese: Breaking up the word, _spät_ means "late" and _lese_ means "picking." Put them together and you have "late picking." That's exactly what this medium-style wine is made of—grapes that were picked after the normal harvest. The extra days of sun give the wine more body and a more intense flavor. Cost: $20–$35.

Auslese: Translated as "out picked," this means that the grapes are selectively picked out from particularly ripe bunches, which yields a medium-to fuller-style wine. You probably do the same thing in your own garden if you grow tomatoes: You pick out the especially ripe ones, leaving the others on the vine. Cost: $25–$50.

Beerenauslese: Breaking the word down, you get _beeren_, or "berries," _aus_, or "out," and _lese_, or "picking." Quite simply (and don't let the bigger names fool you), these are berries (grapes) that are picked out individually. These luscious grapes are used to create the rich dessert wines for which Germany is known. Beerenauslese is usually made only two or three times every ten years. It's not unheard of for a good Beerenauslese to cost up to $250.

Trockenbeerenauslese: A step above the Beerenauslese, but these grapes are dried (_trocken_), so they're more like raisins. These "raisinated" grapes produce the richest, sweetest, honeylike wine—and the most expensive.

Eiswein: A very rare, sweet, concentrated wine made from frozen grapes left on the vine. They're pressed while still frozen. According to Germany's 1971 rules for winemaking, this wine must now be made from grapes that are at least ripe enough to make a Beerenauslese.

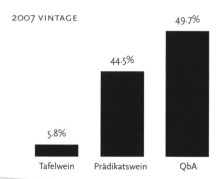

2007 VINTAGE

49.7%

44.5%

5.8%

Tafelwein   Prädikatswein   QbA

FIFTY YEARS AGO, most German wines were dry and very acidic. Even in the finer restaurants, you'd be offered a spoonful of sugar with a German wine to balance the acidity.

A NOTE ON SÜSSRESERVE

A common misconception about German wine is that fermentation stops and the remaining residual sugar gives the wine its sweetness naturally. On the contrary, some wines are fermented dry. Many German winemakers hold back a certain percentage of unfermented grape juice from the same vineyards, the same varietal, and the same sweetness level. This Süssreserve contains all the natural sugar and it's added back to the wine after fermentation. The finest estates do not use the Süssreserve method, but rely on stopping the fermentation to achieve their style.

GIVEN GOOD WEATHER, the longer the grapes remain on the vine, the sweeter they become—but the winemaker takes a risk when he does this because all could be lost in the event of bad weather.

What's the difference between a $100 Beerenauslese and a $200 Beerenauslese (besides a hundred bucks)?

The major difference is the grapes. The $100 bottle is probably made from Müller-Thurgau grapes or Silvaner, while the $200 bottle is from Riesling. In addition, the region the wine comes from will, in part, determine its quality. Traditionally, the best Beerenauslese and Trockenbeerenauslese come from the Rhein or the Mosel.

Quality is higher in wine when:

- The wine is produced from low yields.
- The grapes come from great vineyards.
- The wine is produced by great winemakers.
- The grapes were grown in a great climate or are from a great vintage.

TODAY, MOST German wines, including Beerenauslese and Trockenbeerenauslese, are bottled in spring and early summer. Many no longer receive additional cask or tank maturation, because it has been discovered that this extra barrel aging destroys the fruit.

IN 1921, the first Trockenbeerenauslese was made in the Mosel region.

THE SPÄTLESE RIDER: THE FIRST LATE-HARVEST WINE

The story goes that at the vineyards of Schloss Johannisberg, the monks were not allowed to pick the grapes until the Abbot of Fulda gave his permission. During the harvest of 1775, the abbot was away attending a synod. That year the grapes were ripening early and some of them had started to rot on the vine. The monks, becoming concerned, dispatched a rider to ask the abbot's permission to pick the grapes. By the time the rider returned, the monks believed all was lost, but they went ahead with the harvest anyway. To their amazement, the wine was one of the best they had ever tasted. That was the beginning of Spätlese-style wines.

ONE QUICK way to tell the difference between a Rhein and a Mosel wine on sight is to look at the bottle. Rhein wine comes in a brown bottle, Mosel in a green bottle.

When I'm ordering a German wine in a restaurant or shopping at my local retailer, what should I look for?

The first thing I would make sure of is that it comes from one of the four major regions. These regions are the Mosel, Rheinhessen, Rheingau, and Pfalz, which, in my opinion, are the most important quality wine–producing regions in all of Germany.

Next, look to see if the wine is made from the Riesling grape. Anyone who studies and enjoys German wines finds that Riesling shows the best-tasting characteristics. Riesling on the label is a mark of quality.

Also, be aware of the vintage. It's important, especially with German wines, to know if the wine was made in a good year.

Finally, the most important consideration is to buy from a reputable grower or producer.

What's the difference between Rhein and Mosel wines?

Rhein wines generally have more body than do Mosels. Mosels are usually higher in acidity and lower in alcohol than are Rhein wines. Mosels show more autumn fruits like apples, pears, and quince, while Rhein wines show more summer fruits like apricots, peaches, and nectarines.

Some important villages to look for:

Rheingau: Eltville, Erbach, Rüdesheim, Rauenthal, Hochheim, Johannisberg
Mosel: Erden, Piesport, Bernkastel, Graach, Ürzig, Brauneberg, Wehlen
Rheinhessen: Oppenheim, Nackenheim, Nierstein
Pfalz: Deidesheim, Forst, Wachenheim, Ruppertsberg, Dürkheimer

JOH. JOS. CHRISTOFFEL ERBEN

2001 ÜRZIGER WÜRZGARTEN RIESLING AUSLESE

QUALITÄTSWEIN MIT PRÄDIKAT

GUTSABFÜLLUNG
WEINGUT JOH. JOS. CHRISTOFFEL ERBEN · D-54539 ÜRZIG

PRODUCE OF GERMANY

750 ml e

MOSEL · SAAR · RUWER

alc. 8.0 % by vol

A.P.Nr. 2 602 041 008 02

Can you take the mystery out of reading German wine labels?

German wine labels give you plenty of information. For example, take a look at the label above.

Joh. Jos. Christoffel Erben is the producer.

Mosel is the region of the wine's origin. Note that the region is one of the big four we discussed earlier in this chapter.

2001 is the year the grapes were harvested.

Ürzig is the town and **Würzgarten** is the vineyard from which the grapes originate. The Germans add the suffix "er" to make *Ürziger*, just as a person from New York is called a New Yorker.

Riesling is the grape variety. Therefore, this wine is at least 85 percent Riesling.

Auslese is the ripeness level, in this case from bunches of overripe grapes.

Qualitätswein mit Prädikat is the quality level of the wine.

A.P. Nr. 2 602 041 008 02 is the official testing number—proof that the wine was tasted by a panel of tasters and passed the strict quality standards required by the government.

Gutsabfüllung means "estate-bottled."

WHOSE VINEYARD IS IT, ANYWAY?

Piesporter Goldtröpfchen—350 owners
Wehlener Sonnenuhr—250 owners
Brauneberger Juffer—180 owners

ALL QUALITÄTSWEIN and Prädikatswein must pass a test by an official laboratory and tasting panel to be given an official number, prior to the wine's release to the trade.

IMPRESS YOUR friends with this kind of trivia:
A.P. Nr. 2 602 041 008 02
 2 = the government referral office or testing station
 602 = location code of bottler
 041 = bottler ID number
 008 = bottle lot
 02 = the year the wine was tasted by the board

SINCE THIS wine is a 2001 vintage, the designation is still Qualitätswein mit Prädikat. Starting with the 2007 vintage, this has been changed to Prädikatswein.

THE 2003 harvest was one of the earliest in decades.

AS GERMAN winemakers say, "A hundred days of sun will make a good wine, but 120 days of sun will make a great wine."

PAST GREAT vintages of Beerenauslese and Trockenbeerenauslese: 1985, 1988, 1989, 1990, 1996.

What are the recent trends in the white wines of Germany?

Germany is producing higher-quality wines than ever before, and American interest in these wines has increased at the same time.

I feel the lighter-style Trocken (dry), Halbtrocken (medium-dry), Kabinetts, and even Spätleses are wines that can be easily served as an apéritif, or with very light food and also grilled food, and in particular with spicy or Pacific Rim cuisines. If you haven't had a German wine in a long time, the 2001 through 2006 are spectacular vintages that show the greatness of what German white wines are all about.

And the great news is that those hard-to-read gothic script German wine labels have become more user-friendly—easier to read, with more modern designs.

BEST BETS FOR RECENT VINTAGES IN GERMANY

2001** 2002* 2003* 2004* 2005** 2006* 2007 2008

*Note: * signifies exceptional vintage   ** signifies extraordinary vintage*

FOR FURTHER READING

Gault-Millan Guide to German Wine by Armin Diel and Joel Payne.

WINE AND FOOD

RAINER LINGENFELDER *(Weingut Lingenfelder Estate, Pfalz)*: *With Riesling Spätlese Halbtrocken,* "*We have a tradition of cooking freshwater fish that come from a number of small creeks in the Palatinate forest, so my personal choice would be trout, either herbed with thyme, basil, parsley, and onion and cooked in wine; or smoked with a bit of horseradish. We find it to be a very versatile wine, a very good match with a whole range of white meat. Pork is traditional in the Palatinate region, as are chicken and goose dishes.*"

JOHANNES SELBACH *(Selbach-Oster, Mosel)*: "*What kinds of food do we have with Riesling Spätlese? Anything we like! This may sound funny, but there's a wide variety of food that goes very well with—and this is the key—a fruity, only moderately sweet, well-balanced Riesling Spätlese. Start with mild curries and sesame- or ginger-flavored, not-too-spicy dishes. Or try either gravlax or smoked salmon. You can even have Riesling Spätlese with a green salad in a balsamic vinaigrette, preferably with a touch of raspberry, as long as the dressing is not too vinegary. Many people avoid pairing wine with a salad, but it works beautifully.*

"*For haute cuisine, fresh duck or goose liver lightly sautéed in its own juice, or veal sweetbreads in a rich sauce. Also salads with fresh greens, fresh fruit, and fresh seafood marinated in lime or lemon juice or balsamic vinegar.*

"*With an old, ripe Spätlese: roast venison, dishes with cream sauces, and any white-meat dish stuffed with or accompanied by fruit. It is also delicious with fresh fruit itself or as an apéritif.*"

With Riesling Spätlese Halbtrocken: "*This is a food-friendly wine, but the first thing that comes to mind is fresh seafood and fresh fish. Also wonderful with salads with a mild vinaigrette, and with a course that's often difficult to match: cream soups. If we don't know exactly what to drink with a particular food, Spätlese Halbtrocken is usually the safe bet.*

"*It may be too obvious to say foie gras with Eiswein, but it is a classic.*"

CLASS THREE: THE WHITE WINES OF GERMANY

The Wines of Germany is the third class and the final white-wine tasting before we move on to the reds. It is divided into two parts, a component tasting and then the white wines of Germany.

In the component tasting, you will learn how to identify the four critical components of wine—acid, sugar, tannin, and sulfites—by adding each to water, then to wine. You will get to know your own tolerance thresholds for each as you experience the individual components. This is the ideal introduction to German wines. Why? Because I describe German wine as the perfect balance of residual sugar, fruit, and acid.

White Wines of Germany highlights the stylistic differences between the Mosel and Rhein regions. The wines of the Mosel are generally lower in alcohol and lighter in style than those of the Rhein region.

The real point, of course, is exposing you to the basic characteristics of German white wines.

PART I: PRELUDE: COMPONENT TASTING

What you'll need:

1. Control wine: I recommend either a Gallo Chablis Blanc or a Carlo Rossi Chablis
2. 9 wineglasses
3. Component chart
4. Component tasting worksheet
5. Acids found in wine (a blend of all three, or just one): tartaric, citric, and malic
6. Sugar (superfine)
7. Tannin
8. Sulfur dioxide (sold as potassium metabisulfite in home winemaking shops)

This component tasting will help you understand your own olfactory thresholds for taste (residual sugar and acid), tactile sensation (tannin), and smell (fruit and sulfur dioxide). If you want to try this component tasting at home you can purchase all of the components at home winemaking stores. You'll need nine

2	4	6	8
Acid in Wine	Sugar/Acid in Wine	Tannin in Wine	Sulfur Dioxide in Wine

1	3	5	7
Acid in Water	Sugar/Acid in Water	Tannin in Water	Sulfur Dioxide in Water

glasses: one for the control wine and eight for the components. Whichever control wine you select, use that wine for all of the component tastings.

Control wine

Taste the control wine and record the balance of the wine's components. Did the wine have any residual sugar? Was the wine low, medium, or high in acidity? Was the wine light-, medium-, or full-bodied? Were its components all in balance or was there one that dominated? Although everyone starts with the same wine, it's amazing to see how each taster's threshold for each component differs. In last semester's class one-third of the students rated the acidity as high, one-third felt it was balanced, and another third judged it as low, all of which highlight the fact that everyone has different "taste" thresholds!

Once you've finished discussing the control wine, continue with the component tasting, which is divided into four sections, one for each component.

COMPONENT 1: ADDING ACID

Acid in Water: Add 1½ teaspoons of acid mixture (tartaric, citric, and malic acids) to 1 liter of water.

Pour two ounces of the acid/water blend for each taster and taste; record and compare your reactions. Acidity is usually most strongly felt on the sides of the tongue and in your gums. Pay particular attention to these areas of your mouth as you taste the first two glasses in this trial. By isolating the components in neutral water, you will experience acidity, nothing else, which instantly highlights your acidity threshold: Some people cringe at the sourness while others find it palatable, even pleasant.

COMPONENT TASTING WORKSHEET

Control Wine:

60-Second Wine Expert:

Identify the major component in each time slot.

0–15 seconds_____   30–45 seconds_____

15–30 seconds_____   45–60 seconds_____

Component I:

1. Acid in water: _____

2. Acid in wine: _____

Component II:

3. Sugar/acid in water: _____

4. Sugar/acid in wine: _____

Component III:

5. Tannin in water: _____

6. Tannin in wine: _____

Component IV:

7. Sulphur dioxide in water: _____

8. Sulphur dioxide in wine: _____

Now comes one of the most important lessons of the tasting class: the order in which the wines are served and how one wine can affect another. Go back to the control wine and taste it again. Has the taste changed? Most likely your answer will be an emphatic *yes*! However, the wine hasn't changed, your awareness or perception of acidity has. The high acid water component was so strong that it affected the taste of the control wine, which now seems more acidic than it did on your first taste.

Acid in Wine: Add l teaspoon of acid mixture to l liter of wine.

Pour a two-ounce serving of the acid/wine mix for each taster. By raising the acid level of the wine you've obviously changed the balance of the wine since acidity is wine's strongest component. Taste the wine and record your notes. In class, I've found some students prefer this style over the control wine, while others wanted their money back! Additionally, this tasting will help you understand how adding acid to wine is one way winemakers can affect a wine's style.

COMPONENT II: ADDING SUGAR AND ACID

Sugar and acid to water: Add 8 teaspoons of superfine sugar and l teaspoon of acid to one liter of water.
Sugar and acid to wine: Add 6 teaspoons of superfine sugar and l teaspoon of acid mixture to l liter of wine.

Sweetness is usually tasted on the tip of the tongue; experiment with how your tongue reacts to sweetness. After trying the sugar/acid mixture in water, try the sugar/acid wine. Record your thoughts of both and discuss, then go back and taste the control wine. Since your tongue has adjusted itself to the double whammy of both higher acidity and higher sugar, you'll find the balance of the components in the control wine has completely changed.

COMPONENT III: ADDING TANNIN

Tannin is sold in winemaking stores in a powder form. In order to make the tannin solution, mix three teaspoons of tannin powder with six ounces of warm or hot water, as tannin will not dissolve in cold water.

Tannin to water: Mix 1 teaspoon of tannin solution into 1 liter of water.
Tannin to wine: Add 1 teaspoon of tannin solution to 1 liter of wine.

Tannin affects the balance and taste of wine. As before, taste and discuss the effects to adding tannin to water, then to the control wine. Take notes on each. You'll discover that the astringency of the tannin in both the water and the wine will overpower and dry out your taste buds; your mouth may become so dry that you will lose your saliva, a key element in taste. By this time in the component tasting, the control wine has undergone many "changes" and few traces of its original taste remain. The tannin on your tongue will overpower the sweetness and fruit of the control wine, leaving only acidity and tannin.

COMPONENT IV: ADDING SULFUR DIOXIDE (SO_2)

I'm frequently asked questions about the use of sulfites in wine, usually from people asking why sulfur dioxide (potassium metabisulfite) is added to a wine and if it is healthy. First, all wines contain some SO_2 because it is a natural by-product of fermentation. Second, because SO_2 kills bacteria in wine, prevents unwanted fermentation, and acts as a preservative, it is occasionally added during the winemaking process (see page 10). Many people confuse sulfur dioxide with hydrogen sulfite, which has the smell of rotten eggs; sulfur dioxide is more of a sensation than a smell. Too much sulfur dioxide in wine can produce an itching sensation in your nose, sneezing, and watering of the eyes. Is it healthy? Not really, but it's not unhealthy, either, unless you have a natural allergy to it. Because it is a naturally occurring component in wine, it's important that you understand what your tolerance for it is. I have an extremely low threshold for sulfur dioxide and those who are allergic may have a stronger reaction.

IN MY class, I pre-pour the first 6 of the 8 water/wine components. When my students enter the classroom they often notice that the room has a pleasant wine cellar smell. If I had pre-poured the sulfur dioxide, the classroom would smell more like a laboratory.

Sulfur dioxide to water: Add ⅛ teaspoon of SO_2 to 1 liter of water.
Sulfur dioxide to wine: Add ⅛ teaspoon of SO_2 to 1 liter of wine.

Add the same amount of SO_2 to the water as you do to the wine; first smell the water, then the wine. It is not neccessary to taste it. Interestingly, most students do not experience the sulfur dioxide in water but, due to the alcohol content, many of those same students will understand SO_2 once it's added to the control wine and inhaled; still others won't experience it at all. Individual tolerance depends on personal thresholds. You may find it repugnant (as I do); it may not bother you at all; or you might fall somewhere in between. In any event, if sulfur dioxide dominates a wine, the wine is flawed.

PART II: THE WHITE WINES OF GERMANY

At this point in my class, students need some *real* wine. The refreshing fruit, sweetness, and acidity of good German white wines provide the perfect transition.

I've found that German wines are not as well-known or as well-understood as French or California wines to most Americans. German wines are often dismissed because they seem complicated, and also because they are light-bodied white wines and the best German wines have higher levels of residual sugar. Don't make that mistake. Once you learn the main villages, vineyards, classifications, and a little German pronunciation, you'll find it easy to understand and you'll be able to enjoy the charm and elegance of the great German wines.

Here are the wines I poured in my most recent class:

1. A blind wine: any Qualitätswein from Germany
2. Graacher Himmelreich Riesling Kabinett 2006, J.J. Prüm (Mosel)
3. Niersteiner Brückchen Riesling Kabinett 2006, Strub (Rheinhessen)
4. Wehlener Sonnenuhr Riesling Spätlese 2006, Meulenhof (Mosel)
5. Gleisweiler Holle Riesling Spätlese 2006, Minges (Pfalz)
6. Urziger Wurzgarten Riesling Auslese 2004, J. J. Christoffel Erben (Mosel)
7. Deidesheimer Grainhubel Riesling Auslese 2004, Dr. Deinhard (Pfalz)
8. Tokaji Aszú 5 Puttonyos Disnókő 2000 (Hungary)

There are five sections to this tasting.

SIX GREAT vintages in a row, 2001 to 2006, were exceptional vintages in both the Mosel and the Rhein regions of Germany, a very rare occurrence because of their northerly locations.

SECTION I: IDENTIFYING THE CHARACTERISTICS OF A GOOD QUALITY GERMAN WINE (ONE WINE, TASTED ALONE)

Wine #1 should be tasted blind if you have several people participating in your tasting. I chose a good typical Qualitätswein because it is medium-dry and has a good balance of fruit and acid with a touch of residual sugar. Qualitätswein typifies German wine, so taste it as your control wine, take notes, and pay attention to the fruit, acid, and sugar. As noted on page 101, there are two different levels of German wines moving from the basic classification, Tafelwein, or table wine, to Qualitätswein.

Retail price $15
Ready to Drink

The next six wines are ordered according to their ripeness level. I believe the highest-quality German wines are made with the Riesling grape variety. All of the Prädikatswein recommended for this tasting are produced from 100 percent Riesling.

SECTION II: TASTING AND COMPARING TWO KABINETTS
(TWO WINES, TASTED TOGETHER; WINES SHOULD BE THE SAME VINTAGE OR NO MORE THAN ONE YEAR APART)

Wine #2: Graacher Himmelreich Riesling Kabinett 2006, J.J. Prüm (Mosel)

Wine #2 comes from the Mosel region, the village of Graach and the Himmelreich vineyard. It is classified a Kabinett based on its residual sugar content. The Prüm family owns some of the best vineyard land in all of the Mosel. It is made from 100 percent Riesling and comes from the outstanding 2006 vintage. This Riesling will be the driest and lightest wine of the next six wines and usually has a little *spritzig*, a slight bit of carbon dioxide purposely leftover after fermentation, enhancing the flavor of the refreshing and lively Riesling fruit.

Retail price $25
Ready to drink
Other recommended producers of this style Mosel Kabinett are: Kesselstatt, Bergweiler-Prüm, Jos Christoffel, and Frederich-Wilhelm-Gymnasium.

Wine #3: Niersteiner Brückchen Riesling Kabinett 2006, Strub (Rheinhessen)

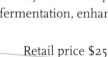

The Niersteiner Brückchen Riesling Kabinett 2006, Strub comes from the Rheinhessen region, the village of Nierstein and the Brückchen vineyard and is classified a Kabinett. Walter Strub is the 11th generation winemaker. All the grapes for this wine are hand-picked, whole bunch pressed, and fermented slowly. This wine has more concentration, body, and depth of Riesling flavor than the Graacher, and a vibrant, balanced structure.

Retail price $18
Ready to drink
Other recommended wines of this style Rheinhessen Kabinett are: Niersteiner Paterberg, Niersteiner Oelber, or Niersteiner Orbel, all from the producer Strub.

Section III: Tasting and Comparing Two Spätlese
(Two wines, tasted together, wines should be of the same vintage or within one year)

Wine #4: *Wehlener Sonnenuhr Riesling Spätlese 2006, Meulenhof (Mosel)*

This wine is from the Mosel region, the village of Wehlen, and from one of the most famous vineyards in Germany-Sonnenuhr, and is classified a Spätlese. The estate has a history going back into the twelfth century. Even though this wine has higher residual sugar content than the Kabinetts, the delicate Riesling fruit and zesty acidity gives this wine a lingering finish.

Retail price $30
Ready to drink, but can age
Other recommended producers of this style of Mosel Riesling Spätlese are: Selbach-Oster, J.J. Prüm, Kesselstatt, S.A. Prüm, Kerpen.

Wine #5: *Gleisweiler Holle Riesling Spätlese 2006, Minges (Pfalz)*

This wine is from the Pfalz region, the village of Gleisweil, and from the Holle vineyard and is classified a Spätlese. The history of this winery is traced back to the fifteenth century and the Minges family ownership is in its sixth generation. The Minges family also owns a fairly large vineyard holding in the Pfalz region. The exotic bouquet combined with its chalkiness and mineral overtones give this Riesling a well-rounded finish.

Retail price $27
Ready to drink, but can age
Another recommended producer of this style of Pfalz Riesling Spätlese is: Weingut Johannishof.

THE RHEINHESSEN, Rheingau, and the Pfalz all produce different style Rieslings coming from different soils, slopes, and proximity to the rivers.

SECTION IV: TASTING OF TWO AUSLESE
(TWO WINES, TASTED TOGETHER, NOT NECESSARY TO HAVE THE SAME VINTAGE, BUT MUST SHOW YOUNGER TO OLDER)

Wine #6: Urziger Wurzgarten Riesling Auslese 2004, J.J. Christoffel Erben (Mosel)

This wine is from the Mosel region, the village of Urgiz and the Wurzgarten vineyard, and is classified an Auslese from the exceptional 2004 vintage. Once we get to the German Auslese classification it's a whole new ball game. We are now into what I would describe as a dessert wine category. The *Weingut* of J.J. Christoffel Erben is small, only producing 2,500 cases a year, all very high quality. This is a wine of great finesse. The immediate sweetness followed by the tropical fruit and juicy acidity give pleasure from first to last taste.

Weingut is the German name for winery.

> Retail price $40
> Ready to drink, but can age
> Other recommended producers of this style of Mosel Riesling Auslese are: Dr. Loosen, Karl Erbes, and Alfred Merkelbach.

Wine #7: Deidesheimer Grainhubel Riesling Auslese 2004, Dr. Deinhard (Pfalz)

This wine is from the Pfalz region, the village of Deidesheim, the Grainhubel vineyard, and is classified an Auslese. Deinhard was founded in 1849 and today is one of the largest producers of Sekt (sparkling wine) in Germany. With over 35 hectares of vineyards, it is the largest estate of all tasted in this class. This Auslese has a drier style than the Urziger, but has a nice harmony of components, dominated by the intensity of the Riesling fruit. The extra two years of aging demonstrate that many German wines have the potential to age.

> Retail price $45
> Ready to drink, but can age
> Other recommended producers of this style of Pfalz Riesling Auslese are: Bassermann-Jordan and Dr. Bürklin-Wolf.

Section V: One of the Greatest Sweet Wines of the World: Tokaji Aszú (one wine, tasted alone)

Wine #8: Tokaji Aszú 5 Puttonyos, Disnókő 2000 (Hungary)

Along with French Sauternes and German Beerenauslese and Trockenbeere-nauslese, the Tokaji Aszú is one of the "classic" sweet dessert wines in the world. The Disnókő estate was created by the Cazes family of Château Lynch Bages in Bordeaux.

My students will either love this wine or want their money back! Its high sugar content (120 grams) is both seductive and delicious. It's sweet but intoxicating because of its near-perfect balance of fruit, acid, and residual sugar. The botrytricized furmint grapes bring out the richness of honeyed apricot flavors.

Retail price $63 (500L)
Should age for 10+ years
Other recommended producers of Tokay are: Château Pajzos, Royal Tokaji Company, Oremus, and Szepsy.

Questions for Class Three:
The White Wines of Germany

12. What are the two main categories of Qualitätswein? 101

13. Name the levels of ripeness of Prädikatswein. 102

14. What does the word *Spätlese* mean in English? 102

15. What is the average range of alcohol levels of German wines? 101

16. What is Eiswein? 102

17. What is Süssreserve? 103

18. What is *Botrytis cinerea* (*Edelfäule*)? 106

19. Match the region to the village. 104

    a. Rheingau   ___Oppenheim

    b. Mosel   ___Rüdesheim

    c. Rheinhessen   ___Bernkastel

    d. Pfalz   ___Piesport

                    ___Johannisberg

                    ___Deidesheim

                    ___Nierstein

20. What does the German term *Gutsabfüllung* indicate? 105

The Red Wines of Burgundy and the Rhône Valley

THE RED WINES OF BURGUNDY · WINE-PRODUCING AREAS · BEAUJOLAIS ·

CÔTE CHÂLONNAISE · CÔTE DE BEAUNE · CÔTE DE NUITS ·

RHÔNE VALLEY

The Red Wines of Burgundy

Now we're getting into a whole new experience in wines—the reds. The complexity, nuances, flavors, and length of taste in red wines evoke a sense of excitement for me and my students, and we tend to concentrate more when we taste red wines.

2,000 YEARS OF EXPERIENCE

Burgundy's reputation for winemaking dates as far back as 51 B.C.

LAND OF 1,000 NAMES

There are more than 1,000 names and more than 110 appellations you must memorize to become a Burgundy wine expert.

What's so different about red wines (beyond their color)?

We're beginning to see more components in the wines—more complexities. In the white wines, we were looking mainly for the acid/fruit balance, but now, in addition, we're looking for other characteristics, such as tannin.

Why is Burgundy so difficult to understand?

Before we go any further, I must tell you that there are no shortcuts. Burgundy is one of the most difficult subjects in the study of wines. People get confused about Burgundy. They say, "There's so much to know," and "It looks so hard." Yes, there are many vineyards and villages, and they're all important. But there are really only fifteen to twenty-five names you should know if you'd like to understand and speak about Burgundy wines intelligently. Not to worry. I'm going to help you decode all the mysteries of Burgundy: names, regions, and labels.

What are the main red wine–producing areas of Burgundy?

Côte d'Or {
Côte de Nuits Beaujolais
Côte de Beaune Côte Châlonnaise

What major grape varieties are used in red Burgundy wines?

The two major grape varieties are Pinot Noir and Gamay. Under Appellation d'Origine Contrôlée laws, all red Burgundies are made from the Pinot Noir grape, except Beaujolais, which is produced from the Gamay grape.

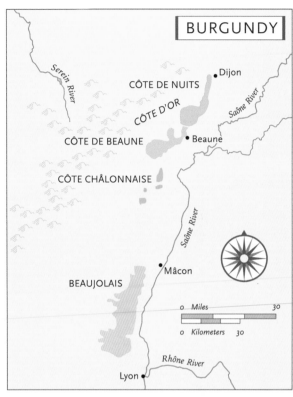

THE CÔTE D'OR is only 30 miles long and half a mile wide.

BLAME NAPOLEON

If you're having trouble understanding the wines of Burgundy, you're not alone. After the French Revolution in 1789, all the vineyards were sold off in small parcels. The Napoleonic Code also called for a law of equal inheritance for the children— continuing to fragment the vineyards even further.

THE MAGNIFICENT AND DIFFICULT PINOT NOIR

The fame of the Pinot Noir has its origins in Burgundy, France. I have a tremendous amount of respect for the individuals who have chosen to plant Pinot Noir since it is a difficult grape to make into a great wine. You have to be really passionate and patient when growing this thin-skinned grape. It is susceptible to many different diseases, and too much sunlight (heat) during the growing season will end the chances of making a balanced wine.

What you will get from a great Pinot Noir is less tannin, less extraction of color, and less body. The best Pinot Noirs in Burgundy are not about muscle and density but rather elegance and finesse.

BEAUJOLAIS

IN AN average year, some 19 million cases of wine are produced in Burgundy. Twelve million cases of that are Beaujolais!

- The wine is made from 100 percent Gamay grapes.
- This wine's style is typically light and fruity. It's meant to be consumed young. Beaujolais can be chilled.
- Beaujolais is the best-selling Burgundy in the United States by far, probably because there is so much of it, it's so easy to drink, and it's very affordable. Most bottles cost between eight and twenty dollars, although the price varies with the quality level.

What are the different quality levels of Beaujolais?

There are three different quality levels of Beaujolais:

Beaujolais: This basic Beaujolais accounts for the majority of all Beaujolais produced. Cost: $.

Beaujolais-Villages: This comes from certain villages in Beaujolais. There are thirty-five villages that consistently produce better wines. Most Beaujolais-Villages are a blend of wines from these villages, and usually no particular village name is included on the label. Cost: $$.

Cru: A cru is actually named for the village that produces this highest quality of Beaujolais. Cost: $$$$.

There are ten crus (villages):

BROUILLY	JULIÉNAS
CHÉNAS	MORGON
CHIROUBLES	MOULIN-À-VENT
CÔTE DE BROUILLY	RÉGNIÉ
FLEURIE	SAINT-AMOUR

What's Beaujolais Nouveau?

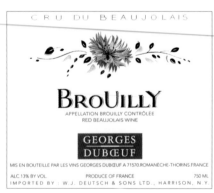

ALL GRAPES in the Beaujolais region are picked by hand.

Beaujolais Nouveau is even lighter and fruitier in style than your basic Beaujolais and it is best to drink it young. Isn't that true of all Beaujolais wines? Yes, but Nouveau is different. This "new" Beaujolais is picked, fermented, bottled, and available at your local retailer in a matter of weeks. (I don't know what you call that in your business, but I call it good cash flow in mine. It gives the wine-maker a virtually instant return.)

There's another purpose behind Beaujolais Nouveau: Like a preview of a movie, it offers the wine-consuming public a sample of the quality of the vintage and style that the winemaker will produce in his regular Beaujolais for release the following spring.

Beaujolais Nouveau is meant to be consumed within six months of bottling. So if you're holding a 2000 Beaujolais Nouveau, now is the time to give it to your "friends."

How long should I keep a Beaujolais?

It depends on the level of quality and the vintage. Beaujolais and Beaujolais-Villages are meant to last between one and three years. Crus can last longer because they are more complex: they have more fruit and tannin. I've tasted Beaujolais crus that were more than ten years old and still in excellent condition. This is the exception, though, not the rule.

Which shippers/producers should I look for when buying Beaujolais?

BOUCHARD   DROUHIN   DUBOEUF
JADOT   MOMMESSIN

BEST BETS FOR RECENT VINTAGES OF BEAUJOLAIS

2002*   2003*   2005*   2006   2007   2008

*Note: * signifies exceptional vintage*

BEAUJOLAIS NOUVEAU MADNESS

The exact date of release is the third Thursday in November, and Beaujolais Nouveau is introduced to the consumer amid great hoopla. Restaurants and retailers all vie to be the first to offer the new Beaujolais to their customers.

ONE-THIRD of the Beaujolais grapes are used to make Beaujolais Nouveau.

"Beaujolais is one of the very few red wines that can be drunk as a white. Beaujolais is my daily drink. And sometimes I blend one-half water to the wine. It is the most refreshing drink in the world."

—DIDIER MOMMESSIN

TO CHILL OR NOT TO CHILL?

As a young student studying wines in Burgundy, I visited the Beaujolais region, excited and naive. In one of the villages, I stopped at a bistro and ordered a glass of Beaujolais. (A good choice on my part, don't you think?) The waiter brought the glass of Beaujolais and it was chilled, and I thought that these people had not read the right books! Every wine book I'd ever read always said you serve red wines at room temperature and white wines chilled.

Obviously, I learned from my experience that when it comes to Beaujolais Nouveau, Beaujolais, and Beaujolais-Villages, it's a good idea to give them a slight chill to bring out the fruit and liveliness (acidity) of the wines. That is why Beaujolais is my favorite red wine to have during the summer.

However, to my taste, the Beaujolais crus have more fruit and more tannin and are best served at room temperature.

WINE AND FOOD

Beaujolais goes well with almost anything—especially light, simple meals and cheeses—nothing overpowering. Generally, try to match your Beaujolais with light food, such as veal, fish, or fowl. Here's what some of the experts say:

GEORGES DUBOEUF: *"A lot of dishes can be eaten with Beaujolais—what you* choose depends on the appellation and vintage. With charcuteries and pâtés you can serve a young Beaujolais or Beaujolais-Villages. With grilled meat, more generous and fleshy wines, such as Juliénas and Morgon crus, can be served. With meats cooked in a sauce (for example, coq au vin), I would suggest a Moulin-à-Vent cru from a good vintage."

ANDRÉ GAGEY (Louis Jadot): *"Beaujolais with simple meals, light cheeses, grilled meat—everything except sweets."*

DIDIER MOMMESSIN: *"Serve with an extremely strong cheese, such as Roquefort, especially when the wine is young and strong enough for it. Also with white meat and veal."*

CÔTE CHÂLONNAISE

Now we're getting into classic Pinot Noir wines that offer tremendous value.

You should know three villages from this area:

Mercurey: 95 percent red

Givry: 90 percent red

Rully: 50 percent red

Mercurey is the most important, producing wines of high quality. Because they are not well known in the United States, Mercurey wines are often a very good buy.

Which shippers/producers should I look for when buying wines from the Côte Châlonnaise?

MERCUREY	FAIVELEY
	DOMAINE DE SUREMAIN
	MICHEL JUILLOT
GIVRY	DOMAINE THENARD
	DOMAINE JABLOT
	LOUIS LATOUR
RULLY	ANTONIN RODET

CÔTE D'OR

Here is the heart of Burgundy. The Côte d'Or (pronounced "coat door") means "golden slope." This region gets its name from the color of the foliage on the hillside, which in autumn is literally golden, as well as the income it brings to the winemakers. The area is very small and its best wines are among the priciest in the world. If you are looking for a $7.99 everyday bottle of wine, this is not the place that will produce it.

What's the best way to understand the wines of the Côte d'Or?

First, you need to know that these wines are distinguished by quality levels—generic, Village, Premier Cru vineyards, and Grand Cru vineyards. Let's look at the quality levels with the double pyramid shown below. As you can see, not much Grand Cru wine is produced, but it is the highest quality and extremely expensive. Generic wine, on the other hand, is more readily available. Although much is produced, very few generic wines can be classified as outstanding.

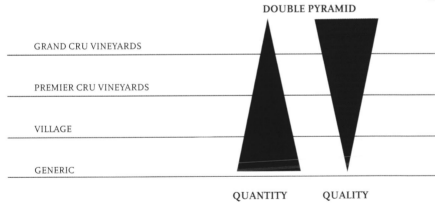

DOUBLE PYRAMID

GRAND CRU VINEYARDS

PREMIER CRU VINEYARDS

VILLAGE

GENERIC

QUANTITY   QUALITY

The Côte d'Or is divided into two regions:

Côte de Beaune: Red and white wines (70 percent red and 30 percent white).

Côte de Nuits: 95 percent red wines, the highest-quality red Burgundy wines come from this region.

Another way to understand the wines of the Côte d'Or is to become familiar with the most important villages, Grand Cru vineyards, and some of the Premier Cru vineyards.

GENERIC WINES are labeled simply "Burgundy" or "Bourgogne." A higher level of generic wines will be labeled Côte de Beaune Villages or Côte de Nuits Villages, being a blend of different village wines.

THERE ARE 32 Grand Cru Vineyards:
8 white
24 red
24 from the Côte de Nuits
8 from the Côte de Beaune

HAS THIS ever happened to you? In a restaurant, you order a Village wine—Gevrey Chambertin, for example—and by mistake the waiter brings you a Grand Cru Le Chambertin. What would you do?

$
Village Only = Village Wine

$$
Village + Vineyard
(Clos Saint-Jacques) = Premier Cru

$$$$
Vineyard Only
(Le Chambertin) = Grand Cru

IT'S THE LAW!

Beginning with the 1990 vintage, all Grand Cru Burgundies must include the words "Grand Cru" on the label.

Why are we bothering with all this geography? Must we learn the names of all the villages and vineyards?

I thought you'd never ask. First of all, the geography is important because it helps make you a smart buyer. If you're familiar with the most important villages and vineyards, you're more likely to make an educated purchase.

You really don't have to memorize all the villages and vineyards. I'll let you in on a little secret of how to choose a Burgundy wine and tell at a glance if it's a Village wine, a Premier Cru, or a Grand Cru—usually the label will tip you off in the manner illustrated here.

This is the method I use to teach Burgundy wine. Ask yourself the following:

Where is the wine from? France

What type of wine is it? Burgundy

Which region is it from? Côte d'Or

Which area? Côte de Nuits

Which village is the wine from? Chambolle-Musigny

Does the label give more details? Yes, it tells you that the wine is from a vineyard called Musigny, which is one of the thirty-two Grand Cru vineyards.

France
Burgundy
Côte d'Or
Côte de Nuits
Chambolle-Musigny
Musigny

* The closer you get to the center of the circle, the better the quality of the wine, and it will likely cost more.

Twenty-five years later in Burgundy

The red wines of Burgundy still remain the benchmark for Pinot Noir throughout the world. Over the last twenty-five years, the great wines of Burgundy have only gotten better (and more expensive!), and the good wines have become more consistent and of higher quality. Better clonal selection vineyard management and a new generation of winemakers will continue to give pleasure for decades to come. Both the shippers' (négociants) wines and the estate-bottled producers are making the best wines that Burgundy has ever known.

Why are the well-known great Burgundies so expensive?

The answer is simple: supply and demand. The Burgundy growers and shippers of the Côte d'Or have a problem all business people would envy—not enough supply to meet the demand. It has been this way for years and it will continue, because Burgundy is a small region that produces a limited amount of wine. The Bordeaux wine region produces three times as much wine as Burgundy does.

IN THE 1960s, Burgundy wines were fermented and vatted for up to three weeks. Today's Burgundy wines are usually fermented and vatted for six to twelve days.

BURGUNDY WINE HARVEST

(average number of cases over a five-year period for red and white)

Regional Appellations	2,136,674
Beaujolais	11,503,617
Côte Châlonnaise	357,539
Côte d'Or (Côte de Nuits)	511,594
Côte d'Or (Côte de Beaune)	1,391,168
Chablis	755,188
Mâconnais	2,136,674
Other Appellations	339,710
Total Burgundy Harvest	19,132,164 cases

BEST BETS FOR RECENT VINTAGES OF CÔTE D'OR

1999*   2002*   2003*   2005**   2006

*Note: * signifies exceptional vintage*

*** signifies extraordinary vintage*

IF YOU DON'T want to be disappointed by the Burgundy wine you select, make sure you know your vintages. Also, due to the delicacy of the Pinot Noir grape, red Burgundies require proper storage, so make sure you buy from a merchant who handles Burgundy wines with care.

HOW IMPORTANT is the producer? Clos de Vougeot is the single largest Grand Cru vineyard in Burgundy, totaling 124 acres, with more than 70 different owners. Each owner makes his own winemaking decisions, such as when to pick the grapes, the style of fermentation, and how long to age the wine in oak. Obviously, all Clos de Vougeot is not created equal.

Who are the most important shippers to look for when buying red Burgundy wine?

BOUCHARD PÈRE ET FILS	**LOUIS JADOT**
JOSEPH DROUHIN	**LOUIS LATOUR**
JAFFELIN	**LABOURÉ-ROI**
CHANSON	

Although 80 percent of Burgundy wine is sold through shippers, some fine estate-bottled wines are available in limited quantities in the United States. Look for the following:

DOMAINE CLERGET	**DOMAINE LOUIS TRAPET**
DOMAINE COMTE DE VOGÜE	**DOMAINE MONGEARD-**
DOMAINE DANIEL RION	**MUGNERET**
DOMAINE DE LA ROMANÉE-CONTI	**DOMAINE PARENT**
DOMAINE DUJAC	**DOMAINE PIERRE DAMOY**
DOMAINE GEORGES ROUMIER	**DOMAINE POTEL**
DOMAINE GROFFIER	**DOMAINE POUSSE D'OR**
DOMAINE HENRI GOUGES	**DOMAINE PRINCE DE MÉRODE**
DOMAINE HENRI LAMARCHE	**DOMAINE TOLLOT-BEAUT**
DOMAINE JAYER	**DOMAINE VINCENT GIRARDIN**
DOMAINE JEAN GRIVOT	**MAISON FAIVELEY**
DOMAINE LEROY	

FOR FURTHER READING

I recommend *The Wines of Burgundy* by Clive Coates, M.W.; *Burgundy* by Anthony Hanson; *Making Sense of Burgundy* by Matt Kramer; *The Great Domaines of Burgundy* by Remington Norman; and *Burgundy* by Robert M. Parker Jr.

WINE AND FOOD

To get the most flavor from both the wine and the food, some of Burgundy's famous winemakers offer these suggestions:

ROBERT DROUHIN: *"In my opinion, white wine is never a good accompaniment to red meat, but a light red Burgundy can match a fish course (not shellfish). Otherwise, for light red Burgundies, white meat—not too many spices; partridge, pheasant, and rabbit. For heavier-style wines, lamb and steak are good choices."* Personally, Mr.

Drouhin does not enjoy red Burgundies with cheese—especially goat cheese.

PIERRE HENRY GAGEY *(Louis Jadot):* *"With red Beaujolais wines, such as Moulin-à-Vent Château des Jacques, for example, a piece of pork like an andouillette from Fleury is beautiful. A Gamay, more fruity and fleshy than Pinot Noir, goes perfectly with this typical meal from our terroir. My favorite food combination with a red Burgundy wine is poulet de*

bresse demi d'oeil. The very thin flesh of this truffle-filled chicken and the elegance and delicacy from the great Pinot Noir, which come from the best terroir, go together beautifully."

LOUIS LATOUR: *"With Château Corton Grancey, filet of duck in a red wine sauce. Otherwise, Pinot Noir is good with roast chicken, venison, and beef. Mature wines are a perfect combination for our local cheeses, Chambertin and Citeaux."*

The Red Wines of the Rhône Valley

As a former sommelier, I was often asked to recommend a big, robust red Burgundy wine to complement a rack of lamb or filet mignon. To the customers' surprise, I didn't recommend a Burgundy at all. The best bet is a Rhône wine, which is typically a bigger and fuller wine than one from Burgundy, and usually has a higher alcoholic content. The reason for these characteristics is quite simple. It all goes back to location and geography.

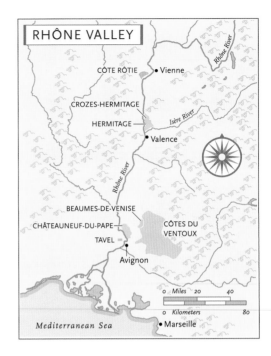

Where's the Rhône Valley?

The Rhône Valley is in southeastern France, south of the Burgundy region, where the climate is hot and the conditions are sunny. The extra sun gives the grapes more sugar, which, as we have discussed, boosts the level of alcohol. The soil is full of rocks that retain the intense summer heat during both day and night.

Winemakers of the Rhône Valley are required by law to make sure their wines have a specified amount of alcohol. For example, the minimum alcoholic content required by the AOC is 10.5 percent for Côtes du Rhône and 12.5 percent for Châteauneuf-du-Pape.

What are the different quality levels of the Rhône Valley?

		% of Production
1.	Côtes du Rhône ($)	58%
2.	Côtes du Rhône Villages ($$)	8%
3.	Côtes du Rhône Crus (specific regions) ($$$$)	10%
	Northern Rhône	
	Southern Rhône	
4.	Other appellations	24%

OF ALL the wines made in the Rhône Valley, 91% are red, 6% are rosé, and 3% are white.

SOME OF the oldest vineyards in France are in the Rhône Valley. Hermitage, for example, has been in existence for more than 2,000 years.

CÔTES DU RHÔNE wine can be produced from grapes grown in either or both the northern and southern Rhône regions. More than 90% of all Côtes du Rhône wines come from the southern region.

What are the winemaking regions in the Rhône Valley?

The region is divided into two distinct areas: northern and southern Rhône. The most famous red wines that come from the northern region are:

CROZES-HERMITAGE (3,000+ ACRES)   **HERMITAGE (324 ACRES)**
CÔTE RÔTIE (555 ACRES)

The most famous red wines from the southern region are:

CHÂTEAUNEUF-DU-PAPE (7,822 ACRES)
GIGONDAS (3,036 ACRES)

Two distinct microclimates distinguish the north from the south. It is important for you to understand that these areas make distinctly different wines because of:

- Soil
- Location
- Different grape varieties used in making the wines of each area

What are the main red-grape varieties grown in the Rhône Valley?

The two major grape varieties in the Rhône Valley are:

GRENACHE   **SYRAH**

Which wines are made from these grapes?

The Côte Rôtie, Hermitage, and Crozes-Hermitage from the north are made primarily from the Syrah grape. These are the biggest and fullest wines from that region.

For Châteauneuf-du-Pape, as many as thirteen different grape varieties may be included in the blend. But the best producers use a greater percentage of Grenache and Syrah in the blend.

What's Tavel?

It's a rosé—an unusually dry rosé, which distinguishes it from most others. It's made primarily from the Grenache grape, although nine grape varieties can be used in the blend. When you come right down to it, Tavel is just like a red wine, with all the red-wine components but less color. How do they make a rosé wine with red-wine characteristics but less color? It's all in the vatting process.

TWO OTHER important red grapes in the Rhône Valley are:

Cinsault
Mourvèdre

THE 13 CRUS OF THE RHÔNE VALLEY

North
Château-Grillet (white)
Condrieu (white)
Cornas
Côte-Rôtie
Crozes-Hermitage
Hermitage
St-Joseph
St-Peray
South
Châteauneuf-du-Pape
Gigondas
Lirac
Tavel (rosé)
Vacqueyras

What's the difference between "short-vatted" and "long-vatted" wines?

When a wine is "short-vatted," the skins are allowed to ferment with the must (grape juice) for a short period of time—only long enough to impart that rosé color. It's just the opposite when a winemaker is producing red Rhône wines, such as Châteauneuf-du-Pape of Hermitage. The grape skins are allowed to ferment longer with the must, giving a rich, ruby color to the wine.

What's the difference between a $25 bottle of Châteauneuf-du-Pape and a $75 bottle of Châteauneuf-du-Pape?

A winemaker is permitted to use thirteen different grapes for his Châteauneuf-du-Pape recipe, as I mentioned earlier. It's only logical, then, that the winemaker who uses a lot of the best grapes (which is equivalent to cooking with the finest ingredients) will produce the best-tasting—and the most expensive—wine.

For example, a $25 bottle of Châteauneuf-du-Pape may contain only 20 percent of top-quality grapes (Grenache, Mourvèdre, Syrah, and Cinsault) and 80 percent of lesser-quality grapes; a $75 bottle may contain 90 percent of the top-quality grapes and 10 percent of others.

BEST BETS FOR RED RHÔNE VALLEY WINES

North 1995 1996 1997 1998 1999* 2000
2001 2003* 2004 2005 2006* 2007 2008
South 1995 1998* 1999 2000* 2001*
2003* 2004* 2005* 2006* 2007** 2008

*Note: * signifies exceptional vintage*

* * signifies extraordinary vintage

How do I buy a red Rhône wine?

You should first decide if you prefer a light Côtes du Rhône wine or a bigger, more flavorful one, such as an Hermitage. Then you must consider the vintage and the producer. Two of the oldest and best-known firms are M. Chapoutier and Paul Jaboulet Aîné. Also look for the producers Guigal, Chave, Beaucastel, Jean-Luc Colombo, Domaine du Vieux Télégraphe, Alain Graillot, Clos des Papes, Roger Sabon & Fils, Mont Redon, Le Vieux Donjon, Domaine du Pégau, and Château Rayas.

TRIVIA QUESTION: What are the 13 grapes allowed in Châteauneuf-du-Pape?

Grenache	Muscardin
Syrah	Vaccarèse
Mourvèdre	Picardin
Cinsault	Clairette
Picpoul	Roussanne
Terret	Bourboulenc
Counoise	

CHÂTEAUNEUF-DU-PAPE means "new castle of the Pope," so named for the palace in the Rhône city of Avignon in which Pope Clément V (the first French pope) resided in the 14th century.

RHÔNE VALLEY vintages can be tricky: A good year in the north may be a bad year in the south, and vice versa.

OLDER GREAT VINTAGES

North: 1983, 1985, 1988, 1989, 1990, 1991
South: 1985, 1988, 1989, 1990

A SIMPLE Côtes du Rhône is similar to a Beaujolais—except the Côtes du Rhône has more body and alcohol. A Beaujolais, by AOC standards, must contain a minimum of 9% alcohol; a Côtes du Rhône, 10.5%.

The first four represent 92% of the grapes used, with Grenache by far the most.

THERE IS no official classification for Rhône Valley wines.

SUNSHINE QUOTIENT

Region	Hours per Year
Burgundy	2,000
Bordeaux	2,050
Châteauneuf-du-Pape	2,750

THE MEDIEVAL papal coat of arms appears on some Châteauneuf-du-Pape bottles. Only owners of vineyards are permitted to use this coat of arms on the label.

A GOOD VALUE is Côtes du Ventoux. One of the most widely available wines to look for in this category is La Vieille Ferme.

When should I drink my Rhône wine?

Tavel: within two years

Côtes du Rhône: within three years

Crozes-Hermitage: within five years

Châteauneuf-du-Pape: after five years, but higher-quality Châteauneuf-du-Pape is better after ten years

Hermitage: seven to eight years, but best after fifteen, in a great year

RHÔNE VALLEY HARVEST	
(average number of cases over a five-year period)	
Côtes du Rhône regional appellation	20.4 million
Northern and southern Crus	4.3 million
Côtes du Rhône-Villages appellation	3.6 million
Total Rhône Valley harvest	28.3 million cases

Twenty-five years later in the Rhône Valley

Twenty-five years ago the Rhône Valley wines were overshadowed by the red wines of Burgundy and Bordeaux. Today they are all equals except that the best quality value of the three is the Rhône. The region has also been blessed with great weather (think great vintages) over the last ten years, especially in the south. This all makes for superb wines at a reasonable cost.

THE RED RHÔNE VALLEY ROUNDUP

NORTHERN WINES Côte Rôtie • Hermitage • Crozes-Hermitage • St. Joseph • Cornas

GRAPE Syrah

SOUTHERN WINES Châteauneuf-du-Pape • Tavel • Côtes du Rhône • Côtes du Rhône-Villages • Côtes du Ventoux • Gigondas

MAJOR GRAPES Grenache • Syrah • Cinsault • Mourvèdre

WINE AND FOOD

JEAN PIERRE AND FRANÇOIS PERRIN *(Château de Beaucastel and La Vieille Ferme):* *"The white wines of Château de Beaucastel can be drunk either very young—in the first three or four years—or should be kept for ten years or more. The combination of white meat with truffles and mushrooms is an exquisite possibility.*

"Red Rhône wines achieve their perfection from ten years and beyond, and are best when combined with game and other meats with a strong flavor.

"A good dinner could be wild mushroom soup and truffles with a white Beaucastel and stew of wild hare à la royale (with foie gras and truffles) served with a red Château de Beaucastel."

MICHEL CHAPOUTIER: *With a Côtes du Rhône wine, he recommends poultry, light meats, and cheese. Côte Rôtie goes well with white meats and small game. Châteauneuf-du-Pape complements the ripest of cheese, the richest venison, and the most lavish civet of wild boar. An Hermitage is suitable with beef, game, and any full-flavored cheese. Tavel rosé is excellent with white meat and poultry.*

FRÉDÉRIC JABOULET: *"My granddad drinks a bottle of Côtes du Rhône a day and he's in his eighties. It's good for youth. It goes with everything except old fish," he jokes.*

More specifically, Mr. Jaboulet says, "Hermitage is good with wild boar and mushrooms. A Crozes Hermitage, particularly our Domaine de Thalabert, complements venison or roast rabbit in a cream sauce, but you have to be very careful with the sauce and the weight of the wine.

"Beef ribs and rice go well with a Côtes du Rhône, as does a game bird like roast quail. Tavel, slightly chilled, is refreshing with a summer salad. Muscat de Beaumes-de-Venise, of course, is a beautiful match with foie gras."

HERMITAGE IS the best and the longest-lived of the Rhône wines. In a great vintage, Hermitage wines can last for fifty years.

U.S. IMPORTS of Rhône wines have risen more than 200% in the last five years.

THE TWO most famous white wines of the Rhône Valley are called Condrieu and Château Grillet. Both are made from the grape variety called Viognier.

THERE IS a white Châteauneuf-du-Pape and a white Hermitage, but only a few thousand cases are produced each year.

FOR THOSE who prefer sweet wines, try Beaumes-de-Venise, made from the Muscat grape.

FOR FURTHER READING

I recommend *The Wines of the Rhône Valley*, by Robert M. Parker Jr.

CLASS FOUR: THE RED WINES OF BURGUNDY AND THE RHÔNE VALLEY

One of the most difficult subjects to teach is the wines of Burgundy. At the beginning stages of this book, my publisher wanted to be convinced that I could write a "simple" guide to wine. He asked me to choose the most difficult wine region to understand and write a simple chapter. I chose Burgundy. He liked what I wrote and the book became a reality. But writing that chapter wasn't easy.

The three most important things to know about Burgundy wine, ranked in order of importance, are: the producer, the vintage, and the classification system. Each of these differences becomes more evident after tasting each flight.

Some of my favorite wines come from the Rhône Valley. From the simple, medium-bodied Côtes du Rhône; to the spicy Crozes-Hermitage; to the big, voluptuous, high-alcohol Châteauneuf-du-Papes, these are some of the greatest wines in the world and still represent one of the best values in all winedom. If I ever add another wine class to the school and to the book, it would be devoted to wines made from the Grenache and Syrah grape varieties, and leading the way would be the wines of the Rhône Valley.

Wines for Class Four

1. Beaujolais Villages, Louis Jadot 2008
2. Fleurie, Georges Duboeuf 2008
3. Mercurey, Domaine de la Croix Jacquelet, Faiveley 2006
4. Pommard, Bouchard Père & Fils 2006
5. Volnay-Santenots, Domaine Ballot-Millot et Fils 2006
6. Chambolle-Musigny, Joseph Drouhin 2006
7. Nuits-St-Georges, Les Haut Pruliers, Domaine Daniel Rion 2006
8. Côtes du Rhône, Perrin 2007 **BEST VALUE**
9. Crozes-Hermitage, Les Jalets, Jaboulet 2006 **BEST VALUE**
10. Châteauneuf-du-Pape, La Bernardine, Chapoutier 2005

There are five parts to this tasting.

Part I: Beaujolais
(two wines tasted together,
and of the same vintage)

When it comes to Burgundy, I start off with the lightest of the red wines: those of the Beaujolais region and made from 100 percent Gamay grapes. These two wines will enhance your understanding of just how important the Burgundy wine producers, or négociants, are. I begin with Beaujolais Villages since it is a lesser appellation than the Fleurie.

Pour the two wines; stand and study both from above. Do you notice a difference in color? Does one wine have a deeper color than the other?

You should notice a slight difference in color: the Beaujolais Villages is usually lighter than the Fleurie even though both wines were made using 100 percent Gamay grapes and both were produced in 2008, a great vintage. This difference in color tells us a lot about the two wines: lighter colors indicate higher acidity, lower tannins, and demonstrates its readiness or drinkability.

Color is dictated by a wine's classification and the winemaker's technique. Because the color of this wine derives entirely from the skin of the grape, the longer a wine ferments with its skin—in a process called "maceration"—the darker its color will be. In our case, the darker red of the Fleurie tells us that it comes from a higher concentration of grapes that spent more time macerating with its skins than did the Villages.

Wine #1: Beaujolais Villages, Louis Jadot 2008

The Beaujolais Villages Jadot smells like fresh grape juice. It reminds me of the smell of a winery during harvest. It has lots of red fruit with raspberry and strawberry smells, very little tannin, and high acidity. The grapes for this wine can only come from designated villages within the Beaujolais district.

    Retail price $10
    Ready to drink
    Other recommended producers of the Beaujolais Villages style wine are: Bouchard, Drouhin, and DuBoeuf.

I USE the producers Louis Jadot and Georges Duboeuf because they are both high-quality wines and also the most widely distributed Beaujolais in the United States.

Wine #2: Fleurie, Georges Duboeuf 2008

The Beaujolais Fleurie Duboeuf 2008 has a more concentrated Gamay bouquet, more tannin, higher alcohol, more fruit, and less acidity than the Beaujolais Villages. The grapes from this wine can only come from the village of Fleurie.

Retail price $15

Ready to drink

If you can't find the Beaujolais from the village of Fleurie try another village such as Brouilly or Moulin-à-Vent. Other recommended producers are: Joseph Drouhin and Louis Jadot.

PART II: THE CÔTE CHÂLONNAISE (ONE WINE, TASTED ALONE)

Wine #3: Mercurey, Domaine de la Croix Jacquelet, Faiveley 2006

We move now to Pinot Noir, whose bouquet and aroma bear little resemblance to that of the Gamay. Pinot Noir is more concentrated, spicy, and seductive. The majority of the Burgundy class is devoted to the wines of the Côte d'Or but I would be remiss were I not to include a tasting of a wine from the Côte Châlonnaise. I choose this Pinot Noir from Burgundy because it is easy to drink, accessible now, will be the lightest and least expensive of all of the Pinot Noirs that we will taste. It also provides an excellent transition between the wines of Beaujolais and the Côte de Beaune, which follows.

This wine is made from grapes picked at their perfect ripeness. It is more complex, fuller in body, and has more integrated fruits and tannins than any of the Beaujolais wines.

Retail price $23

Ready to drink

Other recommended producers of the Mercurey style wines are: Domaine de Suremain and Michel Juillot.

The next four wines are all from the Côte d'Or and I begin with two wines from the Côte de Beaune and then continue with the two wines from the Côte de Nuits. Red wines from the Côte de Beaune have historically been lighter in style than those from the Côte de Nuits.

Part III: A Village Wine and a Premier Cru from the Côte de Beaune (two wines, tasted together, preferably of the same vintage)

The Pommard is a Village wine, while the Volnay is from a Premier Cru vineyard: The Pommard is tasted first. Tasting these two wines together highlights the differences between a Village and a Premier Cru vineyard. The year 2006 was a great vintage in Burgundy.

Wine #4: Pommard, Bouchard Père & Fils 2006

The grapes for this wine can only come from village of Pommard. This Pommard is a well-made, classic-style Pinot Noir with a medium amount of fruit, tannin, and a great balance. It is the perfect restaurant Burgundy, accessible now and reasonably priced.

> Retail price $50
> Ready to drink
> Other recommended négociants for Côte de Beaune style wines are: Joseph Drouhin, Jaffelin, Louis Jadot, and Louis Latour.

Wine #5: Volnay-Santenots, Domaine Ballot-Millot et Fils 2006

The grapes for this wine can only come from the vineyard of Santenots, located in the village of Volnay. Domaine Ballot-Millot specializes in high-quality Premier Cru vineyards in the Côte de Beaune. This is an artisanal-style wine which not only shows the charm of the Pinot Noir grape but of the *terroir*, a French word that loosely translates to mean the combination of soil, climate, and slope of the vineyard site. When I was twenty years old I tasted my first Volnay: I shall never forget its finesse, elegance, and subtlety.

> Retail price $75
> Ready to drink
> Other recommended vineyards in Volnay are: Callieret, Champans, and Clos des Chénes. Other recommended Domaine or estate-bottled producers of the Volnay style wines are: Domaine Clerget, Drouhin, Comte Lafon, and Marquis d'Angerville.

WHAT IS the difference between a négociant and an estate bottled wine? A négociant is a cooperative and buys the grapes or wine directly from a specific appellation. The négociant then bottles the wine they've either bought or made under the négociant name, such as Bouchard Père & Fils. A domaine or estate bottled wine means that the grapes from the village or vineyard listed on the label are owned and grown, and the wine is produced at that property, such as with Ballot-Millot. Most négociants offer a full selection of wine at all different price and quality levels throughout Burgundy. Bouchard is a both a négociant and producer of estate-bottled wines.

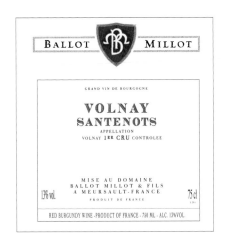

PART IV: THE CÔTE DE NUITS: A VILLAGE AND A PREMIER CRU (TWO WINES TASTED TOGETHER, PREFERABLY OF THE SAME VINTAGE)

Thus far, I've discussed the importance of producers, vintage year, and the different classifications of Burgundy wine. The only real way to understand the differences between a Village classification and a Premier Cru, however, is to taste them together. The next two wines represent some of the best reds produced in Burgundy.

The Côte de Nuit is God's gift to Pinot Noir lovers, and these great Burgundies show the essence of the Pinot Noir taste. These two wines are from outstanding producers: Joseph Drouhin and Daniel Rion. You will taste the differences of soil, vinification, texture, and style in the Village wine of Chambolle-Musigny and a Premier Cru from Nuits St. George. Both are exceptional in their own right, but you should pay particular attention to the differences in appellations and style. As you taste your way through the wines, the differences will become very apparent.

I'm going to begin this tasting by asking you to pour the next five wines—the two Burgundy wines (#6 and #7) in this flight, and the three Rhône Valley wines (#8, #9, and #10). Examine the colors of each. Notice the difference between the lighter colors of the Pinot Noir–based Burgundies and the deeper colors of the Grenache/Syrah-based Rhône Valley wines. The difference in color provides a quick visual demonstration of the differences in texture, intensity, body, and color of the two regions' wines.

Set the three Rhône Valley wines aside and proceed with the two Burgundy wines in this flight.

Wine #6: Chambolle-Musigny, Joseph Drouhin 2006

The Pinot Noir grapes can only come from the village of Chambolle-Musigny. The wine firm of Joseph Drouhin, established in 1756, produces both négociant wines and domaine wines, and is considered one of the top names in all of Burgundy by wine collectors and professional buyers. I begin with this wine because of its Village wine appellation, which should be lighter in style than the next wine. This medium-bodied Chambolle-Musigny is dominated by red fruits and spices with all of the elements of a great Pinot Noir: intensity of fruit, elegance, and a delicate balance of all of its components. It is a superb example of what a Village wine from Côte de Nuits is all about.

Retail price $50
Ready to drink
Other recommended producers of the Chambolle-Musigny style wines
are: Louis Jadot, Georges Roumier, and Robert Groffier.

Wine #7: Nuit-St-Georges, Les Haut Pruliers, Domaine Daniel Rion 2006

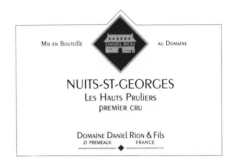

All of the Pinot Noir grapes for this wine come from the Premier Cru vineyard
Les Haut Pruliers in the village of Nuit-St-Georges. Daniel Rion is one of the
top Domaines of Nuits-St-Georges.

The wines of Nuits-St-Georges have a different underlying structure than
other villages of the Côte de Nuits. This wine is dark in color, full, powerful,
firm, concentrated, and tannic—very different in style to the delicate Chambolle-
Musigny. This is the Pinot Noir for those who prefer Cabernet Sauvignon. In
tasting Wines #6 and #7 together, you'll experience the diversity and range of
the Pinot Noir grape wines produced within the Côte de Nuits region.

Retail price $75
Needs more time
Other recommended producers of the Nuit-St-Georges style wines are:
Faiveley, Henri Gouges, Jean Grivot, and Henri Jayer.

PART V: THE CÔTES DU RHÔNE (THREE WINES, TASTED TOGETHER)

After going through all of the major Villages and Premier Crus of Burgundy,
my students and I are thoroughly exhausted and I usually have a mere twenty
minutes to cover one of my favorite regions on earth—the Rhône Valley. Fortunately, the Rhône Valley is far easier to understand than Burgundy.

Compare the lighter colors of Pinot Noir–based Burgundies to the deeper
colors of the Grenache/Syrah-based Rhône Valley wines. You'll get a quick
picture of the differences in texture, intensity, and body, as well as color.

I begin with the lesser appellation Côtes du Rhône then to the medium-
bodied Crozes-Hermitage and end with the higher appellation of Châteauneuf-
du-Pape. The 2007 vintage in the southern Rhône was an excellent vintage
with higher alcohol levels than normal.

Wine #8: Côtes du Rhône, Perrin 2007

Côtes du Rhône would be on my top three lists as best value red wine in the world. They are heavier in body than the Beaujolais wines we had at the beginning of the class with less acidity and more and rounder fruit but still can be consumed young (one to three years). The Perrin Family are the owners of the famous property Beaucastel in Chateauneuf-du-Pape making one of the great Rhône Valley wines.

Retail price $15 **BEST VALUE**
Ready to drink
Other recommended producers of Côtes du Rhône are: Jaboulet, Chapoutier, Chave, and Guigal.

Wine #9: Crozes-Hermitage, Les Jalets, Jaboulet 2006

This wine comes from the northern part of the Rhône Valley and is made with 100 percent Syrah. Jaboulet is one of the Rhône Valley's greatest producers. I personally consume a lot of this wine, finding that it is neither as light as a Pinot Noir nor as heavy as a Cabernet Sauvignon: It's just about perfect. Perhaps a medium-bodied Merlot with a spicy black-pepper character would be a better comparison. However you decide to compare this wine, you'll discover that it's perfect with barbecued meats. This is one of the world's best value wines.

The Burgundy wine prior to these cost more than double the Crozes-Hermitage. Once students discover that this Crozes retails for less than $20, they are ready to buy ten cases!

Retail price $20 **BEST VALUE**
Ready to drink
I would also suggest tasting Crozes-Hermitage Thalabert from Jaboulet.

Note: The order of the wines should change if you substitute an Hermitage for the Crozes-Hermitage: Taste the Châteauneuf-du-Pape first since it would be lighter than the Hermitage.

Wine #10: Châteauneuf-du-Pape, La Bernardine, Chapoutier 2005

This wine is from the southern region of the Rhône Valley and by law is permitted to use thirteen different grape varieties and must have a minimum of 12.5 percent alcohol. Most Châteauneuf-du-Papes will be 13.5 percent alcohol and higher, so you will often see critics describe it as big, bold, powerful, inky, rich, and robust. The La Bernardine is made from the three best grape varieties—Grenache, Syrah, and Cinsault—but is not as big in style as most Châteauneuf-du-Papes. This wine displays a balance of fruits, tannins, and alcohol, with less acidity than the Pinot Noirs.

Retail price $46
Ready to drink, but can still age
Other recommended producers of "big" style Châteauneuf-du-Papes are: Beaucastel, Vieux Télégraphe, Clos des Papes, and Rayas. For a lighter style such as the La Bernardine, try the Mont-Redon, Delas Fréres, or Guigal.

Questions for Class Four: The Red Wines of Burgundy and the Rhône Valley

The Red Wines of Bordeaux

APPELLATIONS · GRAPE VARIETIES · QUALITY LEVELS ·

THE GREAT RED WINES OF BORDEAUX · MÉDOC · GRAVES ·

POMEROL · ST-ÉMILION · CHOOSING A RED BORDEAUX

The Red Wines of Bordeaux

This province of france is rich with excitement and history, and the best part is that the wines speak for themselves. You'll find this region much easier to learn about than Burgundy. For one thing, the plots of land are bigger, and they're owned by fewer landholders. And, as the wine-loving English author Samuel Johnson once said, "He who aspires to be a serious wine drinker must drink claret." That is, the dry red table wine known as Bordeaux.

Some fifty-seven wine regions in Bordeaux produce high-quality wines that are allowed to carry the AOC designation on the label. Of these fifty-seven places, four stand out in my mind for red wine:

> ***Médoc:*** 40,199 acres (produces only red wines)
>
> ***Pomerol:*** 1,846 acres (produces only red wines)

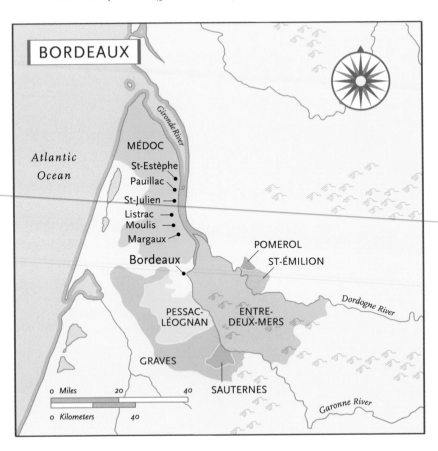

Graves/Pessac-Léognan: 9,855 acres (produces both red and dry white wines)

St-Émilion: 23,384 acres (produces only red wines)

In the Médoc, there are seven important inner appellations you should be familiar with:

HAUT MÉDOC   ST-ESTÈPHE   PAUILLAC   ST-JULIEN

MARGAUX   MOULIS   LISTRAC

Which grape varieties are grown in Bordeaux?

The three major grapes are:

Merlot

Cabernet Sauvignon

Cabernet Franc

Unlike Burgundy, where the winemaker must use 100 percent Pinot Noir to make most red wines (100 percent Gamay for Beaujolais), in Bordeaux the red wines are almost always made from a blend of grapes.

What are the different quality levels of Bordeaux wine?

Bordeaux: This is the lowest level of AOC wine in Bordeaux—wines that are nice, inexpensive, and consistent "drinking" wines. These are sometimes known as "proprietary" wines—wines known by what you could almost call a brand name, such as Mouton-Cadet, rather than by the particular region or vineyard. These are usually the least expensive AOC wines in Bordeaux. Cost: $.

Region: Regional wines come from one of the fifty-seven different regions. Only grapes and wines made in those areas can be called by their regional names: Pauillac and St-Émilion, for example. These wines are more expensive than those labeled simply Bordeaux. Cost: $$.

Region + Château: Château wines are the products of individual vineyards. There are more than 7,000 châteaux in Bordeaux. As far back as 1855, Bordeaux officially classified the quality levels of some of its châteaux. Hundreds have been officially recognized for their quality. In the Médoc, for example, the 61 highest-level châteaux are called Grand Cru Classé. There are also 247 châteaux in the Médoc that are entitled to be called Cru Bourgeois, a step below Grand Cru Classé. Other areas, such as St-Émilion and Graves, have their own classification systems. Cost: $$–$$$$.

THE GRAVES region produces 60% red wine, 40% white wine.

IN 1987, a communal appellation was established to create a higher-level appellation in the northern Graves region. It's called Pessac-Léognan (for both reds and whites).

TAKE A LOOK at the map on page 150. As a general rule of thumb, red wines from the villages and regions on the left bank of the rivers primarily use the Cabernet Sauvignon grape and on the right bank they use Merlot.

IN ALL of Bordeaux, there are some 172,000 acres of Merlot, 72,000 acres of Cabernet Sauvignon, and 33,000 acres of Cabernet Franc.

TWO OTHER grapes that are sometimes used in the blending of Bordeaux wines are Petit Verdot and Malbec.

PROPRIETARY WINES you may be familiar with:

Lauretan   Baron Philippe

Lacour Pavillon   Michel Lynch

Mouton-Cadet

THE MAJOR shippers of regional wines from Bordeaux are:

Barton & Guestier (B & G)

Cordier

Dourthe Kressmann

Eschenauer

Sichel

Yvon Mau

Ets J-P Moueix

Baron Philippe de Rothschild

Borie-Manoux

Dulong

WINES PRICED between $8 and $25 represent 80% of the total production of Bordeaux.

THE TYPICAL Médoc blend can vary from 60% to 80% Cabernet Sauvignon, 25% to 40% Merlot, and 10% to 20% Cabernet Franc.

BORDEAUX (PROPRIETARY)
APPELLATION BORDEAUX
CONTRÔLLÉE

REGIONAL
APPELLATION PAUILLAC
CONTRÔLLÉE

CHÂTEAU
APPELLATION PAUILLAC
CONTRÔLLÉE with
CHÂTEAU NAME

All three of these wines are owned by the same family, the Rothschilds, who also own Château Mouton-Rothschild.

IF YOU see a château on the label, French law dictates that the château really exists and is the château of that winemaker. What you see is what you get.

ACCORDING TO French law, a château is a house attached to a vineyard having a specific number of acres, as well as having winemaking and storage facilities on the property. A wine may not be called a château wine unless it meets these criteria. The terms *domaine*, *clos*, and *cru* are also used.

Here are the major Bordeaux classifications:

Médoc (Grands Crus Classé): 1855; sixty-one châteaux
Médoc (Crus Bourgeois): 1920, revised 1932, 1978, and 2003; 247 châteaux
Graves (Grands Crus Classé): 1959; sixteen châteaux
Pomerol: No official classification
St-Émilion: 1955, revised 1996, revised 2006; fifteen Premiers Grands Crus Classé and forty-six Grands Crus Classé

What is a château?

When most people think of a château, they picture a grandiose home filled with Persian rugs and valuable antiques and surrounded by rolling hills of vineyards. Well, I'm sorry to shatter your dreams (and the dictionary's definition), but most châteaux are not like that at all. Yes, a château could be a mansion on a large estate, but it could also be a modest home with a two-car garage.

Château wines are usually considered the best-quality wines from Bordeaux. They are the most expensive wines; some examples of the best known of the Grand Cru Classé command the highest wine prices in the world!

Let's take a closer look at the châteaux. One fact I've learned from my years of teaching wine is that no one wants to memorize the names of thousands of châteaux, so I'll shorten the list by starting with the most important classification in Bordeaux.

THE GREAT RED WINES OF BORDEAUX

MÉDOC: GRAND CRU CLASSÉ, 1855; 61 CHÂTEAUX

When and how were the château wines classified?

More than 150 years ago in the Médoc region of Bordeaux, a wine classification was established. Brokers from the wine industry were asked by Napoleon III to select the best wines to represent France in the International Exposition of 1855. The top Médoc wines were ranked according to price, which at that time was directly related to quality. (After all, don't we class everything, from cars to restaurants?) According to this new system, the top four (now five, see sidebar below) vineyards—or *crus*—produced "first-growth" wines; the next fourteen best vineyards, second-growth; and so on until you reach the fifth-growth producers. The brokers agreed, provided the classification would never become official. Voilà! Refer to the chart on page 155 for the Official Classification of 1855.

Is there an easier way to understand the 1855 classification?

I've always found the 1855 classification to be a little cumbersome, so one day I sat down and drew up my own chart. I separated the classification into growths (first, second, third, etc.) and then I listed the communes (Pauillac, Margaux, St-Julien, etc.) and set down the number of distinctive vineyards in each one. My chart shows which communes of Bordeaux have the most first growths—all the way down to fifth growths. It also shows which commune corners the market on all growths. Since I was inspired to figure this out during baseball's World Series, I call my chart a box score of the 1855 classification.

A quick glance at my box score gives you some instant facts that may guide you when you want to buy a Bordeaux wine from Médoc.

Tallying the score, Pauillac has three of the five first growths and twelve fifth growths. Margaux practically clean-sweeps the third growths. In fact, Margaux is the overall winner, because it has the greatest number of classed vineyards in all of Médoc. Margaux is also the only area to have a château rated in each category. St-Julien has no first or fifth growths, but is very strong in the second and fourth.

KEVIN ZRALY'S BOX SCORE OF THE 1855 CLASSIFICATION

Commune	1st	2nd	3rd	4th	5th	Total
Margaux	1	5	10	3	2	21
Pauillac	3	2	0	1	12	18
St-Julien	0	5	2	4	0	11
St-Estèphe	0	2	1	1	1	5
Haut-Médoc	0	0	1	1	3	5
Graves	1	0	0	0	0	1
Total Châteaux	5	14	14	10	18	61

GRAND CRU CLASSÉ

CHATEAU LA LAGUNE
HAUT·MÉDOC
APPELLATION HAUT·MÉDOC CONTROLÉE
1995
SOCIÉTÉ CIVILE AGRICOLE DU CHATEAU LA LAGUNE
PROPRIÉTAIRE A LUDON (GIRONDE) FRANCE

PRODUCE OF FRANCE
MIS EN BOUTEILLE AU CHATEAU

GRAND VIN
DE
CHATEAU LATOUR
PREMIER GRAND CRU CLASSÉ
PAUILLAC
1993
12.5 % Vol. 750 ml
DÉPOSÉ APPELLATION PAUILLAC CONTRÔLÉE
STE CIVILE DU VIGNOBLE DE CHATEAU LATOUR PROPRIÉTAIRE A PAUILLAC (GIRONDE) · LG 93

Château
Prieuré-Lichine
GRAND CRU CLASSÉ
1996

MARGAUX
APPELLATION MARGAUX CONTROLÉ
MIS EN BOUTEILLE AU CHATEAU
S.A. CHATEAU PRIEURÉ-LICHINE PROPRIÉTAIRE A CANTENAC · FRANCE
12.5% vol. Cette bouteille porte le N° Lz 249072 750 ml e

1990
CHATEAU DUCRU·BEAUCAILLOU
GRAND CRU CLASSÉ DE MÉDOC EN 1855
SAINT-JULIEN
12.5 % Vol. 750 ml
L. 60 DB APPELLATION SAINT-JULIEN CONTROLÉE
JEAN-EUGÈNE BORIE, PROPRIÉTAIRE A SAINT-JULIEN-BEYCHEVELLE (GIRONDE) PRODUCE OF FRANCE

MIS EN BOUTEILLE AU CHATEAU
CHATEAU MARGAUX
GRAND VIN
1995
PREMIER GRAND CRU CLASSÉ
12.5% vol. 75 cl
MARGAUX
APPELLATION MARGAUX CONTROLÉE
S.C.A. CHATEAU MARGAUX PROPRIÉTAIRE A MARGAUX · FRANCE

GRAND VIN
CHATEAU
LYNCH · BAGES
GRAND CRU CLASSÉ
PAUILLAC
APPELLATION PAUILLAC CONTROLÉE
1995
* CAZES, Propriétaire à PAUILLAC (Gironde) · 12% vol. 300 cl

MIS EN BOUTEILLE AU CHATEAU

GRAND CRU CLASSÉ EN 1855
COS D'ESTOURNEL
SAINT-ESTEPHE
APPELLATION SAINT-ESTEPHE CONTROLEE
1995
DOMAINES PRATS S.A. SAINT-ESTEPHE FRANCE

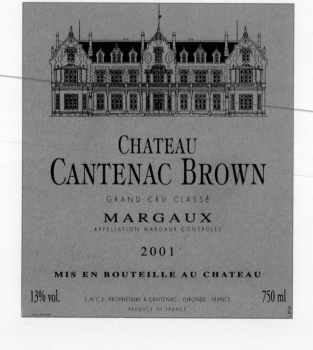

**CHATEAU
CANTENAC BROWN**
GRAND CRU CLASSÉ
MARGAUX
APPELLATION MARGAUX CONTROLÉE
2001
MIS EN BOUTEILLE AU CHATEAU
13% vol. S.N.C.E. PROPRIÉTAIRE A CANTENAC · GIRONDE · FRANCE 750 ml
PRODUCE OF FRANCE

The Official (1855) Classification of the Great Red Wines of Bordeaux

THE MÉDOC

First Growths—Premiers Crus (5)

Vineyard	AOC
Château Lafite-Rothschild	Pauillac
Château Latour	Pauillac
Château Margaux	Margaux
Château Haut-Brion	Pessac-Léognan (Graves)
Château Mouton-Rothschild	Pauillac

Second Growths—Deuxièmes Crus (14)

Vineyard	AOC
Château Rausan-Ségla	Margaux
Château Rausan Gassies	Margaux
Château Léoville-Las-Cases	St-Julien
Château Léoville-Poyferré	St-Julien
Château Léoville-Barton	St-Julien
Château Durfort-Vivens	Margaux
Château Lascombes	Margaux
Château Gruaud-Larose	St-Julien
Château Brane-Cantenac	Margaux
Château Pichon-Longueville-Baron	Pauillac
Château Pichon-Longueville-Lalande	Pauillac
Château Ducru-Beaucaillou	St-Julien
Château Cos d'Estournel	St-Estèphe
Château Montrose	St-Estèphe

Third Growths—Troisièmes Crus (14)

Vineyard	AOC
Château Giscours	Margaux
Château Kirwan	Margaux
Château d'Issan	Margaux
Château Lagrange	St-Julien
Château Langoa-Barton	St-Julien
Château Malescot-St-Exupéry	Margaux
Château Cantenac-Brown	Margaux
Château Palmer	Margaux
Château La Lagune	Haut-Médoc
Château Desmirail	Margaux
Château Calon-Ségur	St-Estèphe
Château Ferrière	Margaux
Château d'Alesme (formerly Marquis d'Alesme)	Margaux
Château Boyd-Cantenac	Margaux

Fourth Growths—Quatrièmes Crus (10)

Vineyard	AOC
Château St-Pierre	St-Julien
Château Branaire-Ducru	St-Julien
Château Talbot	St-Julien
Château Duhart-Milon-Rothschild	Pauillac
Château Pouget	Margaux
Château La Tour-Carnet	Haut-Médoc
Château Lafon-Rochet	St-Estèphe
Château Beychevelle	St-Julien
Château Prieuré-Lichine	Margaux
Château Marquis de Terme	Margaux

Fifth Growths—Cinquièmes Crus (18)

Vineyard	AOC
Château Pontet-Canet	Pauillac
Château Batailley	Pauillac
Château Grand-Puy-Lacoste	Pauillac
Château Grand-Puy-Ducasse	Pauillac
Château Haut-Batailley	Pauillac
Château Lynch-Bages	Pauillac
Château Lynch-Moussas	Pauillac
Château Dauzac	Haut-Médoc
Château d'Armailhac (called Château Mouton-Baron-Philippe from 1956 to 1988)	Pauillac
Château du Tertre	Margaux
Château Haut-Bages-Libéral	Pauillac
Château Pédesclaux	Pauillac
Château Belgrave	Haut-Médoc
Château Camensac	Haut-Médoc
Château Cos Labory	St-Estèphe
Château Clerc-Milon-Rothschild	Pauillac
Château Croizet Bages	Pauillac
Château Cantemerle	Haut-Médoc

ON THE 1945 Mouton-Rothschild bottle there is a big V that stands for "victory" and the end of World War II. Since 1924, and every year since 1945, Philippe de Rothschild asked a different artist to design his labels, a tradition continued by the Baroness Philippine, his daughter. Some of the most famous artists in the world have agreed to have their work grace the Mouton label, including:

Jean Cocteau—1947

Salvador Dalí—1958

Henry Moore—1964

Joan Miró—1969

Marc Chagall—1970

Pablo Picasso—1973

Robert Motherwell—1974

Andy Warhol—1975

John Huston—1982

Saul Steinberg—1983

Keith Haring—1988

Francis Bacon—1990

Setsuko—1991

Antoni Tàpies—1995

Gu Gan—1996

Robert Wilson—2001

HRH Charles, Prince of Wales—2004

Giuseppe Penone—2005

HAVE THERE EVER BEEN ANY CHANGES IN THE 1855 CLASSIFICATION?

Yes, but only once, in 1973. Château Mouton-Rothschild was elevated from a second-growth to a first-growth vineyard. There's a little story behind that.

EXCEPTION TO THE RULE . . .

In 1920, when the Baron Philippe de Rothschild took over the family vineyard, he couldn't accept the fact that back in 1855 his château had been rated a second growth. He thought it should have been classed a first growth from the beginning—and he fought to get to the top for some fifty years. While the baron's wine was classified as a second growth, his motto was:

> *First, I cannot be.*
> *Second, I do not deign to be.*
> *Mouton, I am.*

When his wine was elevated to a first growth in 1973, Rothschild replaced the motto with a new one:

> *First, I am.*
> *Second, I was.*
> *But Mouton does not change.*

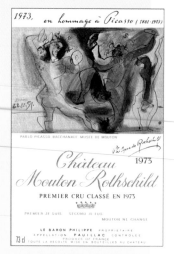

PABLO PICASSO, 1973

Is the 1855 classification still in use today?

Every wine person knows about the 1855 classification, but much has changed over the last century and a half. Some vineyards have doubled or tripled their production by buying up their neighbors' land, which is permitted by law. Obviously the châteaux have seen many changes of ownership. And, like all businesses, Bordeaux has seen good times and bad times.

A case in point was in the early 1970s, when Bordeaux wines were having a difficult time financially, even at the highest level. At Château Margaux, the well-known first-growth vineyard, the quality of the wine fell off from its traditional excellence for a while when the family that owned the château wasn't putting enough money and time into the vineyard. In 1977, Château Margaux was sold to a Greek-French family (named Mentzelopoulos) for $16 million, and since then the quality of the wine has risen even beyond its first-growth standards.

Château Gloria, in the commune of St-Julien, is an example of a vineyard that didn't exist at the time of the 1855 classification. The late mayor of St-Julien, Henri Martin, bought many parcels of second-growth vineyards. As a result, he produced top-quality wine that is not included in the 1855 classification.

It's also important to consider the techniques used to make wine today. They're a lot different from those used in 1855. Once again, the outcome is better wine. As you can see, some of the châteaux listed in the 1855 classification deserve a lesser ranking, while others deserve a better one.

That said, I believe, even after its 150th anniversary, in most cases it is still a very valid classification in terms of quality and price.

MÉDOC CRU BOURGEOIS: 1920, REVISED 1932, 1978, AND 2003; 247 CHÂTEAUX

What does Cru Bourgeois mean?

The Crus Bourgeois of the Médoc are châteaux that were originally classified in 1920, and not in the 1855 classification. In 1932 there were 444 properties listed, but by 1962 there were only 94 members. Today there are 247. The latest classification of Crus Bourgeois of the Médoc and Haut-Médoc was in 2003. Because of the high quality of the 2000, 2003, and 2005 vintages, some of the best values in wine today are in the Cru Bourgeois classification.

The following is a partial list of Crus Bourgeois to look for:

THE CRU BOURGEOIS Château Larose-Trintaudon is the largest vineyard in the Médoc area, making nearly 100,000 cases of wine per year.

CHÂTEAU D'ANGLUDET	CHÂTEAU HAUT-MARBUZET
CHÂTEAU LES ORMES-DE-PEZ	CHÂTEAU PATACHE D'AUX
CHÂTEAU LES ORMES-SORBET	CHÂTEAU LA CARDONNE
CHÂTEAU PHÉLAN-SÉGUR	CHÂTEAU POUJEAUX
CHÂTEAU COUFRAN	CHÂTEAU SIRAN
CHÂTEAU CHASSE-SPLEEN	CHÂTEAU DE PEZ
CHÂTEAU MEYNEY	CHÂTEAU PONTENSAC
CHÂTEAU SOCIANDO-MALLET	CHÂTEAU PIBRAN
CHÂTEAU FOURCAS-HOSTEN	CHÂTEAU MONBRISON
CHÂTEAU LAROSE-TRINTAUDON	CHÂTEAU VIEUX ROBIN
CHÂTEAU GREYSAC	CHÂTEAU LABÉGORCE-ZÉDÉ
CHÂTEAU MARBUZET	CHÂTEAU DE LAMARQUE

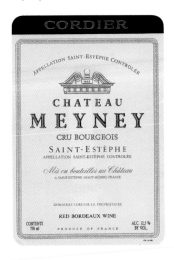

THE RED wines of Pomerol tend to be softer, fruitier, and ready to drink sooner than the Médoc wines.

THE MAJOR grape used to produce wine in the Pomerol region is Merlot. Very little Cabernet Sauvignon is used in these wines.

IT TAKES Château Pétrus one year to make as much wine as Gallo makes in six minutes.

THE VINEYARD at Château Pétrus makes one of the most expensive wines of Bordeaux. It's planted with 95% Merlot.

GRAVES: 1959 GRANDS CRUS CLASSÉ; 12 CHÂTEAUX

The most famous château—we have already seen it in the 1855 classification—is Château Haut-Brion. Other good red Graves classified in 1959 as Grands Crus Classés are:

CHÂTEAU BOUSCAUT
CHÂTEAU HAUT-BAILLY
CHÂTEAU CARBONNIEUX
DOMAINE DE CHEVALIER
CHÂTEAU DE FIEUZAL
CHÂTEAU OLIVIER
CHÂTEAU MALARTIC-LAGRAVIÈRE
CHÂTEAU LA TOUR-MARTILLAC
CHÂTEAU SMITH-HAUT-LAFITTE
CHÂTEAU PAPE-CLÉMENT
CHÂTEAU LA MISSION-HAUT-BRION

POMEROL: NO OFFICIAL CLASSIFICATION

This is the smallest of the top red-wine districts in Bordeaux. Pomerol produces only 15 percent as much wine as St-Émilion; as a result, Pomerol wines are relatively scarce. And if you do find them, they'll be expensive. Although no official classification exists, here's a list of some of the finest Pomerols on the market:

CHÂTEAU PÉTRUS
CHÂTEAU LE PIN
CHÂTEAU LA CONSEILLANTE
CHÂTEAU BEAUREGARD
CHÂTEAU PETIT-VILLAGE
CHÂTEAU NÉNIN
CHÂTEAU TROTANOY
CHÂTEAU LATOUR-À-POMEROL
CHÂTEAU L'ÉVANGILE
CHÂTEAU BOURGNEUF
VIEUX CHÂTEAU-CERTAN
CHÂTEAU CLINET
CHÂTEAU LA POINTE
CHÂTEAU L'ÉGLISE CLINET
CHÂTEAU LAFLEUR
CHÂTEAU PLINCE

CHÂTEAU LA FLEUR-PÉTRUS
CHÂTEAU GAZIN

ST-ÉMILION: 1955, REVISED 1996, REVISED 2006; 15 PREMIERS GRANDS CRUS CLASSÉS AND 46 CHÂTEAUX GRANDS CRUS CLASSÉS

This area produces about two-thirds as much wine as the entire Médoc, and St-Émilion is one of the most beautiful villages in France (in my opinion). The wines of St-Émilion were finally classified officially in 1955, one century after the Médoc classification. There are fifteen first growths comparable to the Cru Classé wines of the Médoc.

THE FIFTEEN FIRST GROWTHS OF ST-ÉMILION (PREMIERS GRANDS CRUS CLASSÉS)

Château Ausone	Château Canon
Château Cheval Blanc	Château Magdelaine
Château Angélus	Château La Gaffelière
Château Beau-Séjour-Bécot	Château Troplong Mondot
Château Beauséjour-Duffau-Lagarrosse	Château Trottevieille
	Château Pavie
Château Belair	Clos Fourtet
Château Figeac	Château Pavie Marquin

Important Grands Crus Classés and other St-Émilion wines available in the United States:

Château Canon-La-Gaffelière	Château Trotanoy
Château La Tour-Figeac	Château Faugères
Château Trimoulet	Château Haut-Corbin
Château Dassault	Château Grand-Mayne
Château Monbousquet	Clos des Jacobins
Château Tertre Roteboeuf	

GRAPE VARIETIES OF ST-ÉMILION

Merlot	70%
Cabernet Franc	25%
Cabernet Sauvignon	5%

SOME OTHER appellations to look for in Bordeaux red wines:
- Fronsac
- Côtes de Blaye
- Côtes de Bourg

THE 1999 VINTAGE was the largest harvest ever in Bordeaux.

ABOUT VINTAGES, Alexis Lichine, a noted wine expert, once said: "Great vintages take time to mature. Lesser wines mature faster than the greater ones. . . . Patience is needed for great vintages, hence the usefulness and enjoyment of lesser vintages." He summed up: "Often vintages which have a poorer rating—if young—will give a greater enjoyment than a better-rated vintage—if young."

DRINK YOUR lighter vintages such as 2001 and 2004 Bordeaux while you wait patiently for your great vintages such as 2000, 2003, and 2005 to mature.

THE EARLIEST harvest since 1893 was 2003.

THE 2003 VINTAGE suffered summer heat waves, fierce storms, and hail, reducing production to the lowest since 1991.

Now that you know all the greatest red-wine regions of Bordeaux, let me take you a step further and show you some of the best vintages.

BORDEAUX VINTAGES

"LEFT BANK"
MÉDOC/ST-JULIEN/MARGAUX/
PAUILLAC/ST-ESTÈPHE/GRAVES

GOOD VINTAGES	GREAT VINTAGES	OLDER GREAT VINTAGES
1994	1990*	1982*
1997	1995	1985
1998	1996	1986
1999	2000*	1989
2001	2003	
2002	2005*	
2004		
2006		
2007		
2008		

"RIGHT BANK"
ST-ÉMILION/POMEROL

GOOD VINTAGES	GREAT VINTAGES	OLDER GREAT VINTAGES
1995	1990	1982
1996	1998*	1989
1997	2000*	
1999	2001	
2002	2005*	
2003		
2004		
2006		
2007		
2008		

*Note: * signifies an exceptional vintage*

How do I buy—and drink—a red Bordeaux?

One of the biggest misconceptions about Bordeaux wines is that they are all very expensive. In reality, there are thousands of Bordeaux wines at all different price ranges.

First and foremost, ask yourself if you want to drink the wine now, or if you want to age it. A great château Bordeaux in a great vintage needs a *minimum* of ten years to age. Going down a level, a Cru Bourgeois or a second label of a great château in a great vintage needs a minimum of five years to age. A regional wine may be consumed within two or three years of the vintage year, while a wine labeled simply Appellation Bordeaux Contrôlée is ready to drink as soon as it's released.

The next step is to be sure the vintage is correct for what you want. If you're looking for a wine you want to age, you must look for a great vintage. If you want a wine that's ready to drink now and you want a greater château, you should choose a lesser vintage. If you want a wine that's ready to drink now and you want a great vintage, you should look for a lesser château.

In addition, remember that Bordeaux wines are a blend of grapes. Ask yourself if you're looking for a Merlot-style Bordeaux, such as St-Émilion or Pomerol, or if you're looking for a Cabernet style, such as Médoc or Graves, remembering that the Merlot is more accessible and easier to drink when young.

What separates a $20 red Bordeaux from a $300 red Bordeaux?

- The place the grapes are grown
- The age of the vines (usually the older the vine, the better the wine)
- The yield of the vine (lower yield means higher quality)
- The winemaking technique (for example, how long the wine is aged in wood)
- The vintage

ON DRINKING THE WINES OF BORDEAUX

"The French drink their Bordeaux wines too young, afraid that the Socialist government will take them away.

"The English drink their Bordeaux wines very old, because they like to take their friends down to their wine cellars with the cobwebs and dust to show off their old bottles.

"And the Americans drink their Bordeaux wines exactly when they are ready to be drunk, because they don't know any better."

—AUTHOR UNKNOWN

A BORDEAUX FOR VALENTINE'S DAY

At one time the Marquis de Ségur owned Château Lafite, Château Latour, and Château Calon-Ségur. He said, "I make my wines at Lafite and Latour, but my heart is at Calon." Hence the label.

Is it necessary to pay a tremendous sum of money to get a great-tasting red Bordeaux wine?

It's nice if you have it to spend, but sometimes you don't. The best way to get the most for your money is to use what I call the reverse pyramid method. For example: Let's say you like Château Lafite-Rothschild, which is at the top of the pyramid at left, but you can't afford it. What do you do? Look at the region. It's from Pauillac. You have a choice: You can go back to the 1855 classification and look for a fifth-growth wine from Pauillac that gives a flavor of the region at a lesser price, though not necessarily one-fifth the price of a first growth. Still too pricey? Drop a level further on the inverted pyramid and go for a Cru Bourgeois from Pauillac. Your other option is to buy a regional wine labeled "Pauillac."

I didn't memorize the seven thousand châteaux myself. When I go to my neighborhood retailer, I find a château I've never heard of. If it's from Pauillac, from a good vintage, and it's twenty to twenty-five dollars, I buy it. My chances are good. Everything in wine is hedging your bets.

Another way to avoid skyrocketing Bordeaux châteaux prices is to take the time to look for their second-label wines. These wines are from the youngest parts of the vineyard and are lighter in style and quicker to mature and are much less expensive than the château wine.

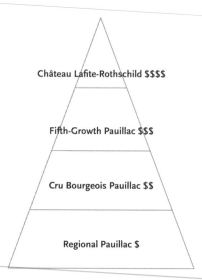

Château Lafite-Rothschild $$$$

Fifth-Growth Pauillac $$$

Cru Bourgeois Pauillac $$

Regional Pauillac $

THE FIRST GROWTHS Château Margaux, Château Latour, Château Lafite Rothschild, and Château Mouton Rothschild use less than 40% of the crop for their wines.

CHÂTEAU	SECOND LABEL WINES
Château Lafite-Rothschild	Carruades de Lafite Rothschild
Château Latour	Les Forts de Latour
Château Haut-Brion	Bahans du Château Haut-Brion
Château Margaux	Pavillon Rouge du Château Margaux
Château Mouton-Rothschild	Petit Mouton
Château Léoville-Barton	La Réserve de Léoville Barton
Château Léoville-Las-Cases	Clos du Marquis
Château Pichon Lalande	Réserve de la Comtesse
Château Pichon Longueville	Les Tourelles de Pichon
Château Palmer	Réserve du Général
Château Lynch-Bages	Château Haut Bages-Averous

Twenty-five years later in Bordeaux

The most dramatic change in the wine world over the last twenty-five years has been the worldwide demand for the best châteaux of Bordeaux. In 1985, the two most important markets for Bordeaux were the United Kingdom and the United States. Today, Asia has become a new and growing market. There has been strong growth in Japan, Hong Kong, South Korea, and China. All of this means higher prices for the best of Bordeaux.

For me it is the end of an era. My first "eureka" moment that wine would become my number-one passion was with a twenty-year-old Bordeaux that cost less than twenty-five dollars. It was a lot of money for a college student but it was worth it. I doubt many young people today can afford the $2,000 price tag for a 2005 Château Latour which probably won't be ready to drink for twenty years! The great châteaux have become wines of prestige and entitlement reserved for the wealthy.

That said, there are still some excellent values for us common folk, from the other seven thousand châteaux. Since 1985, the top châteaux high-quality standard has filtered down to the rest of Bordeaux and as a region they are making the best wines ever in the history of Bordeaux, especially in regions like St-Émilion, Graves, Côtes de Boug, and Côtes de Blaye.

FOR FURTHER READING

I recommend *Grands Vins* by Clive Coates, M.W.; *The Bordeaux Atlas and Encyclopedia of Chateaux* by Hubrecht Duijker and Michael Broadbent; and *Bordeaux* by Robert M. Parker Jr.

WHILE NAPOLEON BONAPARTE preferred the Burgundy Chambertin, the late president Richard Nixon's favorite wine was Château Margaux. Nixon always had a bottle of his favorite vintage waiting at his table from the cellar of the famous "21" Club in New York.

HAD YOU dined at the Four Seasons restaurant in New York when it first opened in 1959, you could have had a 1918 Château Lafite-Rothschild for $18, or a 1934 Château Latour for $16. Or if those wines were a bit beyond your budget, you could have had a 1945 Château Cos d'Estournel for $9.50.

WINE AND FOOD

DENISE LURTON-MOULLE (*Château La Louvière, Château Bonnet*): With Château La Louvière Rouge: *roast leg of lamb or grilled duck breast.*

JEAN-MICHEL CAZES (*Château Lynch-Bages, Château Haut-Bages-Averous, Château Les Ormes-de-Pez*): *"For Bordeaux red, simple and classic is best! Red meat, such as beef and particularly lamb, as we love it in* Pauillac. If you can grill the meat on vine cuttings, you are in heaven."

JACQUES AND FIONA THIENPONT (*Château Le Pin*): *Sunday lunches at Le Pin include lots of local oysters with chilled white Bordeaux followed by thick entrecôte steaks on the barbecue with shallots and a selection of the family's Pomerols, Margaux, or Côtes de France red Bordeaux.*

ANTONY PERRIN (*Château Carbonnieux*): *With red Bordeaux:* magret de canard *(duck breast) with wild mushrooms, or* pintade aux raisins *(Guinea hen with grapes).*

CHRISTIAN MOUEIX (*Château Pétrus*): *With red Bordeaux, especially Pomerol wine: Lamb is a must.*

SINCE 1882, when the venerable French company Guerlain first produced a lip balm containing Bordeaux wine, nursing mothers have used it as a salve for chapped nipples. "It's a wonderfully soothing emollient, and red wine's tannic acid has healing properties," says Elisabeth Sirot, *attaché de presse* at Guerlain's Paris office. "French women have always known this secret." Sirot used it when nursing all four of her children (she learned the tip from her own mother). How sensual—especially considering that the American alternative is petroleum jelly.

CLASS FIVE: THE RED WINES OF BORDEAUX

We now enter the second half of the wine-tasting course and the ideal opportunity to showcase my favorite red wines: those of Bordeaux. Bordeaux has more than seven thousand châteaux, which makes narrowing down to just ten wines very difficult.

The three major grapes cultivated in Bordeaux are Merlot, Cabernet Sauvignon, and Cabernet Franc. Merlot is the most widely planted with almost twice as many vines planted as Cabernet Sauvignon, and three times the number of vines as Cabernet Franc.

Bordeaux wines have a reputation of being expensive and requiring long aging. This is not entirely true: 80 percent of all Bordeaux wines retail between $8 and $25 and most of those can be consumed when you buy them or within two years of purchase.

Wines for Class Five

1. Blind (Appellation Bordeaux Contrôlée 2006)
2. Barton & Guestier Margaux 2006
3. Château Larose Trintaudon 2005 (Haut Médoc) **BEST VALUE**
4. Château Talbot (St-Julien) 2005
5. Clos du Marquis 2004 **BEST VALUE**
6. Château Léoville Las Cases 2004
7. Blind (Cru Bourgeois)
8. Blind (Third, Fourth, or Fifth Growth)
9. Blind (Second Growth)
10. Gruaud Larose 2001 (St-Julien)

There are four parts to this tasting.

PART I: UNDERSTANDING BORDEAUX (FOUR WINES POURED TOGETHER)

Wines #1 through #4 represent the major Bordeaux styles, price, and quality levels, and illustrate the wide diversity of Bordeaux red wines. Tasting these four wines together illustrates how the appellation contrôllée system of Bordeaux works, ranging from the simplest Appellation Bordeaux Contrôlée to the highest Grand Cru Classé classification.

The lowest appellation of these wines is Appellation Bordeaux Contrôlée. The B & G Margaux (Appellation Margaux Contrôlée) is a higher appellation. The next quality level is Château Larose Trintaudon (Château/Haut-Médoc Appellation/Cru Bourgeois), and the highest quality is Château Talbot 2001 (Château/St-Julien Appellation/Grand Cru Classé/Fourth Growth). There are two tasting sections to Part I. The first section compares Wine #1 and Wine #2 and the second compares Wine #3 and Wine #4. Wine #1 and Wine #2 should be from the same vintage, as should Wine #3 and Wine #4.

SECTION I: COMPARING WINES #1 AND #2

By tasting Wine #1 and Wine #2 together, students will experience the texture and taste difference between an Appellation Bordeaux Contrôlée and the higher level Appellation Margaux Contrôlée. The B & G Margaux has much more fruit, is deeper in color, and has more tannin than Wine #1. These regional wines are some of the best value wines in all of Bordeaux; I wish more were available in the United States. Other good appellations to look for are Médoc, Pauillac, and St-Émilion.

Wine #1: Blind (Appellation Bordeaux Contrôlée 2006)

This Appellation Bordeaux Contrôlée wine will show a good Bordeaux wine at a great price. It's an easy-drinking, medium-fruit, balanced-tannin, everyday wine that you can buy for tonight's dinner. Most Appellation Bordeaux Contrôlée wines will be a blend of Merlot, Cabernet Sauvignon, and Cabernet Franc with the primary grape being Merlot.

> Retail price: Most Appellation Bordeaux Contrôlée wines are under $10
> Ready to drink
> Other recommended producers are: Mouton Cadet, Michel Lynch, or Lacour Pavillon.

Wine #2: Barton & Guestier Margaux 2006

The next level of quality in Bordeaux is from one of its fifty-seven different appellations. This wine is from the appellation Margaux, which is a village that produces some of the best wine in Bordeaux. The grapes for this wine can only come from the delimited area of Margaux.

Barton & Guestier is a large négociant who buys grapes or wine from specific appellations and bottles it under their own name. As with the Appellation Bordeaux Contrôlée level, I would buy this wine only in a good to great vintage year.

Retail price $21
Ready to drink, but could age
Another recommended négociant is the Baron Philippe de Rothschild S.A.

Section II: Comparing Wines #3 and #4

Wine #3 and #4 are both classified Château wines. Wine #3, the Haut Médoc is a lesser classification (Cru Bourgeois), and Wine #4, the St-Julien, carries a much higher classification of Grand Cru Classé. 2005 was a great vintage year in Bordeaux.

Wine #3: Château Larose Trintaudon 2005 (Haut Médoc)

This wine comes from the Haut Médoc appellation and is classified as a Cru Bourgeois. Château Larose Trintaudon is the largest vineyard in the Médoc region. The primary grape of this wine is Cabernet Sauvignon blended with Merlot and Cabernet Franc. It is a medium-bodied Bordeaux with great fruit balance, firm tannic structure, and a moderately long finish.

Retail price $20   **BEST VALUE**
Ready to drink, but can age
Other recommended wines for this style are: Château Meyney, Château Les Ormes-de-Pez, Château Greysac, or Château Phélan-Ségur.

Wine #4: Château Talbot 2005 (St-Julien)

This wine is from the St-Julien appellation and is classified a fourth-growth Bordeaux. I often buy château wine from St-Julien for their subtlety and charm. This is a classic Bordeaux with earthy black fruit, medium to full body, soft tannins, and a long finish. I could "suffer" through this wine tonight but it will be at its best in the next five to ten years. The earliest records of the Château Talbot go back to the seventeenth century.

Retail price $60

Needs aging

Other recommended wines of this St-Julien style are: Château Gruaud Larose, Château Léoville Barton, Château Branaire-Ducru, Château LaGrange, or Château Ducru Beaucaillou.

PART II: UNDERSTANDING SECOND LABELS (TWO WINES, TASTED TOGETHER, PREFERABLY OF THE SAME VINTAGE)

Second-label wines are usually produced from a château's youngest vines. The wines they produce are lighter in style and quicker to mature than those made from the grapes of older, classified stock. Second-label wines will cost at least one-third to a half of that of the château wine and are another way of buying good Bordeaux wine without breaking the budget. Although second-label wines are not a new concept in Bordeaux—the Clos du Marquis produced its first second-label wine in 1902—most châteaux began producing second-label wines in the mid-1980s.

By taking the second-label wine of Château Léoville Las Cases, the Clos du Marquis 2004, and tasting it side by side with Léoville Las Cases 2004, you will see the value of looking for second labels.

Wine #5: Clos du Marquis 2004

All the great châteaux of Bordeaux now produce a second label, and Clos du Marquis is considered one of the best and most consistent in quality. It is by no means a "second" wine, and in great years the Clos du Marquis is of the same or better quality than many of the classified growths. The year 2004 was very good in Bordeaux; this wine, five years later, has its components in perfect harmony with firm tannins and forward fruit. (See list of second labels on page 162.)

Retail price $32 **BEST VALUE**

Ready to drink, but will age

Other recommended second-label Bordeaux wines are: Réserve de la Comtesse (Pichon Lalande), Les Tourelles de Pichon (Pichon Longueville), or Réserve du Général (Palmer).

Questions for Class Five:
The Red Wines of Bordeaux

12. What percentage does the Grand Cru Classé Châteaux represent of the total volume of Bordeaux? 153

13. How many châteaux were classified in the official classification of the Mèdoc? 153

14. Name one château from each of the five growths: 155

　　1st _____

　　2nd _____

　　3rd _____

　　4th _____

　　5th _____

15. In what year were the wines of Graves first classified? 158

16. In what year were the wines of St-Émilion first classified? 159

17. What is the primary red grape used in the production of St-Émilion wine? 159

18. Name three great recent vintages from the "left bank" of Bordeaux. 160

19. Name three great recent vintages from the "right bank" of Bordeaux. 160

20. Name two second-label wines of classified châteaux. 162

The Red Wines of California

RED VS. WHITE • MAJOR RED GRAPES OF CALIFORNIA •

RED-GRAPE BOOM • MERITAGE • STYLES • TRENDS

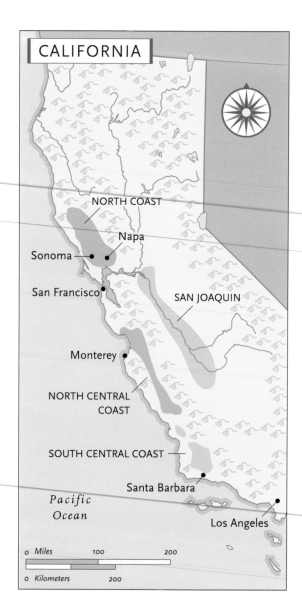

CALIFORNIA

NORTH COAST

Napa

Sonoma

San Francisco

SAN JOAQUIN

Monterey

NORTH CENTRAL
COAST

SOUTH CENTRAL COAST

Santa Barbara

*Pacific
Ocean*

Los Angeles

o Miles   100   200

o Kilometers   200

ACREAGE IN CALIFORNIA

Currently there are 289,401 acres in red
grapes and 182,486 in white grapes planted
in California.

More About California Wines

SINCE WE'VE ALREADY covered the history and geography of California in Class Two, it might be a good idea to go back and review the main viticultural areas of California wine country on page 69, before you continue with the red wines of California. Then, consider the following question that inevitably comes up in my class at the Windows on the World Wine School.

Are Americans drinking more white wine or red?

The chart below shows you the trend of wine consumption in the United States over almost the last forty years. When I first began studying wines in 1970, people were more interested in red wine than white. From the mid-1970s, when I started teaching, into the mid-1990s, my students showed a definite preference for white wine. Fortunately for me (since I am a red wine drinker), the pendulum is surely swinging back to more red wine drinkers.

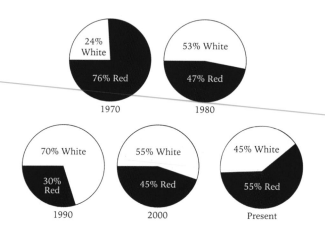

24% White / 76% Red — 1970	53% White / 47% Red — 1980	
70% White / 30% Red — 1990	55% White / 45% Red — 2000	45% White / 55% Red — Present

RED VS. WHITE—CONSUMPTION IN THE UNITED STATES

Why this change?

Looking back at the American obsession with health and fitness in the 1970s and 1980s, we see many people switching from meat and potatoes to fish and vegetables—a lighter diet that called more for white wine than red. "Chardonnay" became the new buzzword that replaced the call for "a glass of white wine." Bars that never used to stock wine—nothing decent, anyway—began to carry an assortment of fine wines by the glass, with Chardonnay, by far, the best-selling wine. Today, steak is back and the new buzzwords are Cabernet Sauvignon, Merlot, and Syrah.

Another major reason for the dramatic upturn in red wine consumption is the power of the media. Television popularized the so-called French Paradox (see box below).

Finally, perhaps the most important reason that red wine consumption has increased in the United States is that California is producing a much better quality red wine than ever before. One of the reasons for improved quality is the replanting of vines over the last twenty years due to the phylloxera problem (see page 79). Some analysts thought the replanting would be financially devastating to the California wine industry, but in reality it may have been a blessing in disguise, especially with regard to quality.

The opportunity to replant allowed vineyard owners to increase their red-grape production. It enabled California grape growers to utilize the knowledge they have gained over the years with regard to soil, climate, microclimate, trellising, and other viticultural practices.

Bottom line: California reds are already some of the greatest in the world, with more and better to come.

THERE ARE more than 30 wine grape varieties planted in California.

CALIFORNIA RED GRAPES IN 2009

Varietal	Acreage
Cabernet	74,643
Zinfandel	49,061
Merlot	48,648

ACCORDING TO the U.S. Dietary Guidelines:

   5 oz. wine = 100 calories

   12 oz. beer = 150 calories

   1.5 oz. distilled spirits = 100 calories

FROM 1991 TO 2008, sales of red wine in the United States grew by more than 125%.

WINE IS fat-free and contains no cholesterol.

THE FRENCH PARADOX

In the early 1990s, the TV series 60 Minutes twice aired a report on a phenomenon known as the French Paradox—the fact that the French have a lower rate of heart disease than Americans, despite a diet that's higher in fat. Since the one thing the American diet lacks, in comparison to the French diet, is red wine, some researchers were looking for a link between the consumption of red wine and a decreased rate of heart disease. Not surprisingly, in the year following this report, Americans increased their purchases of red wines by 39 percent.

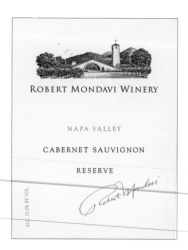

What are the major red grapes in California?

There are five major red grapes grown in California.

Cabernet Sauvignon: Considered the most successful red grape in California, it yields some of the greatest red wines in the world. Cabernet Sauvignon is the predominant variety used in the finest red Bordeaux wines, such as Château Lafite-Rothschild and Château Latour. Almost all California Cabernets are dry, and depending upon the producer and vintage, they range in style from light and ready to drink, to extremely full-bodied and long-lived. California Cabernet has become the benchmark for some of the best California wines.

My favorite California Cabernet Sauvignons are:

ARROWOOD	JOSEPH PHELPS
BEAULIEU PRIVATE RESERVE	LA JOTA
BERINGER PRIVATE RESERVE	LAUREL GLEN
CAKEBREAD	MONDAVI RESERVE
CAYMUS	OPUS ONE
CHAPPELLET	PAUL HOBBS
CHATEAU MONTELENA	PINE RIDGE
CHATEAU ST. JEAN, CINQ CÉPAGES	PRIDE MOUNTAIN
CLOS DU VAL	RIDGE MONTE BELLO
DALLA VALLE	SCHRADER
DIAMOND CREEK	SHAFER HILLSIDE SELECT
DUCKHORN	SILVER OAK
DUNN HOWELL MOUNTAIN	SPOTTSWOOD
GALLO OF SONOMA ESTATE	STAGLIN
GROTH RESERVE	STAG'S LEAP CASK
HEITZ	TREFETHEN
HESS COLLECTION	WHITEHALL LANE
JORDAN	

BEST BETS FOR CABERNET SAUVIGNON (NAPA VALLEY)

1994* 1995* 1996* 1997* 1999* 2001*
2002* 2003 2004 2005* 2006* 2007** 2008

*Note: * signifies exceptional vintage*

*** signifies extraordinary vintage*

"RESERVE" ON the label has no legal meaning. In other words, there is no law that defines it. Some wineries, such as Beaulieu Vineyards and Robert Mondavi Winery, still mark some of their wines Reserve. BV's Reserve is from a particular vineyard. Mondavi's Reserve is made from a special blend of grapes, presumably their best. Other vague terms include "Cask" wines, "Special Selections," or "Proprietor's Reserve." The California Wine Institute has proposed a definition of Reserve to meet the requirement by some export markets.

THERE ARE more than 1,000 different California Cabernet Sauvignons available to the consumer.

MOST CABERNET SAUVIGNONS are blended with other grapes, primarily Merlot. To use the grape variety on the label, the winemaker must use at least 75% Cabernet Sauvignon.

OLDER CABERNET vintages to look for: 1985, 1986, 1987, 1990, and 1991.

CABERNET SAUVIGNON aromas:
Blackberry   Black cherry
Cassis   Eucalyptus

THE 2008 HARVEST was one of the smallest on record.

Pinot Noir: Known as the "headache" grape because of its fragile quality, Pinot Noir is temperamental, high maintenance, expensive, and difficult to grow and make into wine. The great grape of the Burgundy region of France—responsible for such famous wines as Pommard, Nuits-St-Georges, and Gevrey-Chambertin—is also one of the principal grapes in French Champagne. In California, many years of experimentation in finding the right location to plant the Pinot Noir and to perfect the fermentation techniques have elevated some of the Pinot Noirs to the status of great wines. Pinot Noir is usually less tannic than Cabernet and matures more quickly, generally in two to five years. Because of the extra expense involved in growing this grape, the best examples of Pinot Noirs from California may cost more than other varietals. The three top counties for Pinot Noir are Sonoma (11,000 acres), Monterey (6,204 acres), and Santa Barbara (3,401 acres).

My favorite California Pinot Noirs are:

ACACIA	**MARCASSIN**
ARTESA	**MERRY EDWARDS**
AU BON CLIMAT	**MORGAN**
CALERA	**PATZ & HALL**
CLINE	**PAUL HOBBS**
DEHLINGER	**ROBERT MONDAVI**
ETUDE	**ROBERT SINSKEY**
FLOWERS	**SAINTSBURY**
GARY FARRELL	**SANFORD**
J. ROCHIOLI	**SEA SMOKE**
KOSTA BROWNE	**SIDURI**
LITTORAI	**WILLIAMS SELYEM**

BEST BETS FOR PINOT NOIR

Sonoma (Carneros) 2001* 2002* 2003* 2004* 2005* 2006 2007* 2008

Santa Barbara 2003* 2004* 2005 2007 2008

Monterey 2002* 2003* 2004* 2005* 2006 2007 2008

*Note: * signifies exceptional vintage*

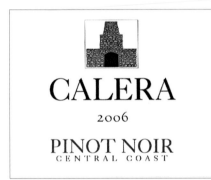

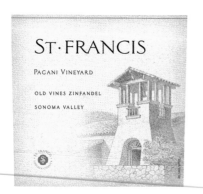

RECENT DNA studies have concluded that Zinfandel is the same grape as the Primitivo in Italy.

WHITE ZINFANDEL, at 35 million cases sold, far outsells red Zinfandel.

SOME ZINFANDELS have more than 16% alcohol.

WHICH TURLEY WAS IT?

In the 2007 vintage, Turley wine cellars made 18 different Zinfandels.

MERLOT MADNESS

There were only two acres of Merlot planted in all of California in 1960. Today there are close to 50,000!

COMMON MERLOT aromas:
Blackberry
Cassis
Cherry
Chocolate
Coffee
Oak

Zinfandel: The surprise grape of California, Zinfandel was used to make "generic" or "jug" wines in the early years of California winemaking. Over the past thirty years, however, it has developed into one of the best red varietal grapes. The only problem in choosing a Zinfandel wine is that so many different styles are made. Depending on the producer, the wines can range from a big, rich, ripe, high-alcohol, spicy, smoky, concentrated, intensely flavored style with substantial tannin, to a very light, fruity wine. And let's not forget white Zinfandel!

My favorite Zinfandels are:

CARLISLE	J. ROCHIOLI
CLINE	ROSENBLUM
DRY CREEK WINERY	ROSHAMBO
FIFE	SEGHESIO
MARTINELLI	SIGNORELLO
MAZZOCCO	ST. FRANCIS
MERRY EDWARDS	TURLEY
RAFANELLI	RIDGE
RAVENSWOOD	

BEST BETS FOR ZINFANDEL (NORTH COAST)

1994*   2001*   2002   2003*   2007

Note: * signifies exceptional vintage

Merlot: For many years Merlot was thought of as a grape only to be blended with Cabernet Sauvignon, because Merlot's tannins are softer and its texture is more supple. Merlot has now achieved its own identity as a super-premium varietal. Of red-grape varietals in California, Merlot saw the fastest rate of new plantings over the last twenty years. It produces a soft, round wine that generally does not need the same aging as a Cabernet Sauvignon. It is a top seller at restaurants, where its early maturation and compatibility with food make it a frequent choice by consumers.

My favorite North Coast Merlots are:

BERINGER HOWELL MOUNTAIN	**MATANZAS CREEK**
CHIMNEY ROCK	**NEWTON**
CLOS DU BOIS	**PALAMO**
DUCKHORN	**PINE RIDGE**
FRANCISCAN	**PRIDE**
HAVENS	**PROVENANCE**
LEWIS CELLARS	**SHAFER**
LUNA	**ST. FRANCIS**
MARKHAM	**WHITEHALL LANE**

BEST BETS FOR MERLOT (NORTH COAST)

2002*   2003   2004*   2005*   2006   2007*   2008

*Note: * signifies exceptional vintage*

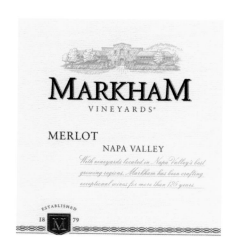

Syrah: The up-and-coming red grape in California is definitely Syrah. I don't know why it's taken so long, since Syrah has always been one of the major grapes of the Rhône Valley in France, making some of the best and most long-lived wines in the world. Further, the sales of Australian Syrah (which they call Shiraz) have been phenomenal in the United States. Americans like the spicy, robust flavor of this grape. It's a perfect grape for California because it thrives in sunny, warm weather.

My favorite Syrahs are:

ALBAN	**NEYERS**
CAKEBREAD	**OJAI**
CLOS DU BOIS	**PAX**
DUMOL	**PEAY**
EDMUNDS ST. JOHN	**PHELPS**
FESS PARKER	**QUPE**
FOXEN	**TABLAS CREEK**
GEYSER PEAK	**VIADER**
JUSTIN	**WILD HORSE**
LAGIER MEREDITH	**ZACA MESA**
LEWIS	

SAN LUIS OBISPO and Sonoma counties have the most acreage of Syrah grapes in California.

BEST BETS FOR SYRAH

South Central Coast   2002*   2003*   2004*   2005   2006
North Coast   2003   2004*   2005   2006*

*Note: * signifies exceptional vintage*

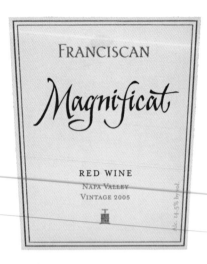

SOME EXAMPLES of Meritage wines of California:
Dominus (Christian Moueix)
Insignia (Phelps Vineyards)
Magnificat (Franciscan)
Opus One (Mondavi/Rothschild)
Cain Five
Trefethen Halo

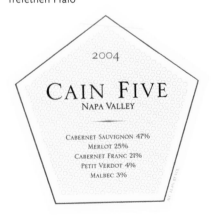

RED-GRAPE BOOM

Look at the chart below to see how many acres of the major red grapes were planted in California in 1970, and how those numbers have increased. Rapid expansion has been the characteristic of the California wine industry!

TOTAL BEARING ACREAGE OF RED-WINE GRAPES PLANTED

GRAPE-BY-GRAPE COMPARISON

GRAPE	1970	1980	1990	2009
Cabernet Sauvignon	3,200	21,800	24,100	74,643
Zinfandel	19,200	27,700	28,000	49,061
Merlot	100	2,600	4,000	48,648
Pinot Noir	2,100	9,200	8,600	24,427
Syrah			400	18,085

What are Meritage wines?

Meritage (which rhymes with *heritage*) is the name for red and white wines made in America from a blend of the classic Bordeaux wine-grape varieties. This category was created because many winemakers felt stifled by the required minimum amount (75 percent) of a grape that must go into a bottle for it to be named for that variety. Some winemakers knew they could make a better wine with a blend of, say, 60 percent of the major grape and 40 percent of secondary grapes. This blending of grapes allows producers of Meritage wines the same freedom that Bordeaux winemakers have in making their wines.

For red wine, the varieties include Cabernet Sauvignon, Merlot, Cabernet Franc, Petit Verdot, and Malbec. For white wine, the varieties include Sauvignon Blanc and Sémillon.

When I buy a Cabernet, Zinfandel, Merlot, Pinot Noir, Syrah, or Meritage wine, how do I know which style I'm getting? Is the style of the wine indicated on the label?

Unless you just happen to be familiar with a particular vineyard's wine, you're stuck with trial-and-error tastings. You're one step ahead, though, just by knowing that you'll find drastically different styles from the same grape variety.

With some 2,200 wineries in California and more than half of them

OPUS ONE

Amid grand hoopla in the wine world, Robert Mondavi and the late Baron Philippe de Rothschild released Opus One. "It isn't Mouton and it isn't Mondavi," said Robert Mondavi. Opus One is a Bordeaux-style blend made from Cabernet Sauvignon, Merlot, and Cabernet Franc grapes grown in the Napa Valley. It was originally produced at the Robert Mondavi Winery in the Napa Valley, but is now produced across Highway 29 in its own spectacular winery.

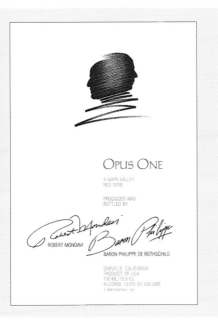

ONE OF THE most memorable tastings I have ever attended in my career was for the fiftieth anniversary of Beaulieu's Private Reserve wine. Over a two-day period, we tasted every vintage from 1936 to 1986 with winemaker André Tchelistcheff. I think everyone who attended the tasting was amazed and awed by how well many of these vintages aged.

GREAT CALIFORNIA ROSÉS
Bonny Doon Vin Gris de Cigare
Frog's Leap La Grenouille
Rouganté
Etude Pinot Noir Rosé
SoloRosa

producing red wines, it is virtually impossible to keep up with the ever-changing styles that are being produced. One of the recent improvements in labeling is that more wineries are adding important information to the back label indicating when the wine is ready to drink, if it should be aged, and many even offer food suggestions.

To avoid any unpleasant surprises, I can't emphasize enough the importance of an educated wine retailer. One of the strongest recommendations I give—especially to a new wine drinker—is to find the right retailer, one who understands wine and your taste.

Do California red wines age well?

Absolutely, especially from the best wineries that produce Cabernet Sauvignon and Zinfandel. I have been fortunate to taste some early examples of Cabernet Sauvignon going back to the 1930s, 1940s, and 1950s, which for the most part were drinking well—some of them were outstanding—proving to me the longevity of certain Cabernets. Zinfandels and Cabernet Sauvignons from the best wineries in great vintages will need a minimum of five years before you drink them, and they will get better over the next ten years. That's at least fifteen years of great enjoyment.

NAPA VALLEY 40 YEARS LATER: 1969–2009

1969: $2,000–$4,000 (cost per acre)
2009: $150,000–$350,000 (cost per acre)

However, one of the things I have noticed in the last ten years, not only tasting as many California wines as I have, but also tasting so many European wines, is that California wines seem to be more accessible when young, as opposed to, say, a Bordeaux. I believe this is one of the reasons California wines sell so well in the United States, especially in restaurants.

What have been the trends in the red wines of California over the last twenty-five years?

One trend has been the association of a specific grape variety with a region (AVA): Cabernet Sauvignon and Merlot are Napa Valley, Pinot Noir is Carneros, Sonoma, Santa Barbara, and Monterey. Syrah is best in the South Central Coast (San Luis Obispo).

Though California winemakers have settled down, they have not given up experimentation altogether, if you consider the many new grape varieties coming out of California these days. I expect to see more wines made with grapes such as the Mourvèdre, Grenache, Sangiovese, and especially Syrah, continuing the trend toward diversity in California red wines.

I personally have an issue with the change in alcohol levels over the past twenty-five years, especially in the red wines. Many winemakers are producing wines with over 15 percent alcohol, which for my own taste changes the balance as the elegance and varietal characteristics are replaced with overpowering alcohols. The reality is most wines around the world have increased in alcohol content but not to the extent that they have in California.

FOR FURTHER READING

I recommend *The Wine Atlas of California* by James Halliday; *Making Sense of California Wine* and *New California Wine* by Matt Kramer; *Wine Spectator's California Wine* by James Laube; and *The Wine Atlas of California and the Pacific Northwest* by Bob Thompson.

DUCKHORN VINEYARDS

2005
NAPA VALLEY
MERLOT

WINE AND FOOD

MARGRIT BIEVER AND ROBERT MONDAVI: *With Cabernet Sauvignon: lamb, or wild game such as grouse and caribou. With Pinot Noir: pork loin, milder game such as domestic pheasant, coq au vin.*

TOM JORDAN: *"Roast lamb is wonderful with the flavor and complexity of Cabernet Sauvignon. The wine also pairs nicely with sliced breast of duck, and grilled squab with wild mushrooms. For a cheese course with mature Cabernet, milder cheeses such as young goat cheeses, St. André and Taleggio, are best so the subtle flavors of the wine can be enjoyed."*

MARGARET AND DAN DUCKHORN: *"With a young Merlot, we recommend lamb shanks with crispy polenta, or grilled duck with wild rice in Port sauce. One of our favorites is barbecued leg of lamb with a mild, spicy, fruit-based sauce. With older Merlots at the end of the meal, we like to serve Cambazzola cheese and warm walnuts."*

JANET TREFETHEN: *With Cabernet Sauvignon: prime cut of well-aged grilled beef; also—believe it or not— with chocolate and chocolate-chip cookies. With Pinot Noir: roasted quail stuffed with peeled kiwi fruit in a Madeira sauce. Also with pork tenderloin in a fruity sauce.*

PAUL DRAPER *(Ridge Vineyards): With Zinfandel: a well-made risotto of Petaluma duck. With aged Cabernet Sauvignon: Moroccan lamb with figs.*

WARREN WINIARSKI *(Stag's Leap Wine Cellars): With Cabernet Sauvignon: lamb or veal with a light sauce.*

JOSH JENSEN *(Calera Wine Co.): "Pinot Noir is so versatile, but I like it best with fowl of all sorts—chicken, turkey, duck, pheasant, and quail, preferably roasted or mesquite grilled. It's also great with fish such as salmon, tuna, and snapper."*

RICHARD ARROWOOD: *With Cabernet Sauvignon: Sonoma County spring lamb or lamb chops prepared in a rosemary herb sauce.*

DAVID STARE *(Dry Creek Vineyard): "My favorite food combination with Zinfandel is marinated, butterflied leg of lamb. Have the butcher butterfly the leg, then place it in a plastic bag. Pour in half a bottle of Dry Creek Zinfandel, a cup of olive oil, six mashed garlic cloves, salt and pepper to taste. Marinate for several hours or overnight in the refrigerator. Barbecue until medium rare. While the lamb is cooking, take the marinade, reduce it, and whisk in several pats of butter for thickness. Yummy!"*

BO BARRETT *(Chateau Montelena Winery): With Cabernet Sauvignon: a good rib eye, barbecued with a teriyaki-soy-ginger-sesame marinade; venison or even roast beef prepared with olive oil and tapenade with rosemary, or even lamb. But when it comes to a good Cabernet Sauvignon, Bo is happy to enjoy a glass with "nothing at all—just a good book."*

PATRICK CAMPBELL *(owner/winemaker, Laurel Glen Vineyard): "With Cabernet Sauvignon, try a rich risotto topped with wild mushrooms."*

JACK CAKEBREAD: *"I enjoy my 1994 Cakebread Cellars Napa Valley Cabernet Sauvignon with farm-raised salmon with a crispy potato crust or an herb-crusted Napa Valley rack of lamb, with mashed potatoes and a red-wine sauce."*

ED SBRAGIA *(winemaker, Beringer Vineyards): "I like my Cabernet Sauvignon with rack of lamb, beef, or rare duck."*

TOM MACKEY *(winemaker, St. Francis Merlot): With St. Francis Merlot Sonoma County: Dungeness crab cakes, rack of lamb, pork roast, or tortellini. With St. Francis Merlot Reserve: hearty minestrone or lentil soup, venison, or filet mignon, or even a Caesar salad.*

CLASS SIX: THE RED WINES OF CALIFORNIA (WITH OREGON AND WASHINGTON)

This is the sixth class and you've tasted more than fifty wines. You've ingested a tremendous amount of information—and wine!—over the last five classes; perhaps too much. So now we relax. Class Six is the "break" class in which we veer away from too many facts and statistics and where I join the class in each 60-second wine expert tasting. I give my personal opinion of each wine as I taste it. It's also the only time in the course that the students observe how a professional wine taster judges wine! This is the class after which I once received the best compliment ever: A student told me that this was the best class of all because she now understood which wines she liked and why. Intrigued, I asked her what about this class was so invaluable. Her answer surprised and delighted me—"Every wine you liked, I hated!" Clearly we were incompatible in our tastes, but she was honest and had discovered more about her own tastes—that's the nature and purpose of wine tasting.

In Class Two we covered the vital information of California and the rest of the United States. In this class I hope you'll learn more about tasting, and further identify your own preferences on wine styles. While I can't be with you as you taste, the notes that follow each tasting are my own.

Wines for Class Six

I am using a Pinot Noir from Oregon and a Merlot from Washington State. These two states are increasingly recognized as producing some of the best wines in the United States.

1. Saintsbury Pinot Noir 2006 (Carneros)
2. Domaine Drouhin Pinot Noir 2006 (Oregon)
3. Ravenswood Zinfandel Sonoma Series 2007
4. Ridge Geyserville Zinfandel 2006
5. Columbia Crest Grand Estates Merlot 2007 (Washington) **BEST VALUE**
6. Clos du Bois Reserve Merlot 2006
7. Louis Martini Cabernet Sauvignon 2005 (Napa Valley) **BEST VALUE**
8. Blind
9. Blind
10. Blind
11. Robert Mondavi Cabernet Sauvignon Reserve 2001

The first six wines are all poured together so that you can clearly see the difference in color between the Pinot Noirs, Zinfandels, and Merlots. The Pinot Noirs are much lighter in color than the Zinfandels and Merlots, and most students judge the Merlot-based wines as the deepest in color. I hope that after you've tasted these first six wines, you will be able to choose the grape variety that best suits your personality: your "eureka" moment.

There are six parts to this tasting.

PART I: PINOT NOIR (TWO WINES TASTED TOGETHER FROM THE SAME VINTAGE)

Within wine circles there is always a heated debate over which state produces the best Pinot Noir: California or Oregon. My answer is always the same: Both states produce some of the best Pinot Noir in the world, but each state produces a different style.

Wine #1: Saintsbury Pinot Noir 2006 (Carneros)

The Saintsbury Winery of Napa, California, was named after the British wine writer George Saintsbury and founded in 1981. Owners Dick Ward and David Graves pioneered growing Chardonnay and Pinot Noir grapes and are well known today for the many different styles they produce of each.

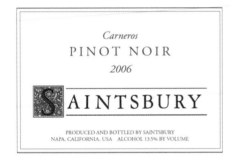

I've used the Saintsbury Pinot Noir many times in my class because of its consistent high quality and reasonable price. This 2006 Pinot Noir is medium in body with a classic Pinot Noir bouquet and hints of spice and black cherry. The complexity of the taste lingers, giving this wine a soft and elegant finish. Although this wine has been aged in small French oak barrels, the oak never dominates the fruit.

Retail price $35
Ready to drink
Other recommended producers are: Acacia, Etude, or Flowers.

Wine #2: Domaine Drouhin Pinot Noir 2006 (Oregon)

I chose the Domaine Drouhin Pinot Noir because of the family's hundreds of years of winemaking expertise in Burgundy, France, where the ultimate expression of Pinot Noir developed. Robert Drouhin visited the Willamette

Retail price $16 **BEST VALUE**
Ready to drink
Another recommended Washington State value Merlot producer is
Hogue Merlot.

Wine #6: Clos du Bois Reserve Merlot 2006

Clos du Bois began thirty-five years ago in 1974. When Windows on the World
opened in 1976, we used their Merlot for wine by the glass and for our banquet customers. It has been up and down in quality over the years, but recently
they have been producing excellent wines, especially the Reserve Merlot. The
grapes for this wine come from the Alexander Valley in Sonoma. The wine is
a blend of 91 percent Merlot, 5 percent Cabernet Sauvignon, and 4 percent
Malbec. The long maceration of the grapes gives a tremendous extraction of
fruit and flavor. This wine was aged in French oak for twenty-one months (half
new oak). This is a blockbuster, full-bodied wine with a long intense finish.

Retail price $22
Ready to drink, but can be aged
Other recommended producers of Merlot are: Markham, Shafer, or
Whitehall Lane.

The next five wines are all made with Cabernet Sauvignon.

PART IV: INTRODUCTION TO CABERNET SAUVIGNON (ONE WINE, TASTED ALONE)

My favorite red grape is Cabernet Sauvignon. It is also one of the best grapes
grown in California, particularly in the Napa Valley. The diversity of style and
price of California Cabernet Sauvignons is abundant. Are you looking to spend
$15 or $150 or $550? There's something for everyone and any occasion.

Wine #7: Louis Martini Cabernet Sauvignon 2005 (Napa Valley)

I've had sentimental feelings for the Louis Martini Winery ever since I created
my first wine list for the Windows on the World restaurant. Louis Martini

Cabernet Sauvignons were featured on every one of my lists for the twenty-five years I worked there as wine director. The Martini family is one of the oldest families of quality winemaking in California. They started their winery in 1922 and moved to the Napa Valley right after prohibition ended. They have always created good quality, primarily red, honest wines at affordable prices. I have been fortunate to have tried many of their early Cabernet Sauvignons going back to the 1940s.

All the grapes for this 2005 Cabernet Sauvignon come from the Napa Valley. The primary grapes are Cabernet Sauvignon (94 percent), Petit Syrah (4 percent), Petit Verdot (.6 percent), Merlot (.5 percent), and Cabernet Franc (.25 percent). Ninety-five percent of the wine was aged in oak barrels for eight months. The wine has an alcohol content of 14.2 percent.

This is not a blockbuster Cabernet Sauvignon, which is the main reason that I use it as my first Cabernet. For as long as I have known the wine, it has been medium in body with really good flavor and structure. It's a great restaurant wine and today remains one of the best values of all of California Cabernet Sauvignons.

Retail price $22 **BEST VALUE**
Ready to drink, but can age
Other recommended producers of this style Cabernet Sauvignon are:
Beringer Founders Estate, Simi, or Gallo of Sonoma.

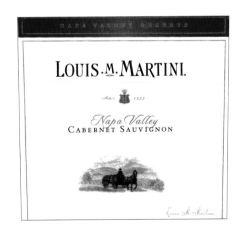

PART V: BLIND (THREE DIFFERENT CABERNET SAUVIGNONS)

Wine #8: Blind

Wine #9: Blind

Wine #10: Blind

This is a very special tasting and much like the tasting we did with the wines of Bordeaux in Class Five. The only thing I let the students know is that these wines are three high-quality Cabernet Sauvignons coming out of my personal wine cellar. The students first discuss the color and the smell, just as they did in the previous class. They now have six minutes in silence to try the three wines. I do this tasting blind because it helps the students concentrate more on the individual characteristics of each wine. Somehow when you see a label, you get a preconceived impression of what the wine should taste like. I also ask the same question as I have in Class Five: Are these Cabernets all from the same vintage or different vintages? See page 176 for a listing of my favorite Cabernets.

Because my students have to read this book for my class, I cannot share with you the three wines I serve. Just use your imagination and think high quality.

PART VI: CABERNET SAUVIGNON RESERVE (ONE WINE, TASTED ALONE)

Wine #11: Robert Mondavi Cabernet Sauvignon Reserve 2001

I would not be writing this chapter, would not have been able to write my wine book, and probably wouldn't have been able to operate my wine school for more than thirty years without the vision of Robert Mondavi. Mondavi set the standards for quality California wine long before anyone was interested, and his insights traveled well beyond the borders of the Napa Valley, California, and the United States. He influenced winemakers throughout the world.

There is no easier way to explain or describe what happens to wine as it gets older or what it tastes like than serving an older Cabernet Sauvignon and allowing you to formulate your own opinion. This 2001 Robert Mondavi Cabernet Sauvignon Reserve is primarily made with Cabernet Sauvignon and most of the grapes come from its To-Kalon Vineyard, arguably the best vineyard in Napa. At eight years old, this wine still has a deep color with earth tones of minerals, and intense flavors of cassis and black fruit. This wine is still in its peak period. It can be consumed now or continue to age.

Retail price $100
Ready to drink, but can age
Other recommended producers of Napa Valley reserve wines are:
Beaulieu Private Reserve, Beringer Private Reserve, Shafer Hillside Select, Silver Oak, or Stag's Leap Cask 23.

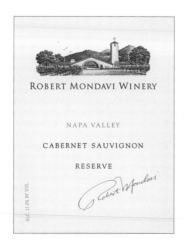

Questions for Class Six:
The Red Wines of California

8. In which two French wine regions would you find Pinot Noir?   177

9. Which county in California has the most plantings of Pinot Noir?   177

10. What grape in California has a similar DNA to the Italian grape Primitivo?   178

11. In which French wine region would you find Syrah?   179

12. In what counties are most of the Syrah grapes planted?   179

13. What was the most planted red grape in California in 1970?   180

14. What is a Meritage wine?   180

15. Name two Meritage wines.   180

The Wines of Spain and Italy

SPAIN • RIOJA • RIBERA DEL DUERO • PENEDÈS • PRIORAT

ITALY • TUSCANY • PIEDMONT • VENETO

ALTHOUGH THERE are nearly 800 different wineries in Spain, about 80% of their production comes from a handful of companies.

The Wines of Spain

SPAIN IS THE WORLD'S third largest producer of wine behind Italy and France. With 2.7 million acres of land planted, Spain has more acreage dedicated to grapevines than any other country in the world.

Despite thousands of years of grape growing and winemaking history, Spain has undergone a radical change over the last twenty-five years. Since joining the European Union in 1986, Spain has benefited from the infusion of capital for its vineyards and wineries. Modern technology, with its stainless steel fermentors and new vineyard trellis systems, has helped create outstanding wines from all of Spain's diverse wine regions. Often beset by a dry climate and frequent droughts, especially in the center and south of the country, irrigation became legal in 1996 for grapevines, which has increased both the quality and volume of Spain's wine production.

What are the major grape varieties planted in Spain?

There are hundreds of grape varieties grown in Spain. Here are the ones you most likely find in the wine store or restaurant:

NATIVE TO SPAIN		INTERNATIONAL	
White	*Red*	*White*	*Red*
Albariño	Tempranillo	Chardonnay	Cabernet
Verdejo	(Tinto Fino)	Sauvignon Blanc	Sauvignon
Macabeo (Viura)	Garnacha		Merlot
Cariñena	Monastrell		Syrah

THERE ARE more than 600 grapes varieties planted in Spain.

What are the major wine regions of Spain?

Spain first established Denominación de Origen (DO) laws in 1982 and revised them in 1970. There were twenty-five DOs in 1982 and today, Spain has seventy-one DO regions and two DOC regions. Similar to the AOC laws of France, Spain's DO laws control a region's boundaries, grape varieties, winemaking practices, yield per acre, and most important, the aging of the wine before it can be released.

My favorite wine regions of Spain with the most important grapes include the following:

Rioja: Tempranillo
Ribera del Duero: Tinto Fino
Priorat: Garnacha, Cariñena
Penedès: Macabeo, Cabernet Sauvignon, Cariñena, Garnacha
Rías Baixas: Albariño
Rueda: Verdejo
Sherry (Jerez): Palomino

YOU WILL find the word *cosecha*, which means "harvest" or "vintage" in Spanish, on some labels. It can also indicate a wine that has little barrel aging, and is often used by producers for their "modern-style" wines.

DOC IS the highest level of quality wine in Spain. As of 2009 there are only two that qualify: Rioja and Priorat.

We'll put aside the region of Jerez for now, since you will become a Sherry expert in a later chapter. Let's begin with Rioja, which is located in northern Spain near the French border. In fact, it's less than a five-hour (two-hundred-mile) drive to Rioja from Bordeaux, which has influenced the style of Rioja winemaking since the 1800s.

During the 1870s the phylloxera blight, traveling from north to south, arrived in Bordeaux and nearly destroyed the wine industry there. Many of Bordeaux's winemakers and owners chose to relocate to Rioja, where the blight had yet to appear and whose climate and growing conditions were similar to that of Bordeaux. As they established their own wineries and vineyards, they influenced how Rioja wine was made. This influence is still apparent in today's Rioja wines.

RIOJA

Despite a surge in diverse and interesting wines from elsewhere in Spain, Rioja still reigns as the principal red-wine-producing region. Rioja offers both quality and quantity and sits comfortably alongside the world's greatest wine-producing regions. In 1985, Rioja had roughly 100,000 acres planted in grapes; in 2009, there were more than 150,000 acres. One of the biggest recent changes in Rioja has been the rejuvenation of its vineyards: 41 percent of all its vines have been planted over the last ten years. Since 1993 the amount of red grapes planted has doubled and now accounts for 90 percent of total grape production.

Rioja continues to innovate within its traditional style and offers consumers a tremendous range of quality at price points appealing to both novices and collectors.

Which red grapes are used in Rioja wines?

TEMPRANILLO   **GARNACHA**

Why are Rioja wines so easy to understand?

All you need to know when buying a Rioja wine is the style (level) and the reputation of the Rioja winemaker/shipper. The grape varieties are not found on the wine labels, and there's no classification to be memorized. The three major levels of Rioja wines are:

Crianza: Released after two years of aging, with a minimum of one year in oak barrels ($)

Reserva: Released after three years of aging, with a minimum of one year in oak barrels ($$)

Gran Reserva: Released after five to seven years of aging, with a minimum of two years in oak barrels ($$$)

How would I know which Rioja wine to buy?

Aside from going with your preferred style and the reputation of the winemaker/shipper, you may also be familiar with a Rioja wine by its proprietary name. The following are some bodegas to look for, along with some of their better-known proprietary names. Also, three of the best U.S. importers for Spanish wine are Steve Metzler (Classical wines), Jorge Ordoñez (Fine Estates from Spain), and Eric Solomon (European Cellars).

BARON DE LEY

BODEGAS BRETÓN

BODEGAS DINASTIA VIVANCO

BODEGAS LAN

BODEGAS MONTECILLO

BODEGAS MUGA—MUGA RESERVA, PRADO ENEA, TORRE MUGA

VINOS DE PAGOS means that the wine comes from a single estate.

SPANISH WINERIES are sometimes called bodegas.

THE BODEGA *Marqués de Cáceres* is owned by a Spaniard who also owns Château Camensac, a fifth-growth Bordeaux.

FINCA means "farm."

MARQUÉS DE Murrieta was the first commercial bodega in Rioja, established in 1852.

SOME OF THE top Rioja winemakers say that the 2001 and 2004 vintages are the best they have ever tasted.

BODEGAS REMÍREZ DE GANUZA

BODEGAS RIOJANAS—MONTE REAL, VIÑA ALBINA

BODEGAS TOBÍA

CUNE—IMPERIAL, VIÑA REAL

CONTINO

EL COTO

FINCA ALLENDE

FINCA VALPIEDRA

LA RIOJA ALTA—VIÑA ALBERDI, VIÑA ARDANZA

LOPEZ DE HEREDÍA

MARQUÉS DE CÁCERES

MARQUÉS DE MURRIETA

MARQUÉS DE RISCAL

MARTÍNEZ BUJANDA—CONDE DE VALDEMAR

PALACIOS REMONDO

REMELLURI

SEÑORIO DE SAN VICENTE

YSIOS

BEST BETS FOR RIOJA

1994* 1995* 2001** 2003 2004** 2005* 2006 2007

Note: *signifies exceptional vintage   ** signifies extraordinary vintage

RIBERA DEL DUERO

When I wrote the original edition of this book, I did not include the Ribera del Duero region. Back then most of the region's wines were made at cooperatives except, arguably, that of the most famous winery of Spain, Bodegas Vega Sicilia, which has been making wine since the 1860s. But one wine does not a region make.

AALTO

One of the newest wineries in Ribera del Duero, Aalto, released its first vintage in 1999. It was created by the former legendary winemaker at Vega Sicilia, Mariano Garcia, and his business partner, Javier Zaccagnini. They presently are making two wines, Aalto and Aalto PS. Judging by the reviews both wines have received, they need to be added to your wine cellar!

In the early 1980s another wine, Pesquera, received great reviews from the wine press, setting the tone for astounding growth and helping stimulate quality wine production in the region. Today there are over 260 wineries there, and a new generation of quality winemakers is emerging.

What are the major red grapes used in Ribera del Duero?

TINTO FINO (AKA TEMPRANILLO)   **MALBEC**

CABERNET SAUVIGNON   **GARNACHA**

MERLOT

BEST BETS FOR RIBERA DEL DUERO

1996*   2001*   2004**   2005*   2006   2007*

Note: *signifies exceptional vintage   ** signifies extraordinary vintage

PENEDÈS

Located just outside of Barcelona, the Penedès region produces a famous sparkling wine called Cava, protected under its own DO. The two best-known names of Spanish sparkling wine in the United States are Codorniu and Freixenet, two of the biggest producers of bottle-fermented sparkling wine in the world. One of the best features of these wines is their reasonable price for a traditional method sparkling wine.

In addition to Cava, the Penedès region is known for high-quality table wine. The major producer is the Torres family, whose name is synonymous with quality. Their most famous wine, Gran Coronas Black Label, is made with

KEVIN ZRALY'S FAVORITE RIBERA DEL DUERO PRODUCERS

Aalto
Vega Sicilia
Pesquera
Viña Mayor
Pago de los Capellanes
Bodegas Emilio Moro
Dominio de Pingus
Abadia Retuerta
Bodegas Felix Callejo
Condado de Haza
Hacienda Monasterio

KEVIN ZRALY'S FAVORITE PENEDÈS PRODUCERS

Torres (Mas La Plana)
Jean Leon
Marques de Monistrol
Albet i Noya

100 percent Cabernet Sauvignon, and is rare and expensive. But the Torres family also produces a full range of fine Spanish wines in all price categories.

What grapes are used in Penedès?

FOR CAVA	FOR RED	FOR WHITE
Macabeo	Tempranillo	Chardonnay
Parellada	Cabernet Sauvignon	Parellada
Xarel-lo	Garnacha	Macabeo
Chardonnay	Merlot	Riesling
		Gewürztraminer

BEST BETS FOR PENEDÈS

2002*   2003*   2004*   2005*   2006   2007

*Note: *signifies exceptional vintage*

PRIORAT WINES must have a minimum of 13.5% alcohol.

MOST VINEYARDS are so steep in Priorat that mechanical equipment is difficult to maneuver, so mules are used instead (just like the old days!).

PRIORAT

1995: 16 wineries
2008: 80 wineries

THE PRIORAT vineyards are located at an altitude of 1,000 to 3,000 feet.

BECAUSE OF extremely low yields and demand, it is difficult to find an inexpensive Priorat. The best easily sell for over $100 a bottle.

PRIORAT

This region, located a few hours south of the Penedès region, epitomizes the renaissance of Spanish wines. The Carthusian monks farmed the vineyards for over eight hundred years until the early 1800s, when the government auctioned off their land to local farmers. In the late 1800s, phylloxera blight forced most farmers to stop planting grapes, and many began to cultivate hazelnuts and almonds. By 1910 most wine was made in cooperatives and, up until twenty-five years ago, Priorat was mostly known for sacramental wine.

In the late 1980s some of the most well-known Spanish wine producers, including René Barbier and Alvaro Palacios, started to revive the old Carthusian vineyards. Today Priorat produces some of the best red wine in Spain. In fact, the Spanish government has awarded Priorat the highest status of DOC. Only two regions in Spain have this rating (the other is Rioja).

What are the grapes used in making Priorat wines?

Native to Spain: Garnacha (Grenache), Cariñena (Carignan)
International: Cabernet Sauvignon, Merlot, Syrah

ALVARO PALACIOS

Alvaro Palacios is one of Spain's wine mavericks. Starting at his family's winery in Rioja, he has expanded into the Priorat and Bierzo regions—two regions that he helped revitalize. His Priorat wine, L'Ermita, is one of the most expensive and highly rated wines in Spain. For better value, try the Finca Dofi and, for the best value, Les Terrasses.

BEST BETS FOR PRIORAT

2004* 2005** 2007*

Note: *signifies exceptional vintage ** signifies extraordinary vintage

WHITE WINES OF SPAIN

Rueda: Located in north-central Spain, Rueda wines have been well-known for centuries. Up until the 1970s, Ruedas were fortified wines whose major grape was Palomino. They were similar to Sherry in style.

The "modern" style of Rueda white wine is dry, fruity, and fresh. It is made from Verdejo, Viura and, occasionally, Sauvignon Blanc grapes.

Rías Baixas: Rías Baixas is located in the northwestern part of Spain in the region of Galicia. Like Rueda, Rías Baixas began to make outstanding white wines in the 1980s. Over 90 percent of the wine is made from the Albariño grape.

FOR FURTHER READING

I recommend *The New Spain* by John Radford; *The New and Classical Wines of Spain* by Jeremy Watson, and *Peñín Guide to Spanish Wine* directed by Jose Penin and produced by Grupo Penin (annual).

KEVIN ZRALY'S FAVORITE
PRIORAT PRODUCERS

Alvaro Palacios
Pasanau
Clos Mogador
Clos Erasmus
Clos Martinet
Clos de L'Obac
Clos Daphne
Mas Igneus

FOR THE PRIORAT TOURIST: Remnants of the priory called Scala Dei (God's Stairway) and a museum devoted to its history are open to the public.

OTHER WINE-PRODUCING
AREAS OF SPAIN

Bierzo
Castilla-La Mancha
Jumilla
Navarra
Toro

The Red Wines of Italy

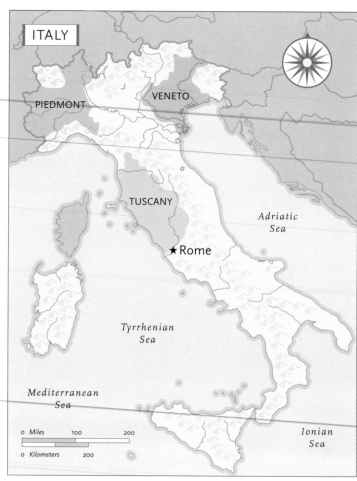

ITALY

PIEDMONT

VENETO

TUSCANY

★Rome

Adriatic Sea

Tyrrhenian Sea

Mediterranean Sea

Ionian Sea

0 Miles 100 200

0 Kilometers 200

TOP THREE REGIONS IN PRODUCTION OF ITALIAN WINES

1. Veneto	17.7%
2. Piedmont	17.1%
3. Tuscany	10.7%

MANY WINE producers in Italy are now making wines from Cabernet Sauvignon, Merlot, and Chardonnay.

ITALY IS THE WORLD'S largest producer of wine as of 2008. It has been producing wine for more than three thousand years, and the vines grow everywhere. As one retailer of fine Italian wine once told me, "There is no country. Italy is one vast vineyard from north to south."

Italian wines are good for any occasion—from quaffing to serious tasting. Some of my favorite wines are Italian. In fact, 25 percent of my personal wine cellar is stocked with them.

There are more than two thousand different wine labels, if you care to memorize them; twenty regions; and ninety-six provinces. But don't worry. If you want to know the basics of Italian wines, concentrate on the three regions listed below, and you'll be well on your way to having Italy in the palm of your hand.

TUSCANY

PIEDMONT

VENETO

What are the major red-grape varieties in Italy?

There are hundreds of indigenous grapes planted throughout Italy. In Tuscany, the major red-grape variety is Sangiovese, in Piedmont it is Nebbiolo, and in Veneto, it is Corvina.

How are Italian wines controlled?

The Denominazione di Origine Controllata (abbreviated DOC), the Italian equivalent of the French AOC, defines where wine is produced and how it can be labeled. Italy's DOC laws went into effect in 1963.

During the 1980s, the Italian agricultural ministry took quality control one step further than the regular DOC, by adding the higher-ranking DOCG. The G stands for *Garantita,* meaning that, tasting-control boards absolutely guarantee the stylistic authenticity of a wine.

As of 2009, the wines from Tuscany and Piedmont that qualified for the DOCG were:

TUSCANY	PIEDMONT
Vernaccia di San Gimignano	Moscato d'Asti/Asti
Chianti	Gattinara
Chianti Classico	Barbaresco
Vino Nobile di Montepulciano	Barolo
Carmignano Rosso	Acqui or Brachetto d'Acqui
Brunello di Montalcino	Ghemme
Morellino di Scansano	Gavi or Cortese di Gavi
	Roero
	Dolcetto di Dogliani Superiore

Nine of the thirty-five Italian DOCG wines are from Piedmont and seven are from Tuscany. Almost half of the DOCGs are located in these two regions, which is why your study of Italian wines should focus on them.

DOC LAWS

The DOC governs:

The geographical limits of each region

The grape varieties that can be used

The percentage of each grape used

The maximum amount of wine that can be produced per acre

The minimum alcohol content of the wine

The aging requirements, such as how long a wine should spend in wood or bottle, for certain wines

THE BIGGEST difference between the AOC of France and the DOC of Italy is that the DOC has aging requirements.

AT PRESENT, there are 35 wines that are entitled to the DOCG designation.

DOCG WINES from regions other than Tuscany and Piedmont include Taurasi, Greco di Tufo, and Fiano di Avellino from Campania; Albana di Romagna from Emilia-Romagna; Torgiano Riserva and Montefalco Sagrantino di Montefalco from Umbria; Franciacorta, Valtellina Superiore, and Sforzato di Valtellina from Lombardy; Recioto di Soave, Bardolino Superiore, and Soave Superiore from Veneto; Vermentino de Gallura from Sardinia; Ramandolo and Colli Orientale del Fruili Picolit from Friuli-Venezia Giulia; Montepulciano d'Abruzzo Colline Teramane from Abruzzi; Conero and Vernaccia di Serrapetrona from Marches; and Cerasvolo di Vittoria from Sicily.

THERE ARE more than 300 DOC wines accounting for 20% of Italy's total wine production.

OF ALL Italian DOC wines, 60% are red.

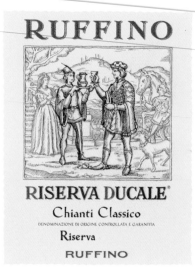

TUSCANY—THE HOME OF CHIANTI

What are the different levels of Chianti?

Chianti: The first level. Cost: $.

Chianti Classico: From the inner historic district of Chianti. Cost: $$.

Chianti Classico Riserva: From a Classico area, and must be aged for a minimum of two years, three months. Cost: $$$$.

How should I buy Chianti?

First of all, find the style of Chianti you like best. There is a considerable variation in Chianti styles. Second, always buy from a shipper or producer whom you know—one with a good, reliable reputation. Some quality Chianti producers are:

ANTINORI	FRESCOBALDI
BADIA A COLTIBUONO	MELINI
BROLIO	MONSANTO
CASTELLO BANFI	NOZZOLE
CASTELLO DI AMA	RICASOLI
FONTODI	RUFFINO

Which grapes are used in Chianti?

According to updated DOCG requirements, winemakers are required to use at least 80 percent Sangiovese to produce Chianti. The DOCG also encourages the use of other grapes by allowing an unprecedented 20 percent nontraditional grapes (Cabernet Sauvignon, Merlot, Syrah, etc.). These changes, along with better winemaking techniques and better vineyard development, have all contributed greatly to improving Chianti's image over the last twenty-five years. A separate DOCG has been established for Chianti Classico, and many producers of this wine now use 100 percent Sangiovese.

Which other high-quality wines come from Tuscany?

Three of the greatest Italian red wines are Brunello di Montalcino, Vino Nobile di Montepulciano, and Carmignano. All of these wines are made with the Sangiovese grape. If you purchase the Brunello, keep in mind that it probably needs more aging (five to ten years) before it reaches peak drinkability. There are more than 150 producers of Brunello. My favorite producers of Brunello di Montalcino are:

CARPINETO	LA FUGA
CONSTANTI	MARCHESI DE FRESCOBALDI
BARBI	POGGIO ANTICO
ALTESINO	COL D'ORCIA
CASTELGIORONDO	CASTELLO BANFI
LA PODERINA	CAPARZO
IL POGGIONE	GAJA
LISINI	SOLDERA

Those of Vino Nobile di Montepulciano are:

AVIGNONESI	DEI
BOSCARELLI	FATTORIA DEL CERRO
FASSATI	POGGIO ALLA SALA

For Carmignano, look for:

VILLA CAPEZZANA	ARTIMINO
POGGIOLO	

BEST BETS FOR WINES FROM TUSCANY

1997** 1999** 2001* 2003
2004** 2005* 2006** 2007

*Note: * signifies exceptional vintage   ** signifies extraordinary vintage*

BRUNELLO IS CHANGING

Beginning with the 1995 vintage, Brunellos are required to be aged in oak for a minimum of two years instead of the previous three. The result? A fruitier, more accessible wine.

BRUNELLO DI MONTALCINO, because of its limited supply, is sometimes very expensive. For one of the best values in Tuscan red wine, look for Rosso di Montalcino.

IN 2008 THE winemakers of Brunello voted to maintain 100% Sangiovese Grosso for their wines and not to blend with other grape varieties.

PIEDMONT—THE BIG REDS

Some of the finest red wines are produced in Piedmont. Two of the best DOCG wines to come from this region in northwest Italy are Barolo and Barbaresco.

The major grapes of Piedmont are:

DOLCETTO

BARBERA

NEBBIOLO

Barolo and Barbaresco, the "heavyweight" wines from Piedmont, are made from the Nebbiolo variety. These wines have the fullest style and a high alcohol content. Be careful when you try to match young vintages of these wines with your dinner; they may overpower the food.

My favorite producers of Piedmont wines are:

ANTONIO VALLANA	**M. CHIARLO**
FONTANAFREDDA	**B. GIACOSA**
GAJA	**MARCHESI DI GRESY**
PIO CESARE	**LUCIANO SANDRONE**
PRUNOTTO	**PAOLO SCAVINO BROGOGNO**
RENATO RATTI	**MARCHESI DI BAROLO**
CERETTO	**VIETTI**
G. CONTERNO	**MARCARINI**
ROBERT VOERZIO	**SANDRONE**
DOMENICO CLERICO	**CONTERNO FANTINA**
A. CONTERNO	**PRODUTTORI D'BARBARESCO**

BEST BETS FOR WINES FROM PIEDMONT

1990*   1996**   1997*   1998*   1999*   2000**   2001**   2003
2004**   2005*   2006*   2007

*Note: * signifies exceptional vintage   ** signifies extraordinary vintage*

THREE REASONS to visit Piedmont in the fall: the harvest, the food, and the white truffles.

APPROXIMATELY 50% of the vineyards in Piedmont are Barbera.

MORE THAN 90% of the Piedmont grapes are planted on hillsides.

PIEDMONT'S PRODUCTION

65% red
18% Spumante (sparkling white)
17% white

IT IS SAID that when you begin drinking the red wines of Piedmont, you start with the lighter-style Barbera and Dolcetto, move on to the fuller-bodied Barbaresco, until finally you can fully appreciate a Barolo. As the late vintner Renato Ratti said, "Barolo is the wine of arrival."

HAVE PIEDMONT wines changed over the last ten years? Many have. The wines of the past were more tannic and difficult to appreciate when young, while many of the present-day wines are easier to drink.

GIUSEPPE COLLA of Prunotto offers his "Best Bets" in the form of advice. His general rule: In a good vintage, set a Barbaresco aside for a minimum of four years before drinking. In the same situation, put away a Barolo for six years. However, in a great vintage year, lay down a Barbaresco for six years and a Barolo for eight years. As they say, "Patience is a virtue"—especially with wine.

OLDER GREAT vintages of Piedmont: 1982, 1985, 1988, 1989

BAROLO VS. BARBARESCO

BAROLO (MORE THAN 8 MILLION BOTTLES)	BARBARESCO (NEARLY 3 MILLION BOTTLES)
Nebbiolo grape	Nebbiolo grape
Minimum 12.5% alcohol	Minimum 12.5% alcohol
More complex flavor, more body	Lighter; sometimes less body than Barolo, but fine and elegant
Must be aged at least three years (one in wood)	Requires two years of aging (one in wood)
"Riserva" = five years of aging	"Riserva" = four years of aging

THE PIEDMONT region had six great vintages in a row: 1996–2001.

IN ONE of the biggest changes in the DOCG regulations, the wines of Barolo now have to be aged in wood for only one year, and the minimum alcohol has been changed to 12.5%. Before 1999, Barolo had a mandatory two years of wood aging and 13% minimum alcohol.

ANOTHER GREAT Piedmont wine is called Gattinara. Look for the Antoniolo Reservas.

THE PRODUCTION of Barolo and Barbaresco at 11 million bottles a year is equivalent to that of only a medium-size California winery!

VENETO—THE HOME OF AMARONE

This is one of Italy's largest wine-producing regions. Even if you don't recognize the name immediately, I'm sure you've had Veronese wines at one time or another, like Valpolicella, Bardolino, and Soave. All three are very consistent, easy to drink, and ready to be consumed whenever you buy them. They don't fit into the category of a Brunello di Montalcino or a Barolo, but they're very good table wines and they're within everyone's budget. The best and most improved of the three is Valpolicella. Look for Valpolicella Superiore made by the *ripasso* method.

RIPASSO: The adding back of grape skins from Amarone wine to Valpolicella, giving it extra alcohol and more flavor.

THE TOP five wines imported to the United States from Italy are:

1. Riunite
2. Casarsa
3. Bolla
4. Cavit
5. Ecco Domani

The above wines equal 43% of all imported table wine in the United States.

Easy-to-find Veneto producers are:

BOLLA   **ALLEGRINI**

FOLONARI   **ANSELMI**

SANTA SOFIA   **QUINTARELLI**

THE NAME "Amarone" derives from *amar*, meaning "bitter," and *one* (pronounced "oh-nay"), meaning "big."

CLASSICO: All the vineyards are in the historical part of the region.

SUPERIORE: Higher levels of alcohol and longer aging.

What's Amarone?

Amarone is a type of Valpolicella wine made by a special process in the Veneto region. Only the ripest grapes (Corvina, Rondinella, and Molinara) from the top of each bunch are used. After picking, they're left to "raisinate" (dry and shrivel) on straw mats. Does this sound familiar to you? It should, because this is similar to the process used to make German Trockenbeerenauslese and French Sauternes. One difference is that with Amarone, the winemaker ferments most of the sugar, bringing the alcohol content to 14 to 16 percent.

My favorite producers of Amarone are:

MASI   **QUINTARELLI**

BERTANI   **TOMMASI**

ALLEGRINI

BEST BETS FOR AMARONE

1990* 1993 1995* 1996 1997* 1998
2000* 2001 2002* 2003* 2005*

*Note: * signifies exceptional vintage*

HOW ITALIAN WINES ARE NAMED

Winemaking regions have different ways of naming their wines. In California, you look for the grape variety on the label. In Bordeaux, most often you will see the name of a château. But in Italy, there are three different ways that wine is named: by grape variety, village or district, or simply by a proprietary name. See the examples below.

GRAPE VARIETY	VILLAGE OR DISTRICT	PROPRIETARY
Barbera	Chianti	Tignanello
Nebbiolo	Barolo	Sassicaia
Sangiovese	Montalcino	Summus
Pinot Grigio	Barbaresco	Ornellaia

IN ITALY, vineyards aren't classified as they are in Bordeaux and Burgundy. There are neither Grands Crus nor Premiers Crus.

Twenty-five years later in Italy

Twenty-five years ago most Italian wine was made to be consumed in Italy, and not for the export market. To the Italians, wine was an everyday thing like salt and pepper on their table to enhance the taste of their food.

But since then, winemaking has become more of a business, and the Italian winemakers' philosophy has changed considerably from making casual-drinking wines to much better-made wines that are also much more marketable around the world. They've accomplished this by using modern technology, modern vinification procedures, and updated vineyard management as a basis for experimentation.

Another area of major experimentation is with nontraditional grape varieties such as Cabernet Sauvignon and Merlot. As a result, the biggest news in the whole wine industry over the last twenty-five years is the change in Italian wines. When I talk about experimentation, you must remember that this isn't California we're talking about, but Italy, with thousands of years of traditions that are being changed. In Italy, the producers have had to unlearn and relearn winemaking techniques in order to make better wines for the export market.

The prices of Italian wines have also increased tremendously over the last twenty-five years—not good news for consumers. Some of the wines from Italy have become among the most expensive in the world. That's not to say they're not worth it, but the pricing situation isn't the same as it was twenty-five years ago.

AN INTERESTING observation in Italy: Bottled water and beer consumption are both increasing, while wine consumption is decreasing.

ONE OF the newest trends in Italy is single-vineyard labeling.

THE 800,000 hectares of vineyards in Italy are owned by more than one million growers.

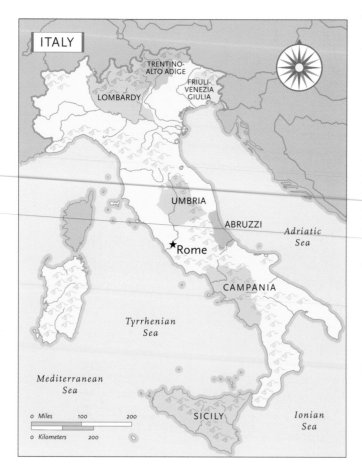

IN THE last 10 years, Italians have become more weight- and health-conscious, so they're changing their eating habits. As a result, the leisurely four-hour lunch and siesta is a thing of the past. Yes, all good things must come to an end.

MY ITALIAN-WINE friends sometimes refer to Veneto as Tri-Veneto, which includes Trentino, Alto-Adige, and Friuli. Some of the best white wines of Italy come from those regions.

A Quick Guide to Other Important Regions

I SOMETIMES WISH THAT it was possible for my book to cover every one of the world's wine regions, especially when it comes to a country like Italy. Of course, that would defeat the purpose of a "simple" guide to wine. But in Italy, where all twenty regions produce good to great wine, it is important that you have a quick look at the less well known regions along with a brief guide to the wines to look for.

ABRUZZI
Grapes: Montepulciano
Best Wine: Montepulciano d'Abruzzo
Favorite Producers: Elio Monti, Emidio Pepe, La Valentina, Masciarelli

FRUILI-VENEZIA GIULIA
Grapes: Pinot Grigio, Pinot Bianco, Chardonnay, Sauvignon Blanc
Favorite Producers: Jermann, Livio Felluga, Marco Felluga, Mario Schiopetto, Vie di Romans

TRENTINO-ALTO ADIGE
Grapes: *White*—Pinot Grigio, Pinot Bianco, Chardonnay, Sauvignon, Gewürztraminer
Red—Cabernet Sauvignon, Cabernet Franc, Lagrein, Merlot
Favorite Producers: Alois Lageder, Cantina di Terlano, Ferrari (Sparkling), Foradori, Tiefenbrunner, Tramin

LOMBARDY
Grapes: Nebbiolo, Trebbiano
Wines: Franciacorta (Sparkling), Lugana, Valtellina (Grumello, Sassella, Inferno, Valgella)
Favorite Producers: Sparkling—Bellavista, Ca' del Bosco
Valtellina—Conti Sertoli, Fay, Nino Negri, Rainoldi

UMBRIA

Grapes: Trebbiano, Sagrantino, Sangiovese
Wines: Orvieto, Sagrantino di Montefalco, Torgiano Rosso Riserva
Favorite Producers: Arnaldo Caprai, Lungarotti, Paolo Bea

CAMPANIA

Grapes: Aglianico, Fiano, Greco, Sangiovese
Best Wines: Greco di Tufo, Fiano di Avellino, Taurasi
Favorite Producers: Feudi di San Gregorio, Mastroberardino, Molettiera, Montevetrano, Mustilli, Villa Matilde

SICILY

Grapes: White—Catarratto, Chardonnay, Grecanico, Inzolia, Malvasia, Moscato
Red—Cabernet Sauvignon, Merlot, Nero d'Avola (Calabrese), Syrah
Best Wines: Marsala, Moscato di Pantelleria, Nero d'Avola
Favorite Producers: De Bartoli, Duca di Salaparuta (Duca Enrico), Gulfi, Morgante, Palari, Planeta, Rapitalà, Regaleai (Rosso del Conte), Santa Anastasia

Italian Whites

I am often asked why I don't teach a class on Italian white wines. The answer is quite simple. Take a look at the most popular white wines: Soave, Frascati, and Pinot Grigio, among others. Most of them retail for less than fifteen dollars. The Italians traditionally do not put the same effort into making their white wines as they do their reds—in terms of style or complexity—and they are the first to admit it.

Plantings of international white varieties such as Chardonnay and Sauvignon Blanc, along with some of the better indigenous grapes, have recently elevated the quality of Italian white wines.

FOR FURTHER READING

I recommend *The Pocket Guide to Italian Wines* and *Wine Atlas of Italy* by Burton Anderson; *Vino Italiano* by Joseph Bastianich and David Lynch; *Italian Wine* by Victor Hazan; and *Italian Wines for Dummies* by Mary Ewing Mulligan and Ed McCarthy.

PINOT GRIGIO is a white-grape variety that is also found in Alsace, France, where it is called Pinot Gris. It is also grown with success in Oregon and California.

IS PINOT GRIGIO HOT?

In 1970, Italy produced only 11,000 cases of Pinot Grigio, and in 2008, Pinot Grigio was the number-one imported Italian varietal in the United States, with more than 10 million cases sold.

FOR GREAT Italian whites, try Gavi from Piedmont, and wines from the Friuli region.

Badia a Coltibuono

CHIANTI CLASSICO
DENOMINAZIONE DI ORIGINE CONTROLLATA E GARANTITA

ESTATE BOTTLED BY TENUTA DI COLTIBUONO S.R.L. · GAIOLE IN CHIANTI · ITALIA

Riserva

Net Cont. 750 ml   PRODUCT OF ITALY   Alc. 13.5 % by vol

"Piedmontese wines show better with food than in a tasting."
—ANGELO GAJA

"When you're having Italian wines, you must not taste the wine alone. You must have them with food."
—GIUSEPPE COLLA of Prunotto

WINE AND FOOD

In Italy, the wine is made to go with the food. No meal is served without wine. Take it from the experts.

The following food-and-wine suggestions are based on what some of the Italian wine producers enjoy having with their wine. You don't have to take their word for it. Get yourself a bottle of wine, a tasty dish, and mangia!

AMBROGIO FOLONARI *(Ruffino):* "*Chianti with prosciutto, chicken, pasta, and of course pizza.*" *When it comes to a Chianti Classico Riserva, Dr. Folonari says,* "*Pair it with a hearty prime-rib dinner or a steak.*"

EZIO RIVELLA *(Castello Banfi):* "*A Chianti is good with all meat dishes, but I save the Brunello for 'stronger' dishes, such as steak, wild boar, pheasant, and other game, as well as Pecorino Toscano cheese.*"

ANGELO GAJA: "*Barbaresco with meat and veal, and also with mature cheeses that are 'not too strong,' such as Emmenthaler and Fontina.*" *Mr. Gaja advises against Parmesan and goat cheese when you have a Barbaresco. And if you're having a Barolo, Mr. Gaja's favorite is roast lamb.*

GIUSEPPE COLLA *(Prunotto):* "*I enjoy light-style Dolcetto with all first courses and all white meat—chicken and veal especially.*" *He prefers not to have Dolcetto with fish.* "*The wine doesn't stand up well to spicy sauce, but it's great with tomato sauce and pasta.*"

RENATO RATTI: *Mr. Ratti once told me that both Barbera and Dolcetto are good with chicken and lighter foods. However, Barolo and Barbaresco need to be served with heavier dishes to match their own body. Mr. Ratti also suggests: a roast in its natural sauce or, better yet, brasato al Barolo—braised in Barolo; meat cooked with wine; pheasant, duck, wild rabbit; and cheeses. For a special dish, try risotto al Barolo (rice cooked with Barolo wine). And when serving wine with dessert, Mr. Ratti recommends* "*strawberries or peaches with Dolcetto wine.*" *The dryness in the wine, contrasted with the natural sweetness of the fruit, makes for a taste sensation!*

LORENZA DE'MEDICI *(Badia a Coltibuono):* Since Tuscan cooking is very simple, she recommends "*an assortment of simple foods.*" *She prefers herbs to heavy sauces. With young Chianti, she suggests* "*roast chicken, squab, or pasta with meat sauce.*" *To complement an older Chianti, she recommends a wide pasta with meat braised in Chianti, pheasant or other game, wild boar, or roast beef.*

PIERO ANTINORI: "*I enjoy Chianti with the grilled foods for which Tuscany is famous, especially its bistecca alla Fiorentina (steak).*" *He suggests poultry and even hamburgers as other tasty possibilities. With Chianti Classico Riserva, Mr. Antinori enjoys having the best of the vintages with wild boar and fine aged Parmesan cheese.* "*The wine is a perfect match for roast beef, roast turkey, lamb, or veal.*"

CLASS SEVEN: THE RED WINES OF SPAIN AND ITALY

I look forward to this class since many of my students know something about French or American wines but very little about Italian or Spanish wines. This is a class of discovery: finding new wine styles made from indigenous grapes such as Nebbiolo, Sangiovese, and Tempranillo. The wines of both countries have improved dramatically over the last twenty-five years.

Wines for Class Seven

1. Cune Viña Real Crianza 2006 **BEST VALUE**
2. Conde de Valdemar Reserva 2004 **BEST VALUE**
3. La Rioja Alta Gran Reserva 2001
4. Chianti Classico Riserva 2006, Antinori
5. Vino Nobile di Montelpulciano, 2005, Avignonesi
6. Brunello di Montalcino 2004, Castello Banfi
7. Barbera d'Asti, Le Orme 2007, Michele Chiarlo **BEST VALUE**
8. Barbaresco 2004, Vietti
9. Barolo 2004, Prunotto
10. Amarone 2003, Allegrini

There are four parts to this tasting.

PART I: RIOJA (THREE WINES TASTED TOGETHER)

Historically, Rioja has been the center of quality winemaking in Spain, and is now producing some of its best wines ever. Not only are the larger, established producers making better wines, but Rioja has enjoyed a surge in small artisan producers as well. The primary grape variety for all of the Rioja wines is the Tempranillo grape.

These three wines are poured together to show the three different quality levels of Rioja. You'll taste in order from the lightest Crianza, to a bigger Reserva, to the best quality level Gran Reserva.

Questions for Class Seven:
Spain and Italy

Champagne, Sherry, and Port

CHAMPAGNE · *MÉTHODE CHAMPENOISE* · STYLES OF CHAMPAGNE ·

OPENING CHAMPAGNE · CHAMPAGNE GLASSES ·

SPARKLING WINE · SHERRY · PORT

SHIPPERS DON'T always agree on the quality of the wines produced in any given vintage, so the years for vintage Champagnes vary from shipper to shipper. Historically, each house usually declares a vintage three years out of each decade.

TWO METHODS of making rosé Champagne: 1) add red wine to the blend; 2) leave the red grape skins in contact with the must for a short period of time.

MOST CHAMPAGNES are fermented in stainless steel.

CLASSIC CHAMPAGNES (non-vintage) must be aged for a minimum of 15 months in the bottle after bottling. Vintage Champagnes must be aged for a minimum of three years after bottling.

DOM PÉRIGNON Champagne is aged six to eight years before it is put on the market.

"My dear girl, there are some things that just aren't done, such as drinking Dom Perignon '53 above the temperature of 38 degrees Fahrenheit. That's just as bad as listening to the Beatles without earmuffs!"
—SEAN CONNERY *as* JAMES BOND, *in Goldfinger (1964)*

Is every year a vintage year?

No, but more recently, 1995*, 1996*, 1998, 1999, 2000, and 2002* were. Note: These were vintage years for most Champagne houses. "Vintage" in Champagne is different from other wine regions, because each house makes its own determination on whether or not to declare a vintage year.

*Note: * signifies exceptional vintage*

How is Champagne made?

Champagne is made by a process called *Méthode Champenoise*. When a similar method is used outside Champagne, it is called *Méthode Traditionnelle* or Classic Method or *Método Tradicional*, etc. The use of the expression *Méthode Champenoise* is not allowed in the European Union outside of Champagne.

MÉTHODE CHAMPENOISE

Harvest: The normal harvest usually takes place in late September or early October.

Pressing the Grapes: Only two pressings of the grapes are permitted. Prestige cuvée Champagnes are usually made exclusively from the first pressing. The second pressing, called the *taille*, is generally blended with the cuvée to make vintage and non-vintage Champagnes.

Fermentation: All Champagnes undergo a first fermentation when the grape juice is converted into wine. Remember the formula: Sugar + Yeast = Alcohol + CO_2. The carbon dioxide dissipates. The first fermentation takes two to three weeks and produces still wines.

Blending: The most important step in Champagne production is the blending of the still wines. Each of these still wines is made from a single grape variety from a single village of origin. The winemaker has to make many decisions here. Three of the most important ones are:

1. Which grapes to blend—how much Chardonnay, Pinot Noir, and Pinot Meunier?

2. From which vineyards should the grapes come?

3. Which years or vintages should be blended? Should the blend be made from only the wines of the harvest, or should several vintages be blended together?

Liqueur de Tirage: After the blending process, the winemaker adds *Liqueur de Tirage* (a blend of sugar and yeast), which will begin the wine's second fermentation. At this point, the wine is placed in its permanent bottle with a temporary bottle cap.

Second Fermentation: During this fermentation, the carbon dioxide stays in the bottle. This is where the bubbles come from. The second fermentation also leaves natural sediments in the bottle. Now the problems begin. How do you get rid of the sediments without losing the carbon dioxide? Go on to the next steps.

Aging: The amount of time the wine spends aging on its sediments is one of the most important factors in determining the quality of the wine.

Riddling: The wine bottles are now placed in A-frame racks, necks down. The *remueur*, or riddler, goes through the racks of Champagne bottles and gives each bottle a slight turn while gradually tipping the bottle farther downward. After six to eight weeks, the bottle stands almost completely upside down, with the sediments resting in the neck of the bottle.

Dégorgement: The top of the bottle is dipped into a brine solution to freeze it, and then the temporary bottle cap is removed and out fly the frozen sediments, propelled by the carbon dioxide.

Dosage: A combination of wine and cane sugar is added to the bottle after *dégorgement*. At this point, the winemaker can determine whether he wants a sweeter or a drier Champagne.

Recorking: The wine is recorked with a real cork instead of a bottle cap.

DOSAGE

The dosage determines whether the wine will be dry, sweet, or any style in between. The following shows you the guidelines the winemaker uses when he adds the dosage.

Brut: *Dry*	**Sec:** *Semisweet*
Extra dry: *Semidry*	**Demi-sec:** *Sweet*

COMMON CHAMPAGNE AROMAS:

Apple	Yeast (bread dough)
Toast	Hazelnuts/walnuts
Citrus	

WOMEN AND CHAMPAGNE

Women, particularly ones attached to royal courts, deserve much of the credit for Champagne's international fame. Madame de Pompadour said that Champagne was the only drink that left a woman still beautiful after drinking it. Madame de Parabère once said that Champagne was the only wine to give brilliance to the eyes without flushing the face.

IT IS RUMORED that Marilyn Monroe once took a bath in 350 bottles of Champagne. Her biographer George Barris said that she drank and breathed Champagne "as if it were oxygen."

WHEN A London reporter asked Madame Lilly Bollinger when she drank Champagne, Madame Bollinger replied: "I drink it when I'm happy and when I'm sad. Sometimes I drink it when I'm alone. When I have company I consider it obligatory. I trifle with it if I'm not hungry and drink it when I am. Otherwise I never touch it—unless I'm thirsty."

R.D. ON a Champagne wine label means that the wine was recently disgorged (dégorgement).

UNTIL AROUND 1850, all Champagne was sweet.

OCCASIONALLY A Champagne will be labeled "extra brut," which is drier still than brut.

BRUT AND EXTRA-DRY are the wines to serve as apéritifs, or throughout the meal. Sec and demi-sec are the wines to serve with desserts and wedding cake!

What accounts for the different styles of Champagne?

Going back to the three grapes we talked about that are used to make Champagne, the general rule is: The more white grapes in the blend, the lighter the style of the Champagne. And the more red grapes in the blend, the fuller the style of the Champagne.

Also, some producers ferment their wines in wood. Bollinger ferments some, and Krug ferments all their wines this way. This gives the Champagne fuller body and bouquet than those fermented in stainless steel.

How do I buy a good Champagne?

First, determine the style you prefer, whether full-bodied or light-bodied, a dry brut or a sweet demi-sec. Then make sure you buy your Champagne from a reliable shipper/producer. Each producer takes pride in its distinctive house style, and strives for a consistent blend, year after year. The following are some brands in national distribution to look for. While it is difficult to be precise, the designations generally conform to the style of the houses.

LIGHT, DELICATE

A. Charbaut et Fils
Jacquesson
Lanson

LIGHT TO MEDIUM

Billecart-Salmon
Deutz
Nicolas Feuillatte
Laurent-Perrier
G.H. Mumm
Perrier-Jouët
Pommery
Ruinart Père & Fils
Taittinger

MEDIUM

Charles Heidsieck
Moët & Chandon
Piper-Heidsieck
Pol Roger
Salon

MEDIUM TO FULL

Henriot
Louis Roederer

FULL, RICH

Bollinger
A. Gratien
Krug
Veuve Clicquot

When is Champagne ready to drink?

As soon as you buy it. Champagne is something you can drink right away. Non-vintage Champagnes are meant to be drunk within two to three years, and vintage and prestige cuvée Champagnes can be kept longer, about ten to fifteen years. So if you're still saving that Dom Pérignon that you received for your tenth wedding anniversary fifteen years ago, don't wait any longer. Open it!

What's the correct way to open a bottle of Champagne?

Before we sip Champagne in class, I always take a few moments to show everyone how to open a bottle of Champagne properly. I do this for a good reason. Opening a bottle of Champagne can be dangerous, and I'm not kidding. If you know the pounds per square inch that are under pressure in the bottle, you know what I'm talking about.

OPENING CHAMPAGNE CORRECTLY

1. It is especially important that the bottle be well chilled before you open it.

2. Cut the foil around the top of the bottle.

3. Place your hand on top of the cork, never removing your hand until the cork is pulled out completely. (I know this may seem a bit awkward, but it's very important.)

4. Undo the wire. Either leave it on the cork or take it off carefully.

5. Carefully put a cloth napkin over the top of the cork; if the cork pops, it will go safely into the napkin.

6. Remove the cork gently, slowly turning the bottle in one direction and the cork in another. The idea behind opening a bottle is to ease the cork out gently rather than cracking the bottle open with a loud pop and letting it foam. That may be a lot of fun, but it does nothing for the Champagne. When you pop off the cork, you allow the carbon dioxide to escape. That carbon dioxide is what gives Champagne its sparkle. If you open a bottle of Champagne in the way I've just described, it can be opened hours before your guests arrive with no loss of carbon dioxide.

"It's not a Burgundy; it's not a Bordeaux; it's a white wine; it's a sparkling wine that should be kept no longer than two to three years. It should be consumed young."
—CLAUDE TAITTINGER

THE TOP FIVE CHAMPAGNE HOUSES IN SHIPMENTS TO THE UNITED STATES IN 2009

1. Moët & Chandon
2. Veuve Clicquot
3. Perrier-Jouët
4. Piper Heidsieck
5. Nicolas Feuillatte

CHAMPAGNE HOUSES market about two-thirds of Champagne's wines, but they own less than 10% of the vineyards.

THE PRESSURE in a bottle of Champagne is close to 90 pounds per square inch (or "six atmospheres," or roughly three times the pressure in your automobile tire). Champagne is put into heavy bottles to hold the pressurized wine. This is another reason why Champagne is more expensive than ordinary wine.

MILLENNIUM MADNESS

In 1999, a record 327 million bottles of Champagne were sold.

Which glasses should Champagne be served in?

AS BEAUTIFUL as Helen was, the resulting glass was admittedly wide and shallow.

No matter which Champagne you decide to serve, you should serve it in the proper glass. There's a little story behind the Champagne glass, dating back to Greek mythology. The first *coupe*, a footed glass with a shallow cup that widens toward the rim, was said to be molded from the breast of Helen of Troy. The Greeks believed that wine drinking was a sensual experience, and it was only fitting that the most beautiful woman take part in shaping the chalice.

Centuries later, Marie Antoinette, Queen of France, decided it was time to create a new Champagne glass. She had coupes molded to her own breasts, which changed the shape of the glass entirely, since Marie Antoinette was, shall we say, a bit more well endowed than Helen of Troy.

The glasses shown to the left are the ones commonly used today—the flute and the tulip-shaped glass. Champagne does not lose its bubbles as

TO EVALUATE Champagne, look at the bubbles. The better wines have smaller bubbles and more of them. Also, with a good Champagne, the bubbles last longer. Bubbles are an integral part of the wines of Champagne. They create texture and mouth feel.

HOW MANY bubbles are in a bottle of Champagne? According to scientist Bill Lembeck, 49 million per bottle!

CHAMPAGNE BOTTLE SIZES

Magnum	2 bottles
Jeroboam	4 bottles
Rehoboam	6 bottles
Methuselah	8 bottles
Salmanazar	12 bottles
Balthazar	16 bottles
Nebuchadnezzar	20 bottles

WINE AND FOOD

Champagne is one of the most versatile wines that you can drink with a number of foods, from apéritif to dessert. Here are some Champagne-and-food combinations that experts suggest:

CLAUDE TAITTINGER: *Mr. Taittinger's general rule is: "Never with sweets." Instead, he suggests "a Comtes de Champagne Blanc de Blancs drunk with seafood, caviar, or pâté of pheasant." Another note from Mr. Taittinger: He doesn't serve Champagne with cheese because, he says, "The bubbles do not go well." He prefers red wine with cheese.*

CHRISTIAN POL ROGER: *With Brut non-vintage: light hors d'oeuvres, mousse of pike. With vintage: pheasant, lobster, other seafood. With rosé: a strawberry dessert.*

quickly in these glasses as it did in the old-fashioned model, and these shapes also enhance the smell and aromas of the wine in the glass.

What's the difference between Champagne and sparkling wine?

As I've already mentioned, Champagne is the wine that comes from the Champagne region of France. In my opinion, it is the best sparkling wine in the world, because the region has the ideal combination of elements conducive to excellent sparkling winemaking. The soil is fine chalk, the grapes are the best grown anywhere for sparkling wine, and the location is perfect. This combination of soil, climate, and grapes is reflected in the wine.

Sparkling wine, on the other hand, is produced in many areas, and the quality varies from wine to wine. The Spanish produce the popular Codorniu and Freixenet—both excellent values and good sparkling wines, known as *cavas*. The German version is called *Sekt*. Italy has *Spumante*, which means "sparkling." The most popular Italian sparkling wine in the United States is Asti Spumante.

New York State and California are the two main producers of sparkling wine in this country. New York is known for Great Western, Taylor, and Gold Seal. California produces many fine sparkling wines, such as Domaine Chandon, Korbel, Piper-Sonoma, Schramsberg, Mumm Cuvée Napa, Roederer Estate, Domaine Carneros, Iron Horse, Scharffenberger, and "J," by Jordan Winery. Many of the larger California wineries also market their own sparkling wines.

Is there a difference between the way Champagne and sparkling wines are made?

Sometimes. All authentic Champagnes and many fine sparkling wines are produced by *Méthode Champenoise,* described earlier in this chapter, and which, as you now know, is laborious, intensive, and very expensive. If you see a bottle of sparkling wine for $3.99, you can bet that the wine was not made by this process. The inexpensive sparkling wines are made by other methods. For example, in one method the secondary fermentation takes place in large tanks. Sometimes these tanks are big enough to produce 100,000 bottles of sparkling wine.

DOMAINE CHANDON is owned by the Moët-Hennessy Group, which is responsible for the production of Dom Pérignon in France. In fact, the same winemaker is flown into California to help make the blend for the Domaine Chandon.

ABOUT 20% OF the sparkling wines made in the United States are made by the *Méthode Champenoise.*

PIPER-HEIDSIECK has sold the Piper-Sonoma and its vineyards to Jordan Winery. Jordan now produces the wines for Piper-Sonoma.

SHERRY

The two greatest fortified wines in the world are Port and Sherry. These wines have much in common, although the end result is two very different styles.

What exactly is fortified wine?

Fortified wine is made when a neutral grape brandy is added to wine to raise the wine's alcohol content. What sets Port apart from Sherry is when the winemaker adds the neutral brandy. It's added to Port during fermentation. The extra alcohol kills that yeast and stops the fermentation, which is why Port is relatively sweet. For Sherry, on the other hand, the brandy is added after fermentation.

Where is Sherry made?

Sherry is produced in sunny southwestern Spain, in Andalusia. An area within three towns makes up the Sherry triangle. They are:

JEREZ DE LA FRONTERA

PUERTO DE SANTA MARÍA

SANLÚCAR DE BARRAMEDA

Which grapes are used to make Sherry?

There are two main varieties:

Palomino: this shouldn't be too difficult for horse lovers to remember
Pedro Ximénez: named after Peter Siemons, who brought the grape from Germany to Sherry

What are the different types of Sherry?

Manzanilla: dry
Fino: dry
Amontillado: dry to medium-dry
Oloroso: dry to medium-dry
Cream: sweet

ANOTHER FORTIFIED wine is Madeira. Although it is not as popular as it once was, Madeira wine was probably the first wine imported into America. It was favored by the colonists, including George Washington, and was served to toast the Declaration of Independence.

TWO OTHER famous fortified wines are Marsala (from Italy) and Vermouth (from Italy and France).

THE NEUTRAL grape brandy, when added to the wine, raises the alcohol content to 15% to 20%.

FOR YOU HISTORIANS, Puerto de Santa María is where Christopher Columbus's ships were built and where all the arrangements were made with Queen Isabella for his journey of discovery.

THE PALOMINO grape accounts for 90% of the planted vineyards in Sherry.

What are the unique processes that characterize Sherry production?

Controlled oxidation and fractional blending. Normally a winemaker guards against letting any air into the wine during the winemaking process. But that's exactly what makes Sherry—the air that oxidizes the wine. The winemaker places the wine in barrels and stores it in a bodega.

What's a bodega?

In Sherry, a *bodega* is an aboveground structure used to store wine. Why do you think winemakers would want to store the wine above ground? For the air. Sherry is an oxidized wine. They fill the barrels approximately two-thirds full, instead of all the way, and they leave the bung (cork) loosely in the barrel to let the air in.

THE ANGEL'S SHARE

When Sherry is made, winemakers let air into the barrels, and some wine evaporates in the process. Each year they lose a minimum of 3 percent of their Sherry to the angels, which translates into thousands of bottles lost through evaporation!

Why do you think the people of Sherry are so happy all the time? Besides the excellent sunshine they have, the people breathe in oxygen and Sherry.

So much for controlled oxidation. Now for fractional blending. Fractional blending is carried out through the Solera System.

What's the Solera System?

The Solera System is an aging and maturing process that takes place through the dynamic and continuous blending of several vintages of Sherry that are stored in rows of barrels. At bottling time, wine is drawn out of these barrels—never more than one-third the content of the barrel—to make room for the new vintage. The purpose of this type of blending is to maintain the "house" style of the Sherry by using the "mother" wine as a base and refreshing it with a portion of the younger wines.

HERE'S ANOTHER abbreviation for you—PX. Do you remember TBA, QbA, AOC, and DOC? If you want to know Sherry, you may have to say "PX," which stands for the Pedro Ximénez grape.

I'M SURE you're familiar with these four top-selling Sherries: Harveys Bristol Cream, Dry Sack, Tio Pepe, and La Ina.

PX IS USED to make Cream Sherry, like Harveys Bristol Cream, among others. Cream Sherry is a blend of PX and Oloroso.

SHERRY ACCOUNTS for less than 3% of Spanish wine production.

IN TODAY'S Sherry, only American oak is used to age the wine.

SOME SOLERAS can be a blend of 10 to 20 different harvests.

TO CLARIFY the Sherry and rid it of all sediment, beaten egg whites are added to the wine. The sediment attaches itself to the egg whites and drops to the bottom of the barrel. The question always comes up: "What do they do with the yolks?" Did you ever hear of flan? That's the pudding-like dessert made from all the yolks. In Sherry country, this dessert is called *tocino de cielo*, which translated means "the fat of the angels."

OF THE SHERRY consumed in Spain, 90% is Fino and Manzanilla. As one winemaker said, "We ship the sweet and drink the dry."

How do I buy Sherry?

Your best guide is the producer. It's the producer, after all, who buys the grapes and does the blending. Ten producers account for 60 percent of the export market. The top Sherry producers are:

CROFT	**OSBORNE**
EMILIO LUSTAU	**PEDRO DOMECQ**
GONZÁLEZ BYASS	**SANDEMAN**
HARVEYS	**SAVORY AND JAMES**
HIDALGO	**WILLIAMS & HUMBERT**

How long does a bottle of Sherry last once it's been opened?

Sherry will last longer than a regular table wine, because of its higher alcoholic content, which acts as a preservative. But once Sherry is opened, it will begin to lose its freshness. To drink Sherry at its best, you should consume the bottle within two weeks of opening it and keep the opened bottle refrigerated. Manzanilla and Fino Sherry should be treated as white wines and consumed within a day or two.

FOR FURTHER READING
I recommend *Sherry* by Julian Jeffs.

WINE AND FOOD

MAURICIO GONZÁLEZ: *He believes that Fino should always be served well chilled. He enjoys having Fino as an apéritif with Spanish tapas (hors d'oeuvres), but he also likes to complement practically any fish meal with the wine. Some of his suggestions: clams, shellfish, lobster, prawns, langoustines, fish soup, or a light fish such as salmon.*

JOSÉ IGNACIO DOMECQ: *He suggests that very old and rare Sherry should be served with cheese. Fino and Manzanilla can be served as an apéritif or with light grilled or fried fish, or even smoked salmon. "You get the taste of the* smoke better than if you have it with a white wine." *Amontillado is not to be consumed like a Fino. It should be served with light cheese, chorizo (sausage), ham, or shish kebab. It is a perfect complement to turtle soup or a consommé. According to Mr. Domecq, dry Oloroso is known as a sporty drink in Spain—something to drink before hunting, riding, or sailing on a chilly morning. With Cream Sherry, Mr. Domecq recommends cookies, pastries, and cakes. Pedro Ximénez, however, is better as a topping for vanilla ice cream or a dessert wine before coffee and brandy.*

PORT

Port comes from the Douro region in northern Portugal. In fact, in recent years, to avoid the misuse of the name "Port" in other countries, the true Port wine from Portugal has been renamed "Porto" (for the name of Oporto, the port city from which it's shipped).

Just a reminder: Neutral grape brandy is added to Port during fermentation, which stops the fermentation and leaves behind up to 9 to 11 percent residual sugar. This is why Port is on the sweet side.

What are the two types of Port?

Cask-aged Port: This includes *Ruby Port*, which is dark and fruity, blended from young non-vintage wines (Cost: $); *Tawny Port*, which is lighter and more delicate, blended from many vintages (Cost: $$); *Aged Tawny*, which is aged in casks—sometimes up to forty years and longer (Cost: $$–$$$); and *Colheita*, which is from a single vintage but wood-aged a minimum of seven years (Cost: $$–$$$$).

Bottle-aged Port: These wines include *Late Bottled Vintage (LBV)*, which is made from a single vintage, bottled four to six years after the harvest, and similar in style to vintage Port, but lighter, ready to drink on release, with no decanting needed (Cost: $$$); *Vintage Character*, which is similar in style to LBV, but is made from a blend of vintages from the better years (Cost: $$); *Quinta*, which is from a single vineyard (Cost: $$$/$$$$); and *Vintage Port*, which is aged two years in wood and will mature in the bottle over time (Cost: $$$$).

PORT WINE has been shipped to England since the 1670s. During the 1800s, to help preserve the Port for the long trip, shippers fortified it with brandy, resulting in Port as we know it today.

PORT IS usually 20% alcohol. Sherry, by comparison, is usually around 18%.

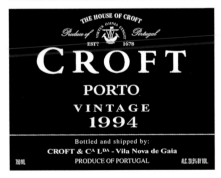

IN A TYPICAL YEAR, 60% of the Port is Tawny and Ruby; 30% is Vintage Character; 7% is Aged Tawny; and 3% is Vintage Port.

WOOD PORT VS. VINTAGE PORT

The biggest difference between cask-aged Port (such as Ruby and Tawny) and bottle-aged Port is this: The cask-aged Port is ready to drink as soon as it is bottled and it will not improve with age. Bottle-aged Port, on the other hand, gets better as it matures in the bottle. A great vintage Port will be ready to drink fifteen to thirty years after the vintage date, depending upon the quality of the vintage.

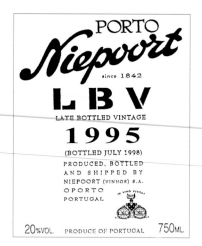

THE BRITISH are known to be Port lovers. Traditionally, upon the birth of a child, parents buy bottles of Port to put away for the baby until its 21st birthday, not only the age of maturity of a child, but also that of a fine Port.

"The 1994 vintage is the greatest for Port since the legendary 1945."
—JAMES SUCKLING, *Vintage Port*

How do I buy Port?

Once again, as with Sherry, Port's grape variety should not dictate your choice. Find the style and the blend you prefer, but even more important, look for the most reliable producers. Of the Port available in the United States, the most important producers are:

A. A. FERREIRA	NIEPOORT & CO., LTD.
C. DA SILVA	QUINTA DO NOVAL
CHURCHILL	RAMOS PINTO
COCKBURN	ROBERTSON'S
CROFT	SANDEMAN
DOW	TAYLOR FLADGATE
FONSECA	W. & J. GRAHAM
HARVEYS OF BRISTOL	WARRE'S & CO.

Should vintage Port be decanted?

Yes, because you are likely to find sediment in the bottle. By making it a practice to decant vintage Port, your enjoyment of it will be enhanced.

How long will Port last once it's been opened?

Port has a tendency to last longer than ordinary table wine because of its higher alcohol content. But if you want to drink Port at its prime, drink the contents of the open bottle within one week.

Is every year a vintage year for Port?

No, it varies from shipper to shipper. And in some years, no vintage Port is made at all. For example, in 1994, 1997, 2000, and 2003, four of the recent vintages for Port, most producers declared a vintage. On the other hand, in 1990 and 1993, Port, in general, was not considered vintage quality.

BEST BETS FOR VINTAGES OF PORT

1963* 1970* 1977* 1983* 1985 1991*
1992 1994* 1997* 2000* 2003*

Note: * signifies exceptional vintage

FOR FURTHER READING

I recommend *The Port Companion* by Godfrey Spence and *Vintage Port: The Wine Spectator's Ultimate Guide* by James Suckling.

CLASS EIGHT: FINAL EXAM, CHAMPAGNE AND PORT

This is our eighth and last class. It's your graduation class and there's no better way to celebrate than by beginning the evening with Champagne and ending the night with Port.

Normally, I begin this class with a final exam during which the students test their olfactory abilities with a blind tasting of four wines, all of which they have had during the semester.

Wines for Class Eight

1. Cristalino Cava Brut NV **BEST VALUE**
2. Roederer Estate Brut NV
3. Domaine Carneros Brut 2005
4. Taittinger Brut La Française NV
5. Veuve Clicquot Brut Yellow Label NV
6. Blind
7. Taylor Fladgate Ruby Port **BEST VALUE**
8. Churchill's Tawny Port: Ten Years Old
9. Warre's 2000 Vintage Porto

There are two parts to this tasting.

PART I: CHAMPAGNES AND SPARKLING WINES

Part I is divided into three sections: the sparkling wines of Spain and the United States, and the Champagnes of France. Most of my readers want to know the best value choices in wine, especially when it comes to expensive wine alternatives. Although French Champagne remains one of the great value wines in the world a non-vintage bottle still costs around $50 a bottle.

Section I: Sparkling Wine: Spain (one wine, tasted alone)

Spain produces some great sparkling wines at unbelievable prices. European Union laws prevent any sparkling wine produced outside of Champagne, France, to be called Champagne. In Germany it is called Sekt, in Italy it is called Spumante, and in Spain it is called Cava.

Wine #1: Cristalino Cava Brut NV

For many years the number-one sparkling wine in my "value" tastings has been Cristalino. It comes from Catalonia, located in northeastern Spain, which is considered to be the best Cava-producing region in the country. It is made with indigenous grapes produced in the same process as French Champagne (*méthode Champenoise*), and is aged for nearly two years in oak. It is great for weddings, special events, and large parties because of its quality and price. This wine has great effervescence (small bubbles) and is light, refreshing, and easy to drink.

> Retail price $10 **BEST VALUE**
> Ready to drink
> Other recommended Cava producers are: Codorniu or Freixenet.

Section II: Sparkling Wines: California (two wines tasted together)

California has been making sparkling wines since the end of Prohibition, but didn't produce a quality sparkling wine until the 1965 introduction of a sparkling wine from the Napa Valley winery Schramsberg. In 1973 the French Champagne producer Moët & Chandon created a Napa Valley sparkling wine, called Domaine Chandon, on a larger scale, and the quality of California sparkling wines has been soaring ever since.

It was difficult to emulate a great French Champagne in California because the climatic conditions of sunny Napa were quite different than the colder climatic conditions of Champagne, France. In all honesty, I did not recommend most California sparkling wines until about fifteen years ago. By then many other sparkling wine producers had joined Domaine Chandon and Schramsberg and, through viticultural research, the major quality grapes

Chardonnay and Pinot Noir are now planted in the right soil and climate to make excellent sparkling wines.

Wine #2: Roederer Estate Brut NV

Many of my readers are familiar with the French Champagne Roederer. Roederer has been involved in fine winemaking for more than two hundred years. They chose to plant their North American vineyards and build their winery in the cooler climate of the Anderson Valley in Mendocino County. The Roederer Estate Brut NV is produced exactly as done in Champagne and is a blend of 60 percent Chardonnay and 40 percent Pinot Noir. All of the grapes used to make Roederer Estate Brut are grown by Roederer in their own vineyards, hence the word "Estate" on the label. The wine is fermented in stainless steel tanks with some oak-aged reserved wines added to the blend to give the wine more intensity and flavor. The winemaker has left some residual sugar in the wine (1.2 percent), which balances out the acidity and combined with the fruit flavors makes this wine very accessible now.

Retail price $34
Ready to drink

Wine #3: Domaine Carneros Brut 2005

This sparkling wine producer was created by another great French Champagne house, Taittinger. I taste the Domaine Carneros after the Roederer for two reasons: This is a vintage sparkling wine; and it contains more red grapes (61 percent Pinot Noir), which gives it more body. All the grapes for this wine come from the Carneros district, the coolest region of Napa/Sonoma, perfect for growing the finicky Pinot Noir. It has also been aged for three years in the bottle and the fruit's acid and carbon dioxide have blended together, making for a clean, crisp, and elegant sparkling wine.

Retail price $29
Ready to Drink
Other recommended California Sparkling Wine producers are:
Domaine Chandon, Piper Sonoma, Mumm Cuvée Napa, Schramsberg, or Iron Horse.

Questions for Class Eight:
Champagne, Sherry, and Port

Austria, Hungary, Greece, Australia, New Zealand, South Africa, Canada, Chile, and Argentina

The Wines of Austria

WHILE AUSTRIAN GRAPE GROWING and winemaking date back to the fourth century B.C., it is only in the past twenty-five years that Austria has been recognized for producing quality wines. Today, Austria produces some of the most elegant and best-tasting white wines—both dry and sweet—in Europe. The Grüner Veltliner and Riesling grapes produce wines that are perfect with food and are one reason for the recent success of Austrian wines in the United States. Both chefs and sommeliers agree that these wines work well with nearly any dish on their menus, from fish and poultry to most meat dishes. And Austrian wines hold their own when paired with Asian spices, too.

What are the wine regions of Austria?

Austria contains four wine regions: Lower Austria (Niederösterreich), Vienna (Wien), Burgenland, and Styria (Steiermark), all located along Austria's eastern borders. The northern wine regions, which include Lower Austria and Vienna, are defined by the Danube River and the fertile valley that surrounds it.

AUSTRIA PRODUCES 70% white wine.

VIENNA, ONE of the world's most beautiful cities, is also classified as an Austrian wine region and is the only major city in the world to be named a wine region.

60% OF ALL AUSTRIAN wines are produced in Lower Austria.

VIENNA DAY TRIP

Visit the village of Klosterneuburg on the Danube River to see a monastery that dates to A.D. 1114. While you are in Klosterneuburg, be sure to taste the Grüner Veltliner of Donauland. The oldest school of enology by the same name, formed in 1860, is also worth a visit.

The two most important regions and their wine districts are:

LOWER AUSTRIA (WHITE WINES): Wachau, Kamptal, Kremstal, Donauland
BURGENLAND (RED AND DESSERT WINES): Neusiedlersee, Mittelburgenland, Neusiedlersee-Hügelland

What are the major grapes grown in Austria?

The main white varieties are:

GRÜNER VELTLINER	**SAUVIGNON BLANC**
RIESLING	**CHARDONNAY**

The main red varieties are:

BLAUFRÄNKISCH	**PINOT NOIR**
ST. LAURENT	

What are the Wine Laws of Austria?

Austria largely follows the same criteria used in other European countries, specifically Germany, with regard to wine labeling, but maintains stricter control. Base quality levels are determined by the ripeness of the grapes and the sugar content of the fermenting grape juice or must.

The three major quality levels are:

TAFELWEIN   **QUALITÄTSWEIN**   **PRÄDIKATSWEIN**

The Austrian wine board tastes and performs a chemical analysis on Qualitätswein and higher levels of wine, giving consumers a guarantee of taste, style, and quality. If a wine lists a specific grape it must contain at least 85 percent of that grape. If a wine has a vintage on the label it must contain a minimum of 85 percent of that vintage. If a wine region is listed, all of the wine (100 percent) must come from that region.

What is the style of Austrian wines?

As with the wines of Germany, Austria's neighbor to the north, most Austrian wines are white. But unlike German wines, most of Austria's wines are dry, with higher alcohol and more body, resembling the wines of Alsace.

GRÜNER VELTLINER accounts for more than one-third of Austrian grape plantings.

IN STYRIA Chardonnay is called Morillon.

THE BEST OF TWO

The Zweigelt grape is a cross between Blaufränkisch and St. Laurent.

ANOTHER NAME for Blaufränkisch is Lemberger.

TRY BLAUFRÄNKISCH blended with Cabernet Sauvignon.

TWO-THIRDS of Austrian wine is Qualitätswein.

ONLY IN THE WACHAU REGION

Steinfeder: maximum alcohol 10.7%
Federspiel: maximum alcohol 11.9%
Smargd: minimum alcohol 11.3%

AUSBRUCH

One of the great dessert wines of the world is Ausbruch, which comes from the village of Rust in Burgenland and has a history that goes back as far as 1617. On a par with a great French Sauternes, German Beeren-auslese, and Hungarian Tokaji, it is made with botrytized grapes and, as with Tokaji, Furmint is its predominate grape variety.

THE WINE GLASS

Even if you haven't yet tasted one of Austria's great white wines, you probably have used a wineglass produced in Austria by Riedel. In the 1960s the Riedel family's glassworks, one of the most famous in the world, began creating wineglasses specifically shaped to enhance the aroma, bouquet, and taste of individual grape varieties. They also own another top wineglass producer, Spiegelau.

SMARGD: a term found on wine labels in the Wachau area made from the highest quality grapes and vinified dry.

Gradation of ripeness is the amount of residual sugar left in the wine after fermentation. It ranges in Austria from the very dry Trocken, to the very sweet Trockenbeerenauslese.

Gradations of Ripeness

DRY	SWEET TO VERY SWEET
Trocken	Tafelwein
Halbtrocken	Landwein
Lieblich	Qualitätswein
	Kabinett
	Prädikatswein
	Spätlese
	Auslese
	Eiswein
	Beerenauslese
	Ausbruch
	Trockenbeerenauslese

Kevin Zraly's Favorite Austrian Wine Producers

ALZINGER	**KRACHER**
BRÜNDLMAYER	**NIGL**
HIRSCH	**PICHLER**
HIRTZBERGER	**PRAGER**
KNOLL	**SCHLOSS GOBELSBURGZ**

BEST BETS FOR AUSTRIAN WINES

2005   2006*   2007

*Note: * signifies exceptional vintage*

FOR FURTHER READING

The Wines of Austria by Philipp Blom and *The Ultimate Austrian Wine Guide* by Peter Moser.

The Wines of Hungary

HUNGARY'S WINE INDUSTRY has thrived culturally and economically for nearly one thousand years and can be traced back as far as the Roman Empire. Tokaji, its most famous and revered wine, has been produced continuously since the sixteenth century. The reputation of Hungarian wine suffered a major decline from 1949 to 1989 under Communist rule, during which time wine production, controlled by a state monopoly, shifted to bulk wine with little regard to maintaining or improving existing quality wines.

Since the end of communism in 1989, Hungary's emphasis has shifted back to quality wines, an effort partially funded by capital from Italian, French, and German winemakers. Today, modern winemaking equipment; new vineyard techniques; and the introduction of Sauvignon Blanc, Chardonnay, and Pinot Gris grapes have helped rebuild Hungary's nearly devastated quality wine industry. The famous vineyards of Tokaj were the first to receive attention, but investment has expanded throughout Hungary, which is once again producing some excellent wines.

What are the major grapes of Hungary?

	NATIVE TO HUNGARY	INTERNATIONAL
White:	Furmint	Sauvignon Blanc
	Hárslevelü	Chardonnay
	Olaszrizling	Pinot Gris (Szürkebarát)
Red:	Kadarka	Cabernet Sauvignon
	Kékfrankos	Merlot
	Portugieser	Pinot Noir

A GRAPE BY ANY OTHER NAME...

The Hungarian language can be difficult for anyone, especially after a glass of wine! Here is a list to help you understand the style of the wine behind the name.

Hungarian name	AKA
Tramini	Gewürztraminer
Szürkebarát	Pinot Gris
Zöld Veltlini	Grüner Veltliner
Kékfrankos	Blaufränkisch

What are the major wine regions of Hungary?

There are twenty-two wine regions in Hungary, seven of which I think you should know. The seven regions, including Tokaj, the most famous and prestigious, along with their most important grapes, are:

BADACSONY (OLASZRIZLING)

EGER (KÉKFRANKOS, PINOT NOIR)

SOMOLÓ (FURMINT)

SOPRON (KÉKFRANKOS)

SZEKSZÁRD (KADARKA, MERLOT, CABERNET SAUVIGNON)

TOKAJ (FURMINT, HÁRSLEVELÜ)

VILLÁNY-SIKLÓS (CABERNET SAUVIGNON, KÉKFRANKOS)

Tokaji Aszú: "The Wine of Kings and King of Wines"

My first taste of the Hungarian sweet wine Tokaji Aszú is one of my fondest wine memories. I was mesmerized by its smell and taste and determined to find out how this "liquid gold" was made.

Tokaji Aszú comes from Tokaj, which is located in Hungary's northeastern corner and is one of the oldest wine regions in the world. Tokaji means from the region of Tokaj (the village) and Aszú refers to the dried, shriveled, and botrytized grapes used in its making. Tokaji Aszú is one of the world's greatest sweet wines and is on a par with French Sauternes and German Trockenbeerenauslese.

Although Tokaji Aszú is usually a blend of four grapes native to Hungary, the primary grape used is Furmint. Throughout the fall harvest season, the grapes affected by the *Botrytis cinerea* mold—or aszú—are picked from the bunch, lightly crushed, and made into an aszú paste. The unaffected grapes are harvested and fermented into a base wine. The aszú paste is collected in baskets called puttonyos, then blended into the base wine according to the desired sweetness. Sweetness is measured in puttonyos, or number of baskets of aszú paste added to the base wine, and you will see the word "Puttonyos" on the label of all Tokaji Aszú. The more botrytis-affected grapes (paste) that are added to the base wine, the sweeter the wine. There are four levels of Puttonyos wine:

3 Puttonyos: 60 grams of sugar per liter
4 Puttonyos: 90 grams of sugar per liter
5 Puttonyos: 120 grams of sugar per liter
6 Puttonyos: 150 grams of sugar per liter

The sweetest of the Tokaj wines are called "Essencia" (or sometimes Eszencia). The Tokaji "Aszú Essencia" contains 180 grams of sugar. Tokaji "Essencia" can have over 800 grams per liter of sugar. It is one of the most unique wines made in the world.

Kevin Zraly's Favorite Tokaji Producers

Chateau Pajzos   **Oremus**

Disznókő   **Royal Tokaji Wine Company**

Hétszőlő   **Szepsy**

BEST BETS FOR TOKAY ASZÚ

2000*   2002   2003   2005*   2006*

Note: *signifies exceptional vintage

FOR FURTHER READING
I recommend *Wine Guide Hungary* by Gabor Rohaly and Gabriella Meszaros.

THE WORLD'S first vineyard classification was for the region of Tokaj in 1700.

THE TRADITIONAL squat Tokay Aszú bottles contain 500 milliliters versus the normal 750 milliliters.

SZAMORODNI IS another style of wine made in Tokaj. It ranges from semidry to semisweet but has fewer grams of sugar than three Puttoynos.

A FRENCH Sauternes has 90 grams of sugar.

A GERMAN Trockenbeerenauslese has 150 grams of sugar.

DUE TO THE high concentration of sugar, it may take years for Essencia to finish fermentation, and then only having an alcohol content of 2% to 5%.

DISZNÓKŐ
TOKAJI ASZÚ
5 PUTTONYOS
2000

The Wines of Greece

As a history major in college, I was fascinated by ancient Greece. I'm sure that coming across wine references in the works of Aristotle, Homer, Plato, and other ancient Greeks; as well as learning about Dionysus, the god of wine, celebration, and fertility, influenced my decision to study wine.

Wine has played an important role in Greek culture and lifestyle since at least as far back as the seventh century B.C. Wine has also always been one of the most traded commodities throughout Greece and the Mediterranean countries.

Prior to 1985, most Greek wines were somewhat ordinary and were exported by large bulk-wine producers to service mainly Greek communities abroad. Over the last twenty-five years, the Greek wine industry has been concentrating on making quality wines. Since Greece entered the European Union in 1981, there has been a tremendous investment in winemaking technology and in Greek vineyards. EU subsidies, together with the winemakers' commitments, have helped finance the building of state-of-the-art wineries throughout Greece.

What is the style of Greek wine?

To understand the difficulty in describing a typical Greek wine, one simply has to look at a map of Greece with its islands, mountains, and proximity to the Aegean and Ionian Seas of the Mediterranean. Greece is the third most mountainous country of Europe, and most of the vineyards are found on the slopes of mountains or on remote islands, with a typical vineyard being smaller in size than one hectare (2.471 acres).

While some of Greece's climate is considered Mediterranean, the mountain regions enjoy a more typically Continental climate with lots of sunshine, mild winters, dry summers, and cool evenings. Some Greek vineyards are picked in August, while others are not harvested until October. The volcanic soils on some of the islands make a very different style of wine depending on whether the vineyards are on flatlands or on steep mountain slopes.

There is a tremendous diversity in the wine regions of Greece. The next ten years will be the defining time for the "New Greece" wines.

"No thing more excellent or more valuable than wine was ever granted mankind by God."

—PLATO

"The wine urges me on, the bewitching wine, which sets even a wise man to singing and laughing gently and rouses him up to dance and brings forth words which were better unspoken."

—HOMER

MEDITERRANEAN CLIMATE: hot summers; a short, mild winter; and long autumns.

"The peoples of the Mediterranean began to emerge from barbarism when they learnt to cultivate the olive and the vine."

—THUCYDIDES

What are the main wine grapes in Greece?

The three major white grapes are:
ASSYRTIKO (A seer' tee ko)
MOSCHOFILERO (Mos ko fee' le ro)
RODITIS (Ro dee' tees)

The two major red grapes are:
AGIORGITIKO (Ah your yee' ti ko)
XINOMAVRO (Ksee no' mav ro)

What are the best winegrowing regions of Greece?

Macedonia (Northern Greece)
Naoussa
Amyndeo
Peloponnese (Southern Greece)
Mantinia
Nemea
Patras
The Islands
Aegean Sea Islands
Santorini
Samos
Rhodes
Crete

ANOTHER WELL-KNOWN grape, found in Patras, is Mavrodaphne.

HISTORIANS HAVE established that wine production in the Peloponnese region began over 7,000 years ago.

THERE ARE over 3,000 islands in Greece and only 63 of them are inhabited.

LOOK FOR the red stripe at the top of the bottle for an OPAP wine and a blue stripe for an OPE wine.

How are the wines of Greece regulated?

Many of the better wines fall under the Greek governmental categories of OPAP (Wines of Appellation of Origin of Superior Quality, which are mostly dry) and OPE (Wines of Appellation of Controlled Origin, which are only sweet). Both designations indicate wines that come from viticultural areas that have been defined since 1971. Nemea is an example of an OPAP wine and Muscat of Patras is an example of an OPE wine.

There is also a designation roughly equivalent of France's Vin de Table, called Epitrapezios Oenos (EO), that does not include an appellation of origin and may be a blend of wines from many different regions.

LIBATION: from the Greek leibein, to pour
SYMPOSIUM: from the Greek symposion,
to drink together
ENOLOGY: from the Greek oinos, wine and
logos, reason or speech

"Shall we not pass a law that, in the first place, no children under eighteen may touch wine at all, teaching that it is wrong to pour fire upon fire either in body or in soul . . . and thus guarding against the excitable disposition of the young? And next, we shall rule that the young man under thirty may take wine in moderation, but that he must entirely abstain from intoxication and heavy drinking. But when a man has reached the age of forty, he may join in the convivial gatherings and invoke Dionysus, above all other gods, inviting his presence at the rite (which is also the recreation) of the elders, which he bestowed on mankind as a medicine potent against the crabbedness of Old Age, that thereby we men may renew your youth, and that, through forgetfulness of care, the temper of our souls may lose its hardness and become softer and more ductile . . ."

— PLATO

ATTICA, ANOTHER wine region in Greece, is known for Retsina and Savatiano. It is also where Dionysus gave wine to the Greeks and the home of some of the most exciting experimentation today.

RETSINA

In 2008, I met at Nemea in the Peloponnese with winemakers from all the main wine regions of Greece. Together we tasted over fifty wines from the major white and red grapes. It was a fascinating tasting of Greece's indigenous grapes such as Moschofilero and Agiorgitiko. The last wine we tasted, Retsina, has been the most famous wine of Greece for thousands of years. One of my friends describes its pungent aroma as an "acquired taste" (think turpentine).

Retsina is made by adding pine resin to wine as a flavoring agent. In ancient times pine resin was used on amphorae to create an airtight seal in order to keep the wine from oxidizing during storage. Resin would sometimes leak into the wine, and eventually the Greeks became used to the pine flavor.

I really think that my Greek winemaker friends wanted to remind me that Retsina, though important, is a wine of the past. The future belongs to the quality wines we had just tasted.

Achaia Clauss	1861
Boutari	1879
Kourtakis	1895

Kevin Zraly's Favorite Greek Producers

ALPHA ESTATE	OENOFOROS
DRIOPI	PAVLIDIS
GAIA ESTATE	SAMOS COOPERATIVE
GEROVASSILIOU	SEMELI
KIR YIANNI	SIGALAS
MANOUSSAKIS	SKOURAS
MERCOURI	TSELEPOS

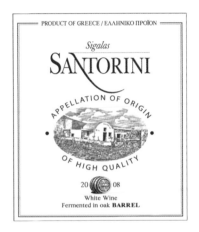

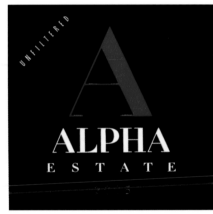

BEST BETS FOR WINES FROM GREECE

2005   2007   2008*

*Note: * signifies exceptional vintage*

FOR FURTHER READING

The Wines of Greece by Konstantinos Lazarakis and *The Illustrated Greek Wine Book* by Nico Manessis.

The Wines of Australia

The WINE INDUSTRY is not new to Australia: Wine, mostly fortified, was produced as early as the late 1700s. Many of Australia's leading wine companies were established more than 175 years ago. Lindemans, Penfolds, Orlando (whose main brand is Jacob's Creek), Henschke, and Seppelt are just a few of the companies that were founded during the nineteenth century. They are now among Australia's largest or most prestigious firms, and continue to produce excellent wines.

In the sixties, Australia was better known for its kangaroos and surfing than for its wine. Today it is the sixth largest producer of wine in the world. The change toward quality varietal wines began in the seventies and then, with tremendous speed and drive, grape acreage increased from 171,782 acres in 1980 to 322,697 acres in 2000 (and 429,456 acres in 2008). From 1988 to 2008, exports of Australian wines increased 98.2% and in 2008 exports exceeded $3 billion dollars.

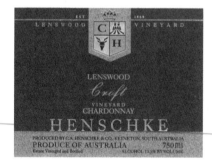 

What are the main grape varieties of Australia?

RED	WHITE
Shiraz (25%)	Chardonnay (19%)
Cabernet Sauvignon (16%)	Sémillon (4%)

THE AUSTRALIAN wine industry began in 1788.

IN 2008, Australia registered 2,299 wineries.

AUSTRALIAN WINE EXPORTS TO THE UNITED STATES

1990: 578,000 cases
2008: 21,000,000 cases

AUSTRALIA is now the third largest importer of wine to the United States. (France is the largest.)

AMERICANS LIKE YELLOW TAIL

Australia's Yellow Tail is the number-one imported wine in the United States. Sales rocketed from 200,000 cases in 2001 to nearly 8 million cases in 2008.

THE VINTAGE in Australia occurs in the first half of the year. Grapes are harvested from February to May.

AUSSIE REDS ON THE MOVE

Only a few years ago, 65% of Australian wine grapes were white varieties. Today, white wines account for 42% of, and reds 58% of, the annual harvest.

What are the main wine regions of Australia?

There are over sixty-four wine-growing regions in Australia, which are called Geographical Indications. Do you need to know them all? Probably not, but to begin your Australian wine journey, you should be familiar with the best districts in four of Australia's six states and what they are known for. They are:

SOUTH AUSTRALIA
    Adelaide Hills: Chardonnay,
        Sauvignon Blanc
    Clare Valley: Riesling
    Barossa Valley: Shiraz, Grenache
    McLaren Vale: Shiraz, Grenache
    Coonawarra: Cabernet Sauvignon

NEW SOUTH WALES
    Hunter Valley: Sémillon

VICTORIA
    Yarra Valley: Chardonnay,
        Pinot Noir

WESTERN AUSTRALIA
    Margaret River: Cabernet Sauvignon,
        Chardonnay, Sauvignon
        Blanc/Sémillon

MORE THAN 100 different grape varieties are grown in Australia.

TWO OTHER REGIONS OF AUSTRALIA

Tasmania, known for sparkling wines
Rutherglen, known for fortified wines

What are the wine laws of Australia?

The Australian wine industry's Label Integrity Program (LIP) took effect with the 1990 vintage. Although the LIP does not govern as many aspects of wine production as France's AOC laws, the LIP does regulate and oversee vintage, varietal, and Geographical Indication claims. To conform to LIP and other regulations set by the Australian Food Standards Code, Australian wine labels must provide a great deal of information.

FORTY-THREE PERCENT of Australian wines are produced in South Australia. South Australia is one of the few wine regions in the world that has never been affected by phylloxera, so many growers still plant using the vines' own rootstock.

CABERNET SAUVIGNON vine cuttings from Château Haut-Brion in Bordeaux were planted near Melbourne in the 1830s. In 1832, James Busby brought Shiraz cuttings from the Chapoutier vineyards in the Rhône Valley, France, which he planted in the Hunter Valley.

PRODUCED FROM ORGANICALLY GROWN GRAPES

EST 1844

Penfolds

CLARE VALLEY
CABERNET SAUVIGNON - SHIRAZ - PETIT VERDOT

Organically grown grapes from Penfolds Clare Valley Vineyard in South Australia
have been vintaged to produce this full bodied red wine in the Penfolds tradition.
Blending Cabernet Sauvignon, Shiraz and Petit Verdot the winemakers have produced
a wine with ripe berry characters, subtle oak and an appealing lingering finish.

750 ml 13.0% alc./vol.

PRODUCED BY PENFOLDS WINES, PENFOLD ROAD, MAGILL, SOUTH AUSTRALIA, AUSTRALIA 5072.
RED WINE PRODUCT OF AUSTRALIA   VIN ROUGE PRODUIT D'AUSTRALIE
61% CABERNET SAUVIGNON - 31% SHIRAZ - 8% PETIT VERDOT

OVER 75% of Australian wine is now
bottled with a screw-cap.

SOME OF the oldest Shiraz (Syrah) grape
vines in the world, many of which are
over 100 years old, are found in Australia.

Take a look at the label on the left. One of most important pieces of information is the producer's name. In this case, the producer is Penfolds. In a blend listing the varieties, as in the example of this wine label, the percentages of each varietal must be shown, with the first grape listed having the highest percentage. If the label specifies a particular wine-growing district—Clare Valley in our example—at least 85 percent of the wine must originate there. If a vintage is given, 95 percent of the wine must be of that vintage.

WHAT IS IN A NAME?

Australia and most other wine countries have been conforming to a 1994 European Union Wine Agreement that states, in part, that countries must end the use of borrowed generic names such as "Burgundy," "Champagne," "Port," and "Sherry." The most famous wine of Australia has arguably been Penfolds Grange Hermitage. In order to conform to the Wine Agreement, Penfolds dropped the word "Hermitage," which is a wine produced in France's Rhône Valley, and shortened the name of their wine to "Grange." Even with its "new" name, Penfolds Grange remains one of the greatest wines of Australia.

THE JIMMY WATSON MEMORIAL TROPHY
The Competitive Aussie

Australians speak as much about rugby as they do about wine. Walking into an Australian winery is sometimes like walking into a college gymnasium: There are trophy cases with all the awards that their wines have won. The most coveted wine award was established in 1962 after an Australian wine lover named Jimmy Watson. It is awarded to the best one-year-old red wine each year. It is interesting to note that the first fifteen awards were given to wines that were labeled "Burgundy type" or "Claret type." It wasn't until 1976 that a wine labeled as a varietal won the trophy.

Kevin Zraly's Top 25 Australian Wine Producers and Some Favorite Wines

CAPE MENTELLE (CABERNET SAUVIGNON)

CULLEN WINES (DIANA MADELINE)

D'ARENBERG (THE DEAD ARM SHIRAZ)

DE BORTOLI (NOBLE ONE)

GRANT BURGE (MESHACH SHIRAZ)

HARDY'S (CHATEAU REYNELLA CELLAR NO. ONE SHIRAZ)

HENSCHKE (CYRIL CABERNET SAUVIGNON, HILL OF GRACE)

KATNOOK (ODYSSEY CABERNET SAUVIGNON)

LEEUWIN ESTATE (ART SERIES CHARDONNAY OR CABERNET SAUVIGNON)

MOUNT MARY (QUINTET)

PENFOLDS (GRANGE, BIN 707 CABERNET SAUVIGNON)

PETALUMA (ADELAIDE HILLS SHIRAZ)

PETER LEHMANN (RESERVE RIESLING OR SEMILLON)

SHAW & SMITH (M3 VINEYARD ADELAIDE HILLS CHARDONNAY)

TAHBILK (ERIC STEVENS PURBRICK SHIRAZ OR CABERNET SAUVIGNON)

TORBRECK VINTNERS (RUN RIG)

TURKEY FLAT (BAROSSA VALLEY SHIRAZ)

VASSE FELIX (MARGARET RIVER CHARDONNAY AND SÉMILLON)

VOYAGER (MARGARET RIVER SAUVIGNON BLANC/SÉMILLON)

WIRRA WIRRA (RSW SHIRAZ AND ANGELUS CABERNET SAUVIGNON)

WOLF BLASS (BLACK LABEL SHIRAZ)

YALUMBA (THE MENZIES COONAWARRA CABERNET SAUVIGNON)

YERING STATION (SHIRAZ VIOGNIER)

BEST BETS FOR WINES FROM AUSTRALIA (BAROSSA, MCLAREN VALE, COONAWARRA)

2004** 2005** 2006* 2008*

Note: * signifies exceptional vintage ** signifies extraordinary vintage

WHAT A difference a year makes:
2007 was the earliest harvest ever
2006 was the latest harvest ever

FOR FURTHER READING

James Halliday's Australian Wine Companion and www.langtons.com.au/Tools/VintageReport.aspx.

The Wines of New Zealand

THE FIRST recorded vintage of New Zealand wine was produced in 1836.

GOVERNED BY THE SEA

NINETY-FIVE PERCENT of New Zealand's population is within a 30-mile drive to the ocean.

IN 1985 New Zealand listed 100 wineries. There were 616 wineries in 2008.

RENT A SHEEP

Besides wine, New Zealand is famous for its dairy products and wool. Wineries let sheep graze freely throughout the vineyards during the winter to keep the fields clear of grass and weeds.

NINETY-THREE PERCENT of New Zealand wines are sealed with screw-caps.

TWENTY-FIVE YEARS ago Sauvignon Blanc represented less than 4% of New Zealand's total grape crop.

IN 1996 ONLY 1,000 acres of Pinot Noir were planted in New Zealand. In 2008 there were over 11,000 acres planted.

NEW ZEALAND'S NATURALLY BEAUTIFUL coastline, magnificent mountains, rolling hills, and outstanding weather are showcased best in the movie trilogy *The Lord of the Rings*. New Zealand is also the home of bungee jumping, which pretty much describes the vitality and exuberance of its young wine industry. Over the last twenty years the wines and vineyards of New Zealand have grown by leaps and bounds. Today, New Zealand's Sauvignon Blanc and Pinot Noir wines are acknowledged by the international wine community to be world-class.

The frenzy has calmed down somewhat lately, but New Zealand wines are still evolving. With over twenty-five different grape varieties planted, winemakers are just beginning to fully understand the potential of New Zealand's soil and weather. Think of the winemakers and vineyard owners of New Zealand as both first generation and the new kids on the block and you'll have a fairly good idea of the potential this country has to produce even more world-class wines. (Look for Pinot Gris and Syrah over the next few years.) The New Zealand public-relations theme, "The best is yet to be discovered" pretty much says it all.

What are the most planted grapes in New Zealand?

SAUVIGNON BLANC (42%)

PINOT NOIR (17%)

CHARDONNAY (14%)

What are the major wine regions of New Zealand?

There are ten wine regions in New Zealand. The five most important regions, and what they are known for, are:

NORTH ISLAND
Hawke's Bay: Bordeaux blends, Chardonnay, Syrah
Martinborough/Wairarapa: Pinot Noir
Gisborne: Chardonnay

SOUTH ISLAND
Central Otago: Pinot Noir
Marlborough: Sauvignon Banc, Pinot Noir

NINETY PERCENT of New Zealand Sauvignon Blanc comes from Marlborough.

THE MOST SOUTHERLY grapes harvested in the world come from Central Otago.

MORE THAN 50% of New Zealand's vineyards are located in Marlborough.

NEW ZEALAND'S WINE PRODUCTION

80% white wines
20% red wines

THE PERFECT SUNRISE

Because of its proximity to the International Date Line, New Zealand grapes are the first in the world to bask in a new day's sun.

NEW ZEALAND

Auckland

NORTH ISLAND

Tasman
Sea

GISBORNE

HAWKE'S BAY

MARTINBOROUGH/
WAIRARAPA
Wellington

MARLBOROUGH

SOUTH ISLAND

Pacific
Ocean

CENTRAL OTAGO

0 Miles   300

0 Kilometers   300

FELTON ROAD
ESTABLISHED 1991

PINOT NOIR
CENTRAL OTAGO
2007

PRODUCED AND BOTTLED BY
FELTON ROAD WINES LTD
BANNOCKBURN

GRAPES GROWN AT OUR BANNOCKBURN VINEYARDS

750 ml   *Wine of New Zealand*   Alc. 14.0% Vol.

SEVENTY PERCENT of New Zealand vines are ten or less years in age.

TOTAL ACRES OF GRAPES BY YEAR

1985	15,000 acres of grapes
1986	11,000 acres of grapes (Vine Pull)
2008	60,000 acres of grapes

SAUVIGNON BLANC—THE "WILD GRAPE"

New Zealand touts itself as "the Sauvignon Blanc capital of the world." So what makes this grape so appealing (or unappealing)? It's all about aromatics, a word that is used a lot in the Marlborough region. The aroma of a New Zealand Sauvignon Blanc is often described by wine writers as pungent, assertive, vibrant, herbaceous, racy, having grapefruit and lime citrus flavors, tropical fruit flavors, or even smelling like cat pee! What's not to like?

What are the Wine Laws of New Zealand?

As of the 2007 vintage, if a grape variety, specific region, or a vintage is listed on the label, it must apply to 85 percent of that wine. Also, if more than one grape is used, the grapes must be listed in decreasing order on the label (i.e., the first grape would be the highest percentage, etc.).

VINE PULL 1986

In 1985 there were approximately 15,000 acres of vines planted in New Zealand. The majority of these grapes (Müller Thurgau being the most widely planted) produced large volumes of low-end wines but few wines of quality. In fact, so much wine was produced that there was a huge surplus of unsold wine and the government offered cash to any grower who agreed to uproot a quarter of his vineyard (also know as the vine pull). This massive purge of inferior wine grapes led to a resurgence of interest in high-quality wine grapes and to widespread plantings of Sauvignon Blanc, Chardonnay, and Pinot Noir. This marked the New Zealand wine industry's new beginning and a significant shift toward quality wine production.

Kevin Zraly's 25 Favorite New Zealand Wineries

AMISFIELD	HUNTER'S
BABICH	KIM CRAWFORD
CARRICK	KUMEU RIVER
CHURCH ROAD	MATUA VALLEY
CLEARVIEW	MILLS REEF
CLOUDY BAY	BRANCOTT (MONTANA)
CRAGGY RANGE	PEREGRINE
DOG POINT	SACRED HILL
DRY RIVER	SERESIN
ESK VALLEY	SAINT CLAIR
FELTON ROAD	TE MATA
FORREST	TRINITY HILL
FROMM	VILLA MARIA

BEST BETS FOR WINES FROM NEW ZEALAND
NORTH ISLAND (HAWKE'S BAY AND MARTINBOROUGH)

2005   2006*   2007*   2008

SOUTH ISLAND (CENTRAL OTAGO AND MARLBOROUGH)

2006*   2007*   2008

*Note: * signifies exceptional vintage*

FOR FURTHER READING
Buyer's Guide to New Zealand by Michael Cooper.

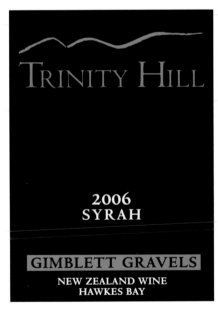

THE YEAR 2008 produced the largest grape crop ever recorded in New Zealand.

The Wines of South Africa

CAPE TOWN was founded in 1652.

SOUTH AFRICA, with the world's oldest wine-growing geology, was settled by the Dutch and by French Huguenots, and has grown grapes and made wine for some 350 years. Until recently, most of its wine was sold domestically or in Europe, and was not available in the United States.

With the democratic election of Nelson Mandela as president in 1994, South Africa's isolation and apartheid officially came to an end, and its wines finally became available to world markets.

THE FIRST South African grape harvest was in 1659.

There were a few producers making very good wine prior to 1994, but for the most part South African wines were ordinary and production emphasized brandy and fortified wines. These were produced by large cooperatives that based output on a quota system and valued quantity over quality.

Over the last sixteen years, however, South African wines have improved dramatically. Many of them now share center stage with some of the best wines produced in the world. And the best is yet to come, since many of South Africa's vineyards are relatively new—one-third of all vineyards have been replanted since 1994—and a vine's age plays a decisive role in the quality of the wine produced. Today, the industry calls for quality over quantity, and has one foot firmly planted in the new world of winemaking and the other foot still rooted in the old paradigm of creating uniquely South African styles of wine. The "new" South African winemakers have begun making up for lost time and now produce some of the world's great quality value wines in one of the most beautiful wine regions on earth.

THERE ARE over 560 wineries in South Africa.

SOUTH AFRICAN soil is among the oldest in the world.

SOUTH AFRICA WINE PRODUCTION

Current (2008):	56% white wine
	44% red wine
Future:	50% white wine
	50% red wine

With over 250,000 acres of vineyards, there is a wide diversity of terrain, with four main soil types. Vineyards are found at altitudes from 300 to 1,300 feet. There are cool coastal vineyards and vineyards whose summer days exceed 100 degrees Fahrenheit. Therefore there is no "recipe viticulture"; all wine production is specific to its site. It is a land of contrast, alive with possibilities.

What are the major grapes grown in South Africa?

The major white varieties are:

CHENIN BLANC

SAUVIGNON BLANC

CHARDONNAY

The major red varieties are:

SHIRAZ/SYRAH

CABERNET SAUVIGNON

BORDEAUX BLENDS (CABERNET SAUVIGNON, MERLOT, AND CABERNET FRANC)

CHENIN BLANC is sometimes labeled as Steen.

THE JURY IS still out on whether South Africa's benchmark white wine will be Chenin Blanc or Sauvignon Blanc. Historically it has been Chenin Blanc, whose South African vines can be more than one hundred years old. Some producers prefer to age it in oak, others age it unoaked, and several winemakers employ both methods. Personally, I believe that the world's best Chenin Blancs come from either South Africa or from the Loire Valley in France.

KEVIN ZRALY'S FAVORITE SOUTH AFRICAN CHENIN BLANCS

Rudera
Cederberg
De Trafford
Kanu
Groote Post
Iona

RETHINKING PINOTAGE

The first South African wine I ever tasted was made from a grape variety called Pino- tage. In 1925 a viticulturist from Stellenbosch University created this grape variety by crossing two grapes, Pinot Noir and Cinsault. Unfortunately, it has never had a single flavor profile. Pinotage can produce an inexpensive, light, somewhat insipid wine smelling of spray paint, acetate, or banana with a very strong, acrid aftertaste; or it can become a big, full-bodied, luscious, and well-balanced wine with tremendous fruit extraction and a long graceful finish that can age for twenty or more years.

I have found that the best producers of Pinotage have a similar formula:

1. *Grapes come from vines at least fifteen years old and planted in cooler climates*
2. *The per-acre crop yield must be low*
3. *The grapes need long skin contact (maceration in open fermentors)*
4. *The wine requires prolonged oak aging (at least two years)*
5. *The Pinotage grape is blended with Cabernet Sauvignon*
6. *The wine needs at least ten years of aging*

My favorite producers of Pinotage are:

KANONKOP   **FAIRVIEW**
L'AVENIR   **SIMONSIG**

What are the main wine regions of South Africa?

South Africa is divided into two main geographic areas: the Western Cape and the Northern Cape. These are further divided into regions, districts, and wards. The most important region is the Coastal Region. Three of the most historically important wines of origin (WO) within the Coastal Region, and the grape varietal that each region specializes in, are:

> *Constantia (1652):* Sauvignon Blanc, Muscat
> *Stellenbosch (1679):* Chardonnay, Cabernet Sauvignon, Pinotage,
>   Bordeaux blends
> *Paarl (1687):* Chardonnay, Shiraz, Chenin Blanc

Other important wine areas of South Africa are:

Swartland: Shiraz, Pinotage	*Walker Bay:* Chardonnay, Pinot Noir
Durbanville: Sauvignon Blanc	*Robertson:* Chardonnay, Shiraz
Darling: Sauvignon Blanc	*Franschhoek:* Cabernet Sauvignon, Syrah
Elgin: Riesling, Sauvignon Blanc, Pinot Noir	

THE WESTERN Cape produces 97% of all South African wines.

THE CAPE wine lands are the only ones in the world influenced by two oceans, the Atlantic and the Indian.

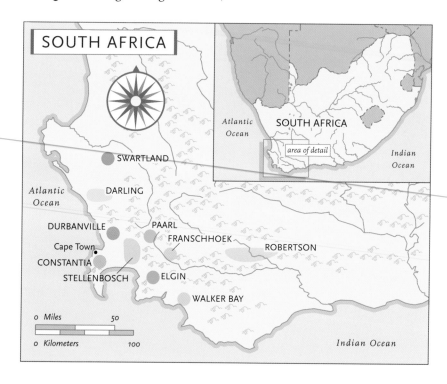

SOUTH AFRICAN DESSERT WINES

Long before Sauternes from France's Bordeaux region and Germany's Trockenbeeren-auslese were first produced, Hungary (Tokaj) and South Africa (Constantia) produced the two greatest sweet wines in the world. Since the eighteenth century, Constantia has been producing wines using the aromatic and fragrant Muscat grape. The original wine style (of grapes that are dried, not botrytized) is still produced at the wine estate Klein Constantia.

How are the wines of South Africa regulated?

In 1973, the Wine of Origin (WO) system defined South Africa's wine-producing areas by three categories:

GEOGRAPHIC: for example, Western Cape
REGION: for example, Coastal Region
DISTRICT: for example, Stellenbosch

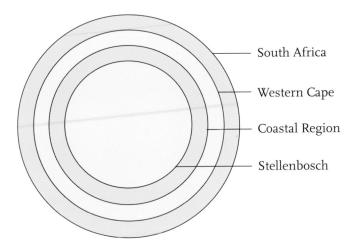

- South Africa
- Western Cape
- Coastal Region
- Stellenbosch

Other controls set by the WO include vintage dating and varietal labeling. A vintage designation means that 85 percent of the grapes used in its making must be from the stated vintage. A varietal designation means that the wine must contain at least 85 percent of the named grape varietal.

FOR THE TOURIST: Most Western Cape wine regions are within a two-hour drive of Cape Town.

FOR SOCCER FANS: The 2010 World Cup will be held in South Africa.

TIME LINE

1652	The Dutch arrive in Cape Town
1659	The first wine is produced
1688	The French Huguenots arrive
1788	Constantia's sweet wines become legendary
1886	Phylloxera destroys South African vineyards
1918	The Cooperative Wine Growers Association (KWV) is established to control the pricing and production of wine throughout South Africa
1918–1995	The KWV produces mostly brandy and fortified wines
1973	The Wines of Origin (WO) system is implemented
1990	Nelson Mandela is released from prison and trade sanctions end
1994	Nelson Mandela is elected president
1994	A new era of South African wine begins
1997	The KWV is transformed from a cooperative into a group of companies

If a wine label states that it is estate bottled, 100 percent of the grapes must be from that estate. If a place of origin is listed on the label, 100 percent of the grapes must come from that region. The two major things not controlled by the WO are the yield per hectare and irrigation.

My Favorite South African Wine Producers

Stellenbosch

Anwilka	Morgenster
De Toren	Mulderbosch
De Trafford	Neil Ellis
Glenelly	Raats Family
Jordan (available as Jardin in the United States)	Rudera
	Rustenberg
Kanonkop	Simonsig
Ken Forrester	Thelema
L'Avenir	Vergelegen
Meerlust	Vriesenhof
Morgenhof	Waterford

Paarl

Fairview	Vilafonté
Glen Carlou	Veenwouden
Nederburg	

Franschhoek

Boekenhoutskloof	Graham Beck
Boschendal	

Swartland

Sadie Family

FOREIGN INVESTMENT IN SOUTH AFRICA WINE

Anwilka: Bruno Prats, former owner of Château Cos d'Estournel; and Hubert de Boüard of Château Angelus (Bordeaux, France) with Lowell Jooste of Klein Constantia

Glen Carlou: Donald Hess (California, Australia, and Argentina)

L'Avenir: Michel Laroche (Chablis, France)

Morgenhof: Anne Cointreau-Huchon (France)

Morgenster: Pierre Lurton, Château Cheval Blanc (Bordeaux, France)

Vilafonté: Zelma Long (formerly of Simi) and Phil Freese (formerly of Mondavi)

Glenelly: May de Lencquesaing, Château Pichon-Lalande (Bordeaux, France)

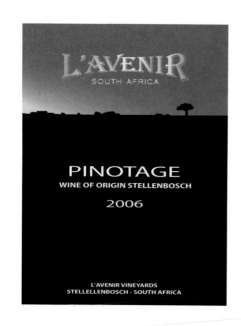

IN 1685, the Constantia wine estate was established.

Constantia

CONSTANTIA UITSIG   **STEENBERG**

KLEIN CONSTANTIA

Elgin

PAUL CLUVER

BEST BETS FOR SOUTH AFRICAN WESTERN CAPE WINES
2005* 2006 2007 2008
*Note: * signifies exceptional vintage*

The Wines of Canada

COMMERCIAL WINEMAKING in Canada began in the early 1800s.

THE WINE HISTORY OF CANADA is not that much different from that of my own state, New York: Both Canada and New York began winemaking by concentrating on growing the winter-hardy *labrusca* grapes (Concord, Catawba, and Niagara). Like New York, many of Canada's wineries specialized in producing fortified wines. These were often bottled using the borrowed European names *port* and *sherry*. The first major change in Canadian viticulture occurred during the 1970s, when several small producers began to experiment with French hybrid grapes. Over the last twenty-five years, the best wines of Canada have been made with European *vinifera* grapes.

QUEBEC AND Nova Scotia also grow grapes, primarily hybrids.

ONTARIO

20,000 acres	125 wineries

BRITISH COLUMBIA

9,000 acres	144 wineries

What are the most important grapes grown in Canada?

The major white grapes are:

CHARDONNAY	**GEWÜRZTRAMINER**
PINOT GRIS	**VIDAL**
RIESLING	

The major red grapes are:

PINOT NOIR	**CABERNET FRANC**
CABERNET SAUVIGNON	**SYRAH**
MERLOT	

What are the major wine regions of Canada?

Canada has two major wine-producing regions: British Columbia on the Pacific Coast, and Ontario in the eastern Great Lakes region.

Ontario/Niagara Peninsula: Chardonnay, Riesling, Pinot Noir, Vidal, Cabernet Franc
British Columbia/Okanagan Valley: Chardonnay, Pinot Gris, Merlot, Cabernet Sauvignon, Syrah, Gewürztraminer, Pinot Noir

How are the wines of Canada regulated?

The Vintners Quality Alliance (VQA) was created to regulate the wines of Ontario in 1988 and British Columbia in 1990. A VQA designation stipulates that the wine must be made using 100 percent *vinifera* varieties and controls varietal percentages. If a wine has the grape variety listed on the label it must contain a minimum of 85 percent of that variety. If a designated viticultural area (DVA) is listed, 95 percent must come from that area. If a vineyard is listed, it must be 100 percent from that vineyard. Over one hundred wineries produce VQA wines.

Kevin Zraly's Favorite Canadian Wineries

CHÂTEAU DES CHARMES

HENRY OF PELHAM

INNISKILLIN

JACKSON-TRIGGS

LE CLOS JORDANNE

MISSION HILL

SUMAC RIDGE

BEST BETS FOR WINES FROM CANADA

Ontario 2005   2006*   ***British Columbia*** 2005   2006

*Note: *signifies exceptional vintage*

FOR FURTHER READING

The Wine Atlas of Canada; Vintage Canada; and *Canadian Wine for Dummies,* all by Tony Aspler.

CANADIAN ICE WINE

The first great Canadian wine I ever tasted was an Ice Wine—or Eiswein—made by the Inniskillin Winery. Inniskillin, founded in 1975, was the first new winery founded in Ontario since 1927 and they produced their first Ice Wine in 1984 after a very cold Canadian winter.

To make Ice Wine, grapes are allowed to freeze on the vine before being picked by hand. The grapes are then carefully pressed while still frozen, yielding a small amount of concentrated juice that is high in sugar and other components. Canadian law dictates that Ice Wine can be made using only vinifera grapes (usually Riesling) and the French hybrid Vidal. It must also contain at least 125 grams of residual sugar per liter. Most Ice Wines are expensive and are sold in half bottles.

CANADA, LIKE the United States, had a period of national prohibition. Canada's prohibition began in 1916 and ended in 1927 (the United States' was from 1920 to 1933).

SIXTY PERCENT of VQA wines are white grapes.

THE LAKE EFFECT

Many people erroneously think that Canada is too far north and too cold to make great wine. Just like in other cool-climate wine regions such as Germany, most of the best vineyards are planted near water, which tempers the climate. Ontario has Lake Ontario and Lake Erie, and British Columbia has Okanagan Lake.

CANADIANS DAN Aykroyd and Wayne Gretzky both have invested in Canadian wineries.

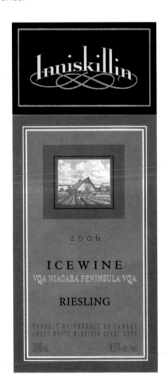

The Wines of Chile

CHILE IS a melting pot of German, French, Spanish, and English.

THE HIGHEST PEAK of the Andes Mountains is called Aconcagua and is over 22,000 feet high.

TIME LINE IN CHILE

1551: Spanish plant first grapes

1850s: Wineries such as Cousiño Macul (1856) are established; pre-phylloxera vines imported from Europe

1870s: Chilean wines become more important for export because of the phylloxera epidemic in Europe and United States

1930s to 1970s: Wines go from quality to ordinary

Mid-1970s: Export market grows

1980s to 1990s: Better-quality wines after big investments in wineries and winemaking equipment

2000 to present: Big investment in vineyards; great world-class wines at reasonable prices.

AFTER A LONG day of tasting Chilean wines, it is a tradition to end with Chile's national drink—a Pisco Sour, a brandy mixed with lemon and/or lime juice, simple syrup, egg white, and a dash of Angostura bitters. The longer the day, the more Pisco you must have!

I WAS IMPRESSED with some of the wineries, and some of the wines I tasted, when I first visited Chile in 1997. It was a country on the verge of producing world-class wine, primarily reds, with the best varietal being Cabernet Sauvignon. Back in those days I called Chile "a work in progress."

On my 2008–2009 world wine tour I spent ten days in Chile, first as a judge for over 400 wines and then visiting wineries throughout the country. What a difference twelve years can make, and not just in better wines! Chile's infrastructure, especially with its new hotel construction and highways, has transformed this country into a big-time tourist destination.

With over 2,500 miles of Pacific coastline and being, on average, only 109 miles wide, Chile has many different climates, from desertlike conditions in the north to glaciers in the south. In the middle of the country within 150 miles of Santiago, its capital, you will find the perfect Mediterranean climate for growing outstanding wine grapes: warm days, cool nights, and ocean winds.

And one cannot write about Chile without mentioning the majestic snow-capped Andes, which supply all the necessary water through both flood and drip irrigation. The peaks average over 13,000 feet. It is the world's longest mountain range—over 4,000 miles extending into seven countries.

Chile has been making wine since the first grapes were planted there in 1551. The first wine was produced in 1555, and in the mid-1800s, French varietals such as Cabernet Sauvignon and Merlot were imported.

But all this progress came to a grinding halt in 1938 when the government of Chile decreed that no new vineyards could be planted. This law lasted until 1974. The renaissance of the modern wine industry of Chile really only began in the early 1980s. The new technology of stainless-steel fermentors, the old technology of French oak barrels, better vineyard management, and drip irrigation were combined to produce higher-quality wines. Even though Chile is still learning and experimenting in its vineyards and in its winemaking, *its red wines are the best values in the world* in the $15-$25 range!

What are the main grape varieties planted in Chile?

The major white grapes are:

SAUVIGNON BLANC (21,490 acres)   **CHARDONNAY** (21,122 acres)

The major red grapes are:

CABERNET SAUVIGNON (100,789 acres)   **CARMÉNÈRE** (17,750 acres)

MERLOT (33,032 acres)   **SYRAH** (8,327)

RETHINKING CARMÉNÈRE

Bordeaux winemaking was influential in the early days of Chile's wine industry. That is why Cabernet Sauvignon is the country's number one red varietal. In the 1850s, Chileans planted other Bordeaux grapes such as Merlot and Cabernet Franc.

In 1994, DNA analysis revealed that a substantial amount of grapes that had been produced and sold as Merlot were actually another Bordeaux grape called Carménère.

What could have been a marketing disaster turned into a positive new identity for Chile. Carménère is now one of the top varietals in Chile and it is the only country in the world to produce it as a single varietal.

When I first visited Chile in 1997, there was a lack of consistency in Carménère from winery to winery; most tasted green and herbaceous. When I revisited Chile in 2009, the quality had changed dramatically. My own tasting experience has shown that to make a great wine from Carménère:

- *It must be planted in a clay, well-drained soil*
- *It needs good weather conditions since it is a late-ripening grape. In the early days it was picked too early—the reason for those herbaceous characteristics.*
- *It is better when blended with Cabernet Sauvignon or Syrah*
- *Oak aging is necessary for at least twelve months to integrate the fruit, tannins, and acidity*
- *Older vines make for better Carménère*
- *At the end of the harvest, it is necessary to pull off the Carménère vines' grape leaves and expose the grapes to as much sunlight as possible*
- *Carménère is a thick-skinned grape that has soft, sweet tannins and low acidity. It is wine that you can enjoy young (three to seven years). The best will cost you $20 or more... still a great value!*

NEW PLANTINGS of Malbec, Carignan, Pinot Noir, and Cinsault will add diversity to Chilean wines over the next ten years.

CABERNET SAUVIGNON accounts for 46% of the total acreage of premium grapes planted in Chile.

WATCH OUT ARGENTINA!

In the 2009 Wines of Chile Awards, for which I was one of the nine American judges, we tasted over 400 wines. The Best of Show wine for 2009—Cabernet Sauvignon? No. Carménère? No. It was a Malbec! Odfjell Vineyards's Orzada Orgánico 2006.

Some foreign investors in Chile include:

Quintessa, California	Veramonte
Torres Winery, Spain	Miguel Torres Winery
Antinori, Italy	Albis
O. Fournier, Spain	O. Fournier
Dan Odfjell, Norway	Odfjell Vineyards

THE FRENCH CONNECTION (FRENCH INVESTMENT IN CHILE)

French Investor	Chilean Winery
Grand Marnier	Casa Lapostolle
Château Lafite Rothschild	Los Vascos
Bruno Prats & Paul Pontallier	Aquitania
William Fèvre	Fèvre
Château Larose Trintaudon	Casas del Toqui
Baron Philippe de Rothschild	Almaviva

MODERN TECHNOLOGY like fermentation in stainless steel vats was introduced to Chile by the Spanish wine family Torres in 1979.

CHILE IS the fourth largest exporter of wine to the United States.

EXPORTS TO THE UNITED STATES

In 1996, Chile exported 100,000 cases of wine to the United States. Since then, Chilean wine exports have increased to more than 7 million cases.

THE LARGEST planting of Cabernet Sauvignon in Chile is in the Colchagua Valley.

OTHER REGIONS OF CHILE

Limari: Cabernet Sauvignon
Aconcagua: Cabernet Sauvignon
San Antonio: Chardonnay
Curicó: Cabernet Sauvignon,
    Sauvignon Blanc
Cachapoal: Cabernet Sauvignon
Maule: Cabernet Sauvignon
Bío Bío: Pinot Noir

**THE SEVEN LARGEST WINERIES
IN CHILE**

WINERY	DATE FOUNDED
Concha y Toro	1883
San Pedro	1865
Errazuriz	1870
Santa Carolina	1875
Santa Rita	1880
Undurraga	1885
Canepa	1930

What are the major winemaking regions in Chile?

This is a little difficult to answer since you have a country that is so narrow. Maybe the best way is to look at the country in an east-west and north-south division. From the east to the west, you have three different climatic conditions:

Coastal: cool climat
Central valley: warm climate
Andes mountains: cool or warm climate

From a north-to-south perspective, the most important regions are:

Casablanca Valley: Sauvignon Blanc, Chardonnay, Pinot Noir
Maipo Valley: Cabernet Sauvignon
Rapel Valley/ Colchagua: Cabernet Sauvignon, Merlot, Carménère

What are the wine laws of Chile?

After the restrictive laws of the seventies were repealed, Chile really began opening up its wine industry. In general, the winemakers have a lot of freedom. Wineries adhere to the label requirements of the EU. The wine must contain 85% of the grape variety, vintage, or domaine of origin (D.O.) that appears on the label.

Kevin Zraly's Favorite Chilean Producers
(With Some of Their Best Wines)

ALMAVIVA
ANAKENA (ONA)
AQUITANIA
ARBOLEDA
CALITERRA (CENIT)
CARMEN (GRANDE VIDURE)
CASA LAPOSTOLLE (CUVÉE
    ALEXANDRE, CLOS APALTA)
CASA SILVA
CHADWICK
CONCHA Y TORO (DON MELCHOR)
CONO SUR (OCIO)
COUSIÑO MACUL (FINIS TERRAE, ANTIGUAS RESERVAS, LOTA)
DE MARTINO
ECHEVERRIA
EMILIANA ORGÁNICO
ERRAZURIZ (DON MAXIMIANO)
LEYDA
LOS VASCOS (LE DIX DE LOS VASCOS)
MATETIC (EQ)
MONTES (ALPHA M, FOLLY)
MORANDÉ
MIGUEL TORRES
ODFJELL
O. FOURNIER (CENTAURI)
SANTA CAROLINA (VIÑA CASABLANCA)
SANTA RITA (CASA REAL)
SEÑA
TARAPACA (RESERVA PRIVADA)
UNDURRAGA (ALTAZOR)
VALDIVIESO (CABALLO LOCO, ECLAT)
VERAMONTE (PRIMUS)

OVER 40% of all winemakers in Chile are women.

THE NUMBER ONE Chilean wine imported into the United States is Concha y Toro. It is also one of the oldest wineries, started in 1883.

KEVIN ZRALY'S CHOICES

THE BEST OF CHILE
Almaviva
Alpha M (Montes)
Seña
Le Dix de Los Vascos
Don Maximiano (Errazuriz)
Antiquas Reservas (Cousiño Macul)
Clos Apalta (Casa Lapostolle)
Don Melchor (Concha y Toro)
Casa Real (Santa Rita)

IN 1995, there were only 12 wineries in Chile. Today there are more than 100.

BEST BETS FOR CHILE

Maipo 2005* 2007* **Casablanca** 2006 2007
Colchagua 2005* 2007*

*Note: * signifies exceptional vintage*

FOR FURTHER READING
The Wines of Chile, by Peter Richards.

JUST A COINCIDENCE?

The best recent vintages in Chile have occurred in odd years: 1997, 1999, 2001, 2003, 2005, and 2007.

The Wines of Argentina

MY WINE STUDENTS are always asking me what country is on the horizon for new wines and wine regions. My answer: Argentina.

There are many reasons for feeling this way. One is great climatic conditions and soil, especially for red wines. Another is the size of Argentina: the second largest country in South America has thousands more acres that can be planted. But the most important reason is tremendous new investment, not only financial but also of world-renowned experts owning their own vineyards and wineries.

Argentina's tradition of making and consuming wine goes back to the colonization by the Spanish in the 1500s. As with many of the great-wine producing countries, it was missionaries (Jesuits, in the case of Argentina) who planted and cultivated vines in Mendoza and to the north in San Juan.

Originally, Argentina never needed to export wine since most of the wine production, which was well made and inexpensive, was consumed domestically. But over the last twenty years, much has changed in Argentina. Annual domestic consumption dropped from twenty-four gallons of wine per person a year to eight gallons. In 2001, with the devaluation of the peso, exporting became more profitable. With foreign investment and winemaking consultants already in place, the timing was perfect for Argentina to enter the export market, with the

THE FLYING WINEMAKER LANDS IN ARGENTINA!

The most famous wine consultant in the world, Frenchman Michel Rolland, has invested his winemaking expertise into an estate of five wineries called Clos de los Siete, all located within eyesight of each other. His partners include top winemakers and viticulturists. The Wine Advocate wrote of the 2007 vintage that "there may be no finer red wine value in Argentina." The four other wineries involved in the group are Monteviejo, Flechas de los Andes, Cuvelier los Andes, and Diamandes.

THE BORDEAUX INVESTMENT CONNECTION
Monteviejo (Château Le Gay, Pomerol)
Cuvelier los Andes (Château Léoville Poyferre, St-Julien)
Bodegas Diamandes (Château Malartic-Lagraviere, Pessac-Léognan)
Flechas de los Andes (Château Clarke, Listrac; and Château Dassault, St-Émilion)
Clos de los Siete (Château le Bon Pasteur, Pomerol)

"unique" grape Malbec giving a wine identity for the country. The quality/price ratio is also one of the best in the world!

With the size of the country and the speed of their winemaking success, look for even more and better wines over the next twenty years.

What are the main grape varieties of Argentina?

The major white grapes are:

Torrontés Riojano (20,300 acres)   **Chardonnay** (14,200 acres)

The major red grapes are:

Malbec (60,300 acres)   **Merlot** (18,300 acres)

Cabernet Sauvignon (43,700 acres)   **Tempranillo** (15,775 acres)

Syrah (30,630 acres)

What are the main wine regions of Argentina?

North
Salta: Torrontés Riojano, Cabernet Sauvignon
  Cafayate

Cuyo
Mendoza: Malbec, Tempranillo, Cabernet Sauvignon
  Uco Valley
  San Juan: Bonarda, Syrah

Patagonia
Rio Negro: Pinot Noir, Torrontés Riojano
Neuquén

Kevin Zraly's Favorite Producers of Argentina wines

Achaval Ferrer (Finca Mirador)
Alta Vista (Alto)
Bodega Norton (Perdriel Single Vineyard)
Catena Zapata (Adrianna Vineyard)
Cheval des Andes
Clos de los Siete

MALBEC IS ALSO known as Cot and makes some full-bodied wines in the Cahors region of France.

THE BLENDING grape of Argentina is Barnardo. There are 45,500 acres of Barnardo grown in Argentina, but primarily because of its low tannins it is usually blended with Malbec and Cabernet Sauvignon, and is rarely used as a single variety.

THE REGION OF Mendoza is about the size of Germany.

FOR THE TOURIST

Take the family to Patagonia, where the most dinosaur fossils in the world are located.

FOR THE GOURMET

The national dish is beef. Argentineans consume about half a pound of beef per person per day. Also, many of the wineries have exceptional restaurants, from Francis Mallman 1884, to the new Urban at O. Fournier.

ALL ARGENTINEAN varietal wines are 100% of the grape named on the label.

FOR THE DANCER

Even if you don't know how to tango, you will love watching this sensual dance all over Argentina.

UP AND COMING wine region: Salta.

OVER 70% OF the 500,000 acres of vineyards planted in Argentina are in Mendoza—about 350,000 acres.

THERE ARE 960 wineries in Argentina, with over 600 located in Mendoza.

COBOS (MARCHIORI VINEYARD)
CUVELIER LOS ANDES (GRAND MALBEC)
ENRIQUE FOSTER (MALBEC FIRMADO)
ETCHART
FINCA FLICHMAN
FINCA SOPHENIA
KAIKEN
LUCA (NICO BY LUCA)
LUIGI BOSCA (ICONO)
FRANCOIS LURTON (CHACAYES)
MENDEL (FINCA REMOTA)
O. FOURNIER (ALFA CRUX MALBEC)
SALENTEIN (PRIMUM MALBEC)
TERRAZAS (MALBEC AFINCADO)
TIKAL (LOCURA)
TRAPICHE
VAL DE FLORES
WEINERT

FOREIGN INVESTMENT IN ARGENTINA

With an average price of $30,000 per acre, no wonder so many influential wine personalities and companies have invested in Argentina over the last 10 years.

WINERY	COUNTRY	ARGENTINEAN WINERY
O. Fournier	Spain	O. Fournier
Cordorniú	Spain	Séptima Winery
Pernod Ricard	France	Etchart Winery
Lurton	France	François Lurton
Chandon	France	Bodegas Chandon
Château Cheval Blanc	France	Cheval des Andes
Sogrape Vinhos	Portugal	Finca Flichman
Concha y Toro	Chile	Trivento, San Martin
Hess	Switzerland	Colomé Winery
Paul Hobbs	U.S.	Viña Cobos

BEST BETS FOR MENDOZA

2005*   2006**   2007   2008**

*Note: * signifies exceptional vintage*   *Note: ** signifies extraordinary vintage*

FOR FURTHER READING

Wines of Argentina, by Michel Rolland and E. Chrabolowsky.

Questions for Wines of the World: The Wines of Austria, Hungary, Greece, Australia, New Zealand, South Africa, Canada, Chile, and Argentina

AUSTRIA	REFER TO PAGE
1. What are the four wine regions of Austria?	250
2. Name three major white grapes and three major red grapes grown in Austria.	251
3. What are the three major quality levels of Austrian wine?	251
4. What is Austria's great dessert wine?	252
5. What three qualities of wine are Riedel glasses shaped to enhance?	252

HUNGARY	REFER TO PAGE
1. Name three major white grapes and three major red grapes grown in Hungary.	253
2. Name three major wine regions of Hungary.	254
3. How is Tokaji made?	254–255
4. What are the four levels of Puttonyos wine?	255
5. What is the name of the sweetest of the Tokaji wines?	255

GREECE	REFER TO PAGE
1. In what century did Greek winemaking begin?	256
2. What are three attributes of the Mediterranean climate?	256
3. How is Greek winemaking terrain unique, compared to the rest of the Mediterranean?	256
4. Name the three major white grapes and two major red grapes grown in Greece.	257
5. Name two of the most important winemaking regions of Greece.	257

AUSTRALIA

NEW ZEALAND

REFER TO PAGE

SOUTH AFRICA

REFER TO PAGE

The Greater World of Wine

THE PHYSIOLOGY OF TASTING WINE • MATCHING WINE AND FOOD

WITH ANDREA ROBINSON • WINE-BUYING STRATEGIES FOR YOUR WINE CELLAR •

FREQUENTLY ASKED QUESTIONS ABOUT WINE

The Physiology of Tasting Wine

ONE OF THE MOST WONDERFUL things about wine is its ability to bring us to our senses. While all of our senses factor into the enjoyment of wine, none does so powerfully or pleasurably as olfaction, our sense of smell combined with our sense of taste.

Happily, most wine tasters regularly experience what evolving scientific understanding also proves: the importance of smell and its impact on everything from learning and loving to aging and health.

How do our sense of smell and taste work, why is smell so emotionally evocative, and why is it so critical to our enjoyment?

HOW DO WE SMELL?

With each inhalation, the nose gathers essential information about the world around us—its delights, opportunities, and dangers. We can shut our eyes, close our mouths, withdraw our touch, and cover our ears, but the nose, with notable exceptions, is always working, alerting us to potential danger and possible pleasure.

Our sense of smell also enhances learning, evokes memory, promotes healing, cements desire, and inspires us to action. It is so important to the preservation and sustenance of life that the instantaneous information it gathers bypasses the thalamus, where the other senses are processed, and moves directly to the limbic system. The limbic system controls emotions, emotional responses, mood, motivation, and our pain and pleasure sensations, and it is where we analyze olfactory stimuli. Memory stored in the limbic system uniquely links emotional state with physical sensation, creating our most important and primitive form of learning: working memory. We remember smell differently than we recall sight, sound, taste, or touch because we often respond to smell the same way we respond to emotion: an increased heart rate, enhanced sensitivity, and faster breathing. It is this emotional connection that gives smell the power to stimulate memory so strongly and why a single smell can instantly transport us back to a particular time and place.

AS PROOF of the evolutionary importance of smell, 1 to 2% of our genes are involved in olfaction, approximately the same percent that is involved in the immune system.

OLFACTORY BULB

LIMBIC SYSTEM

IMPLICIT MEMORIES are perceptual, emotional, sensory, and are often unconsciously encoded and retrieved. Explicit memories are factual, episodic, temporal, and require conscious coding and retrieval. A good wine, well perceived and described, lives on in both forms of memory.

In 2004, the Nobel Prize in Medicine was awarded to Columbia University Professor Richard Axel and Hutchinson Cancer Research Center Professor Linda B. Buck for their breakthrough discoveries in olfaction. Axel and Buck discovered a large family of genes in the cells of the epithelium, or lining, of the upper part of the nose that control production of unique protein receptors, called olfactory receptors. Olfactory receptors specialize in recognizing, then attaching themselves to, thousands of specific molecules of incoming odorants. Once attached, the trapped chemical molecules are converted to electrical signals. These signals are relayed to neurons in the olfactory bulbs (there is one in each nasal cavity) before being carried along the olfactory nerve to the primary olfactory cortex, in the brain's limbic system, for analysis and response. By the time the electrical signals of smell are directed to the limbic system, the component parts of a smell—wet leather, wildflowers, golden apples, and river rocks—have already been identified and translated into electric signals. The limbic system recombines these components for analysis by scanning its vast memory data bank for related matches. Once analysis is completed, the limbic system triggers an appropriate physiological response: danger or pleasure, fight or flight. Taste a Puligny-Montrachet,

NUMEROUS STUDIES have proven the power of scents to affect mood and memory. Lavender has the power to calm. Citrus enhances alertness and, as a result, is occasionally broadcast in office buildings in Japan. And, as Shakespeare writes in *Hamlet*, "There's rosemary, that's for remembrance. Pray thee, love, remember."

ALLERGIES, INJURY, illness, and sexual activity are just some of the reasons our noses can become temporarily or permanently clogged or occluded.

SIZE AND SHAPE do matter. Deep, good wineglasses, such as Riedel's lines of stemware, do much to enhance varietal aroma.

THE OLFACTORY PATHWAY OF PULIGNY-MONTRACHET FROM BOTTLE TO BRAIN

We can trace the olfactory pathway of a Puligny-Montrachet from bottle to brain, through the following steps:

- *We open the bottle, in happy anticipation.*
- *We pour the wine into a proper glass.*
- *We swirl the glass to release the wine's aromas.*
- *We inhale the wine's bouquet deeply and repeatedly.*
- *Chemical components—esters, ethers, aldehydes, etc.—in the wines swirl upward through the nostrils on currents of air.*
- *Midway up the nose, millions of olfactory receptor neurons (olfactory epithelium), with their specialized protein receptors, bind the odorants that form the components of the specific wine profile.*
- *Interaction of the specific odor molecules matched with the right receptor causes the receptor to change shape.*
- *This change gives rise to an electrical signal that goes first to the olfactory bulbs and then to the areas of the brain that convert the electrical signal to the identification of a smell, or group of smells.*
- *The brain associates the smell(s) with perception, impressions, emotions, memories, knowledge, and more.*

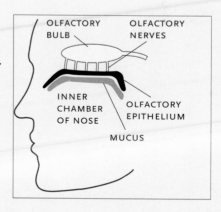

for example, and the limbic system might recognize it as a pleasant white wine made from Chardonnay grapes. More experienced wine tasters, with a more highly developed memory data bank, connect the wine to other Puligny-Montrachets and will recognize it as Puligny. Expert tasters might be able to recall the vineyard, maker, and year. The more we taste, test, and study, the better we become at identification.

Dr. Alan Hirsch of the Smell & Taste Treatment and Research Foundation and experts from the Monell Chemical Senses Center have shed additional light on the evolution and devolution of smell over a lifetime by describing the changes that occur at various periods in the life cycle.

Early childhood: As a child grows, so does his or her ability to recognize and remember different odors, especially those that are paired with an emotional event. At this point in their development, children usually have a hard time describing smells in words, but they are forming lifelong positive and negative sensory and emotional impressions. For example, smelling roses in the garden with Mom will have a far different impact on the feeling the scent elicits later in life than if a child first smells roses at the funeral of a loved one.

Puberty: The sense of smell is at its most acute in both men and women, although women surge further ahead at the onset of menstruation. This heightened sensitivity to smell will persist throughout their fertile years.

Adulthood: Women consistently outscore men in their ability to put names to smells in adulthood, and women give higher ratings on pleasure and intensity, lower ratings on unpleasant aromas. Women's sense of smell is particularly acute at ovulation and during pregnancy.

Midlife: Men and women slowly begin to lose their acuity of smell between the ages of 35 and 40, though the ability to identify and remember smells can continue to improve over the course of a lifetime.

Age 65: By the time they reach age 65, about half the population will experience a decline of, on average, 33 percent in their olfactory abilities. A quarter of the population has no ability to smell after 65.

Age 80: A majority of the population will show losses of up to 50 percent in olfactory abilities by age 80.

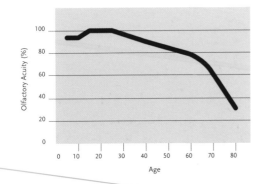

OLFACTORY ACUITY is at its peak in young adulthood.

IT'S A GOOD THING WE HAVE TWO!

The septum, made up of cartilage, divides the nose into two separate chambers, or nostrils, each with discreetly wired epithelium and olfactory bulbs. Each nostril serves a different function and operates at peak capacity at different times. It is rare for both nostrils, even in the healthiest noses, to work at full capacity simultaneously, and people with a deviated septum often report being able to breathe out of only one nostril. Jacobson's Organ author Lyall Watson reports, "A three-hour cycle of alternation between left and right nostrils goes on night and day. At night it contributes to sleep movements." Watson hypothesizes that by day, when we are conscious, right and left nostrils direct information to accordant parts of the brain—the right being the side that perceives, intuits, encodes, and stores implicitly; the left being the side that explicitly analyzes, names, records, and retrieves. "Ideally, we need both. . . . But if a situation is strange and requires action based more on prediction than precedent, you would be better off facing it with a clear left nostril."

WHAT ARE OUR wine senses? Hearing (as in corks popping, wine pouring), seeing, smelling, tasting, feeling, and reflecting, to be sure—but also more. Scientists and experts agree that smell accounts for up to 90% of what many perceive as taste and mouthfeel.

HOW DO WE TASTE?

Like smell, taste belongs to our chemical sensing system. Taste is detected by special structures called taste buds, and we have, on average, between five thousand and ten thousand of them, mainly on the tongue but with a few at the back of the throat and on the palate. Taste buds are the only sensory cells that are regularly replaced throughout a person's lifetime, with total regeneration taking place approximately every ten days. Scientists are examining this phenomenon, hoping that they will discover ways to replicate the process, inducing regeneration in damaged sensory and nerve cells.

Clustered within each taste bud are gustatory cells that have small gustatory hairs containing gustatory receptors. The gustatory receptors, like the olfactory receptors, are sensitive to specific types of dissolved chemicals. Everything we eat and drink must be dissolved—usually by the saliva—in order for the gustatory receptors to identify its taste. Once dissolved, the gustatory receptors read then translate a food's chemical structure before converting that information to electrical signals. These electrical signals are transmitted, via the facial and glossopharyngeal nerves, through the nose and on to the brain where they are decoded and identified as a specific taste.

FIRST IMPRESSIONS? A well-crafted wine's aroma evolves in the glass and our noses quickly become inured to smell. This is why it's advisable to revisit wine's aroma a few times in any given tasting or flight. Tasters can take a cue from the old perfumer's trick of sniffing their sleeves between the many essences/elixirs they may smell on a given day. In other words, they turn to something completely different—balancing sense with non-sense.

MUCH OF what is commonly described as taste—80 to 90% or more—is aroma/bouquet as sensed and articulated by our olfactory receptors, and mouthfeel and texture as sensed by surrounding organs.

OUR SALIVATION

TASTING AND CHEWING increase the rate of salivary flow.

Saliva is critical not only to the digestion of food and to the maintenance of oral hygiene, but also to flavor. Saliva dissolves taste stimuli, allowing their chemistry to reach the gustatory receptor cells.

Remember being told to chew your food slowly so that you would enjoy your meal more? It's true. Taking more time to chew food and savor beverages allows more of their chemical components to dissolve and more aromas to be released. This provides more material for the gustatory and olfactory receptors to analyze, sending more complex data to the brain, which enhances perception. Taste and smell intensify.

While the majority of our taste buds are located in the mouth, we also have thousands of additional nerve endings—especially on the moist epithelial surfaces of the mouth, throat, nose, and eyes—that perceive texture, temperature, and assess a variety of factors, which recognize sensations like the prickle of sulfur, the coolness of mint, and the burn of pepper. While humans can detect an estimated ten thousand smells and smell combinations, we can taste just four or five basic flavors—sweet, salty, sour, bitter, and umami (savory). Of these, only sweet, sour, and occasional bitterness are applicable to wine tasting.

BITTERNESS IN wine arises from a combination of high alcohol and high tannin.

Mouthfeel

Mouthfeel is literally how a wine feels in the mouth. These feelings are characterized by sensations that delight, prick, and/or pain our tongue, lips, and cheeks, and that often linger in the mouth after swallowing or spitting. They can range from the piquant tingle of Champagne bubbles to the teeth-tightening astringency of tannin; from the cool expansiveness of menthol/eucalyptus to the heat of a high-alcohol red; and from the cloying sweetness of a low-acid white to the velvet coating of a rich Rhône. The physical feel of wine is important to mouthfeel, and includes: body, thin to full; weight, light to heavy; and texture, austere, unctuous, silky, and chewy. Each contributes to wine's overall balance. More than just impressions, these qualities can trigger a physical response—drying, puckering, and salivation—which can literally have wines dancing on the tongue and clinging to the teeth.

SMELL AND TASTE TOGETHER

Recent research presents additional proof that taste seldom works alone (something wine tasters have known for centuries) and provides the first clear scientific evidence that olfaction is uniquely "dual." We often smell by inhaling through both nose and mouth simultaneously, adding to smell's complexity. There are two paths by which smells can reach the olfactory receptors:

ORTHONASAL STIMULATION: Odor compounds (smells) reach the olfactory bulb via the "external nares" or nostrils.

RETRONASAL STIMULATION: Odor compounds reach the olfactory bulb via the "internal nares," located inside the mouth (the respiratory tract at the back of the throat). This is why even if you pinch your nose shut, a strong cheese inhaled through the mouth may still smell. Molecules that stimulate the olfactory receptors float around in your mouth, up through your internal nares, and stimulate the olfactory neurons in the olfactory bulb. According to an article in the journal *Neuron*, researchers reported that the smell of chocolate stimulated different brain regions when introduced into the olfactory system through the nose (orthonasally) than it did when introduced through the mouth (retronasally). The study suggests that sensing odor through the nose may help indicate the availability of food while identification through the mouth may signify receipt of food.

The overall word for what we perceive in food and drink through a combination of smelling, tasting, and feeling is flavor, with smell being so predominant of the three that I often say that wine tasting is actually "wine smelling," and some chemists describe wine as "a tasteless liquid that is deeply fragrant." It is flavor that lets us know whether we are eating an apple or a pear, drinking a Puligny-Montrachet or an American Chardonnay. Anyone doubting the importance of smell in determining taste is encouraged to hold his or her nose while eating chocolate or cheese, either of which will tend to taste like chalk.

DAYTIME DRINKING

No scientific evidence shows that our olfactory abilities change over the course of a day, although many winemakers and wine professionals believe their senses to be keener and their palates cleaner in the morning. When evaluating wines for my wine class and books, I prefer to taste around 11 A.M. Others prefer tasting wine with a slight edge of hunger, which seems to enhance their alertness. Get to know your own cycles!

THIRTY-FIVE PERCENT of women and 15 percent of men are super-tasters.

SUPER-TASTERS have more than 10,000 taste buds.

SENSORY OVERLOAD

Super-tasters can be supersensitive, and they may find wines with tannin and high alcohol too bitter; so Cabernet Sauvignon, for example, may not be to their liking. They may also be put off by any sweetness in wine. Non-tasters are the opposite; they might not be bothered by tannin or high alcohol, and sweet wines would probably be perfectly acceptable.

LANGUAGE OF TASTE AND SMELL

Finding the language to describe what we taste and smell, and how what we taste and smell affects us, evolves over our lifetime, with women being slightly better at it than men.

DIFFERENT TASTES and smells of wine come from:
The grape
The winemaking
The aging

WHERE DO YOU EXPERIENCE BITTERNESS?

The back of the tongue
On the sides
In the throat

WHO ARE YOU?

According to Janet Zimmerman, writing in Science of the Kitchen: Taste and Texture, *approximately one-quarter of the population are "super-tasters," one-quarter are "non-tasters," and the remaining half are "tasters." Super-tasters have a significantly higher number of taste buds than tasters, and both groups outnumber non-tasters for taste buds. The averages for the three groups are 96 taste buds per square centimeter for non-tasters, 184 for tasters, and a whopping 425 for super-tasters. Super-tasters tend to taste everything more intensely. Sweets are sweeter, bitters are bitterer, and many foods and beverages, including alcohol, taste and feel unpleasantly strong. Non-tasters are far from picky, and seem less conscious of and therefore less engaged with what they eat and drink. Tasters, the largest and least homogeneous group, vary in their personal preferences but tend to enjoy the widest array of food and drink and relish the act of eating and drinking the most of the three groups.*

TOWARD A COMMON LANGUAGE OF TASTE AND SMELL

Smell is a relatively inadequate word for our most primitive and powerful sense. It means both the smells that emanate from us (we are what we eat and drink) as well as the smells we perceive. Throughout history, wine tasters have done much to create a common language, and to savor the intersection where enlivened and articulated senses meet memory, anticipation, association, and personal preferences throughout history.

Like colors, aroma can be broken down into basic categories which, when combined, yield the rich symphony that is wine. The University of California, Davis's Wine Aroma Wheel categorizes basic fruit aromas as citrus (grapefruit, lemon), berry (blackberry, raspberry, strawberry, black currant), tree (cherry, apricot, peach, apple), tropical (pineapple, melon, banana), dried (raisin, prune, fig), and others. Likewise, vegetative aromas can be categorized as fresh (stemmy, grassy, green, eucalyptus, mint), canned (asparagus, olive, artichoke), and dried (hay, straw, tea, tobacco). Other aroma categories include nutty, caramelized, woody, earthy, chemical, pungent, floral, and spicy.

Still, no two people are alike in either how they smell and taste or what smells and tastes they experience. It is deeply personal and experiential. So, here's to your health and happiness, and to savoring wine and life in and with every sense!

Matching Wine and Food

BY KEVIN ZRALY AND ANDREA ROBINSON

You've tasted your way through eight classes in this book and discovered at least a shopping cart's worth of wines to really enjoy. And for what purpose? Food! The final stop on the wine odyssey—and the whole point of the trip—is the dinner table. Quite simply, wine and food were meant for each other. Just look at the dining habits of the world's best eaters (the French, the Italians, the Spanish): Wine is the seasoning that livens up even everyday dishes. Salt and pepper shakers are a fixture of the American table, but in Europe it's the wine bottle.

ANDREA ROBINSON worked with Kevin at Windows on the World. She is one of only fifteen women in the world to hold the title of Master Sommelier, awarded by the Court of Master Sommeliers. She has written several books on wine and food, and was named Outstanding Wine & Spirits Professional by the James Beard Foundation.

WINE-AND-FOOD MATCHING BASICS

First, forget everything you've ever heard about wine-and-food pairing. There's only one rule when it comes to matching wine and food: The best wine to pair with your meal is whatever wine you like. No matter what!

If you know what you want, by all means have it. Worried that your preference of a Chardonnay with a sirloin steak might not seem "right"? Remember, it's your own palate that you have to please.

ARE YOU a menu maven or a wine-list junkie? Personally, I look at the wine list first, choose my wine, and then make my meal selection.

What's wine-and-food synergy?

Sounds like a computer game for gourmets, right? If up until now you haven't been the wine-with-dinner type, you're in for a great adventure. Remember, the European tradition of wine with meals was not the result of a shortage of milk or iced tea. Rather, it results from what I call wine-and-food synergy— when the two are paired, both taste better.

How does it work? In the same way that combining certain foods improves their overall taste. For example, you squeeze fresh lemon onto your oysters, or grate Parmesan cheese over spaghetti marinara, because it's the combination of flavors that makes the dish.

CHARDONNAY IS a red wine masquerading as a white wine, which, in my opinion, makes it a perfect match for steak.

HOW DO I make my wine and food decision?
What kind of wine do I like?
Texture of food (heavy or light)
Preparation (grilled, sautéed, baked, etc.)
Sauce (cream, tomato, wine, etc.)

Apply that idea to wine-and-food pairing; foods and wines have different flavors, textures, and aromas. Matching them can give you a new, more interesting flavor than you would get if you were washing down your dinner with, say, milk (unless you were dining on chocolate-chip cookies). The more flavorful the food, the more flavorful the wine should be.

Do I have to be a wine expert to choose enjoyable wine-and-food matches?

Why not just use what you already know? Most of us have been tasting and testing the flavors, aromas, and textures of foods since before we got our first teeth, so we're all food experts! As we'll show you, just some basic information about wine and food styles is all you'll need to pick wines that can enhance your meals.

What about acidity?

Acid acts as a turbocharger for flavor. A high-acid wine is a good choice for dishes with cream or cheese sauces. It enhances and lengthens the flavor of the dish. Watch television's Food Network. The TV chefs are always using lemons and limes—acidic ingredients. Even dishes that aren't "sour" have a touch of an acid ingredient to pump up the flavor. As chef Emeril Lagasse says, "Kick it up a notch!"

What role does texture play?

There's an obvious difference in the texture or firmness of different foods. Wine also has texture, and there are nuances of flavor in a wine that can make it an adequate, outstanding, or unforgettable selection with the meal. Very full-style wines have a mouth-filling texture and bold, rich flavors that make your palate sit up and take notice. But when it comes to food, these wines tend to overwhelm most delicate dishes (and clash with boldly flavored ones). Remember, we're looking for harmony and balance. A general rule is: The sturdier or fuller in flavor the food, the more full-bodied the wine should be. For foods that are milder the best wines to use would be medium- or light-bodied.

A FAIL-SAFE food: When in doubt, order roast chicken, which acts as a blank canvas for almost any wine style—light-, medium-, or full-bodied.

DO YOU drink your tea with milk or lemon? The milk coats your mouth with sweetness, whereas the lemon leaves your tongue with a dry crispness.

KEEP IT SIMPLE

Probably one of the reasons that classic French cuisine is noted for its subtlety is because the French want to let their wines "show off." This is an especially good idea if the wine is a special or "splurge" bottle.

Once you get to know the wines, matching them with food is no mystery. Here are two lists (one for red, one for white) with some suggestions based on the texture of the wines and the foods they can match.

White Wines

MY FAVORITE white wine for picnics is German Riesling Kabinett/Spätlese. On a hot summer day, I can think of no better white wine than a chilled German Riesling. The balance of fruit, acid, and sweetness as well as the lightness (low alcohol) make these wines a perfect match for salads, fruits, and cheese. For those who prefer a drier-style Riesling, try Alsace, Washington State, or the Finger Lakes region of New York.

LIGHT-BODIED WHITES	MEDIUM-BODIED WHITES	FULL-BODIED WHITES
Alsace Pinot Blanc	Pouilly-Fumé	Chardonnay*
Alsace Riesling	Sancerre	Chablis Grand Cru
Chablis	White Graves	Meursault
Muscadet	Chablis Premier Cru	Chassagne-
German Kabinett	Mâcon-Villages	Montrachet
and Spätlese	Pouilly-Fuissé	Puligny-Montrachet
Sauvignon Blanc*	St-Véran	Viognier
Orvieto	Montagny	
Soave	Sauvignon Blanc*/	
Verdicchio	Fumé Blanc	
Frascati	Chardonnay*	
Pinot Grigio	Gavi	
Pinot Gris	Gewürztraminer	
	Gruner Veltliner	

Matching Foods

Sole	Snapper	Salmon
Flounder	Bass	Tuna
Clams	Shrimp	Swordfish
Oysters	Scallops	Lobster
	Veal paillard	Duck
		Roast chicken
		Sirloin steak

Note that starred wines are listed more than once. That's because they can be vinified in a range of styles from light to full texture, depending on the producer. When buying these, if you don't know the style of a particular winery, it's a good idea to ask the restaurant server or wine merchant for help.

MY FAVORITE red wine for picnics is Beaujolais. I'll never forget my first summer in France, sitting outside a bistro in Paris and being served a Beaujolais. A great Beaujolais is the essence of fresh fruit without the tannins, and its higher acidity blends nicely with all picnic fare. For barbecued shrimp in the middle of the summer, I opt for chilled Beaujolais.

MY FAVORITE red wine for lunch is Pinot Noir. Since most of us have to go back to work after lunch, the light, easy-drinking style of a Pinot Noir will not overpower the usual luncheon fare of soups, salads, and sandwiches.

MY FAVORITE wine for lamb is Bordeaux or California Cabernet Sauvignon. In Bordeaux they have lamb with breakfast, lunch, and dinner! Lamb has such a strong flavor, it needs a strong wine. The big, full-bodied Cabernet Sauvignons from California and Bordeaux blend in perfectly.

PINOT NOIR is a white wine masquerading as a red wine, which makes it a perfect wine for fish and fowl. Other choices include Chianti Classico and Spanish Riojas (Crianza and Reserva).

BITTERNESS IN wine comes from the combination of high tannin and high alcohol, and these wines are best served with food that is either grilled, charcoaled, or blackened.

COOKING WITH WINE

Try to use the same wine or style that you are going to serve.

Red Wines

LIGHT-BODIED REDS	MEDIUM-BODIED REDS	FULL-BODIED REDS
Bardolino	Cru Beaujolais	Barbaresco
Valpolicella	Côtes du Rhône	Barolo
Chianti	Crozes-Hermitage	Bordeaux
Rioja-Crianza	Burgundy Premiers	(great châteaux)
Beaujolais	and Grands Crus	Châteauneuf-du-Pape
Beaujolais-Villages	Bordeaux (Crus Bourgeois)	
Burgundy (Village)	Cabernet Sauvignon*	Hermitage
Bordeaux (proprietary)	Merlot*	Cabernet Sauvignon*
Pinot Noir*	Zinfandel*	Merlot*
	Chianti Classico Riserva	Zinfandel*
	Dolcetto	Syrah/Shiraz*
	Barbera	Malbec*
	Rioja Reserva and	
	Gran Reserva	
	Syrah/Shiraz*	
	Pinot Noir*	
	Malbec*	

Matching Foods

Salmon	Game birds	Lamb chops
Tuna	Veal chops	Leg of lamb
Swordfish	Pork chops	Beefsteak (sirloin)
Duck		Game meats
Roast chicken		

> "I cook with wine; sometimes I even add it to food."
> —W. C. FIELDS

No-Fault Wine Insurance

Drinking wine with your meals should add enjoyment, not stress, but it happens all too often. You briefly eye the wine list or scan the wine-shop shelf, thinking well, maybe . . . a beer. In the face of so many choices, you end up going with the familiar. But it can be easy to choose a wine to enjoy with your meal.

From endless experimentation at home and in the restaurant, I've come up with a list of "user-friendly" wines that will go nicely with virtually any dish. What these wines have in common is that they are light- to medium-bodied, and they have ample fruit and acidity. The idea here is that you will get a harmonious balance of flavors from both the wine and the food, with neither overwhelming the other. Also, if you want the dish to play center stage, your best bets are wines from this list.

User-Friendly Wines

ROSÉ WINES	WHITE WINES	RED WINES
Virtually any rosé or white Zinfandel	Pinot Grigio	Chianti Classico
	Sauvignon Blanc/ Fumé Blanc	Rioja Crianza
	German Riesling, Kabinett, and Spätlese	Beaujolais-Villages
	Pouilly-Fumé and Sancerre	Côtes du Rhône
	Mâcon-Villages	Pinot Noir
	Champagne and sparkling wines	Merlot

These wines work well for what I call "restaurant roulette"—where one diner orders fish, another orders meat, and so on. They can also match well with distinctively spiced ethnic foods that might otherwise clash with a full-flavored wine. And, of course, all these wines are enjoyable to drink on their own.

Do sauces play a major role when you're matching wine and food?

Yes, because the sauce can change or define the entire taste and texture of a dish. Is the sauce acidic? Heavy? Spicy? Subtly flavored foods let the wine play the starring role. Dishes with bold, spicy ingredients can overpower the flavor nuances and complexity that distinguish a great wine.

Let's consider the effect sauces can have on a simple boneless breast of chicken. A very simply prepared chicken paillard might match well with a light-bodied white wine. If you add a rich cream sauce or a cheese sauce, then you might prefer a high acid, medium-bodied or even a full-bodied white wine. A red tomato-based sauce, such as a marinara, might call for a light-bodied red wine.

Wine and Cheese—Friends or Foes?

As in all matters of taste, the topic of wine and food comes with its share of controversy and debate. Where it's especially heated is on the subject of matching wine and cheese.

Wine and cheese are "naturals" for each other. For me, a good cheese and a good wine will enhance the flavors and complexities of both. Also, the protein in cheese will soften the tannins in a red wine.

The key to this match is in carefully selecting the cheese; therein lies the controversy. Some chefs and wine-and-food experts caution that some of the most popular cheeses for eating are the least appropriate for wine because they overpower it—a ripe cheese like Brie is a classic example.

The "keep-it-simple" approach applies again here. I find that the best cheeses for wines are the following: Parmigiano-Reggiano, fresh mozzarella, Pecorino, Taleggio, and Fontina from Italy; Chèvre, Montrachet, Tomme, and Gruyère from France; Dutch Gouda; English or domestic Cheddar; domestic aged or fresh goat cheese and Monterey Jack; and Manchego from Spain.

My favorite wine-and-cheese matches:

Chèvre/fresh goat cheese: Sancerre, Sauvignon Blanc

Montrachet, aged (dry) Monterey Jack: Cabernet Sauvignon, Bordeaux

Pecorino or Parmigiano-Reggiano: Chianti Classico Riserva, Brunello di Montalcino, Cabernet Sauvignon, Bordeaux, Barolo, and Amarone

Manchego: Rioja, Brunello di Montalcino

What to drink with Brie? Try Champagne or sparkling wine. And blue cheeses, because of their strong flavor, overpower most wines except—get ready for this—dessert wines! The classic (and truly delicious) matches are Roquefort cheese with French Sauternes, and Stilton cheese with Port.

MY FAVORITE cheese with wine is Parmigiano-Reggiano. Now we are really getting personal! I love Italian food, wine, and women (I even married one), but Parmigiano-Reggiano is not just to have with Italian wine. It also goes extremely well with Bordeaux, California Cabernets, and even the lighter Pinot Noirs.

SWEET SATISFACTION:
WINE WITH DESSERT, WINE AS DESSERT

I remember my first taste of a dessert wine—a Sauternes from France's Bordeaux region. It was magical! Then there are also Port, Sherry, and Beerenauslese, to name a few—all very different wines with one thing in common: sweetness. Hence the name "dessert" wines—their sweetness closes your palate and makes you feel satisfied after a good meal. But with wines like these, dessert is just one part of the wine-and-food story.

"Wine with dessert?" you're thinking. At least in this country, coffee is more common, a glass of brandy or liqueur if you're splurging. But as more and more restaurants add dessert wines to their by-the-glass offerings, perhaps the popularity will grow for these kinds of wine. (Because they're so rich, a full bottle of dessert wine isn't practical unless several people are sharing it. For serving at home, dessert wines in half-bottles are a good alternative.)

I like a dessert wine a few minutes before the dessert itself, to prepare you for what is to come. But you certainly can serve a sweet dessert wine with the course.

Here are some of my favorite wine-and-dessert combinations:

MY FAVORITE wine for chocolate is Port. For me, both chocolate and Port mean the end of the meal. They are both rich, sweet, satisfying, and sometimes even decadent together.

Port: dark chocolate desserts, walnuts, poached pears, Stilton cheese

Madeira: milk chocolate, nut tarts, crème caramel, coffee- or mocha-flavored desserts

Pedro Ximénez Sherry: vanilla ice cream (with the wine poured over it), raisin-nut cakes, desserts containing figs or dried fruits

Beerenauslese and Late Harvest Riesling: fruit tarts, crème brûlée, almond cookies

Sauternes: fruit tarts, poached fruits, crème brûlée, caramel and hazelnut desserts, Roquefort cheese

Muscat Beaumes-de-Venise: crème brûlée, fresh fruit, fruit sorbets, lemon tart

Asti Spumante: fresh fruits, biscotti

Vouvray: fruit tarts, fresh fruits

Vin Santo: biscotti (for dipping in the wine)

Often, I prefer to serve the dessert wine as dessert. That way I can concentrate on savoring the complex and delicious flavors with a clear palate. It's especially convenient at home—all you have to do to serve your guests an exotic dessert is pull a cork! And if you're counting calories, a glass of dessert wine can give you the satisfying sweetness of dessert with a lot less bulk (and zero fat!).

How much wine should I order for my dinner party?

At a dinner party where several wines will be served, I allow one bottle for every five people, which equals approximately one five-ounce glass per person.

What's the best wine to serve with hors d'oeuvres for my dinner reception?

Champagne. One of the most versatile wines produced in the world, Champagne has a "magical effect" on guests. Whether served at a wedding or a dinner at home, Champagne remains a symbol of celebration, romance, prosperity, and fun.

FOR FURTHER READING

I recommend *Perfect Pairings* by Evan Goldstein and *Great Wine & Food Made Simple* by Andrea Robinson.

12 BOTTLES OF wine = 1 case

BOTTLE SIZES

375 ml = 12.7 oz = half-bottle
750 ml = 25.4 oz = full bottle
1.5 liters = 50.8 oz = magnum (two bottles)
3 liters = 101.6 oz = double magnum
   (4 bottles)
6 liters = 203.2 oz = Imperial (8 bottles)
9 liters = 304.8 oz = Salamanazar
   (12 bottles)

Wine-Buying Strategies for Your Wine Cellar

Buying and selecting wines for your cellar is the most fun and interesting part of wine appreciation—besides drinking it, of course! You've done all your studying and reading on the wines you like, and now you go out to your favorite wine store to banter with the owner or wine manager. You already have an idea what you can spend and how many bottles you can safely store until they're paired with your favorite foods and friends.

Wine buying has changed dramatically over the last twenty years. Many liquor stores have become wine-specialty stores, and both the consumer and retailer are much more knowledgeable. Even twenty years ago, the wines of South Africa, Spain, New Zealand, Australia, and Chile were not the wines the consumer cared to buy. Back then, the major players were the wines of California, France, and Italy. Today there's so much more diversity in wine styles and wine prices, it's almost impossible to keep up with every new wine and new vintage that comes on the market. You can subscribe, among many publications, to *Wine Spectator, The Wine Enthusiast, Wine & Spirits,* or *Wine Advocate,* Robert M. Parker Jr.'s newsletter, to help you with your choices, but ultimately you'll find the style of wine to suit your own personal taste.

In this book I don't recommend specific wines from specific years because I don't believe that everyone will enjoy the same wines, or that everyone has the same taste buds as I do. I think it's very important that every year the consumers have a general knowledge of wineries that have consistently made great value wine, and know what's hot and what's not. Here are some of my thoughts and strategies for buying wine this year.

There is, and will continue to be, an abundance of fine wine over the next few years. The vintage years of 2000, 2003, and 2005 in Bordeaux; 2001, 2004, 2005, and 2006 in Piedmont and Tuscany; 2003, 2004, 2005, and 2006 in Germany; 2003, 2005, and 2006 in the Rhône Valley; 2002, 2003, and 2005 in Burgundy reds; 2005 and 2007 in Chile; 2006 and 2008 in Argentina; and 2004, 2005, and 2008 in Australian Shiraz will give us great wines to drink over the next few years. The 2002, 2005, 2006, and 2007 vintages for California Cabernet Sauvignon, and 2005 and 2007 Chardonnays are generally excellent. The 1994, 2000, and 2003 vintage Ports are readily available. Although many of the wines from these regions

TOP VALUE WINE REGIONS

Rías Baixas (Spain)
Mendoza (Argentina)
Marlborough (New Zealand)
Chianti (Italy)
Côtes du Rhône (France)
Maipo (Chile)

WHAT KIND OF WINE BUYER ARE YOU?

"Enthusiast"
"Image Seeker"
"Savvy Shopper"
"Traditionalist"
"Satisfied Sipper"
"Overwhelmed"
—FROM CONSTELLATION WINES U.S.

are high-priced, there still remain hundreds of wines under twenty dollars that you can drink now or cellar for the future.

Anyone can buy expensive wines! In an average year I taste some three thousand wines. This past year I tasted over six thousand wines! The real challenge is finding the best values—the ten-dollar bottle that tastes like a twenty-dollar bottle. The following is a list of my buying strategies for my own wine cellar. This is by no means a complete roster of great wines, but most are retasted every year and have been consistently good.

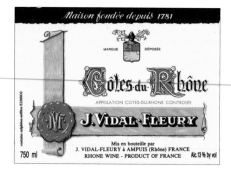

Everyday Wines
($10 and under)

Argentina
Alamos Malbec and Bonarda
Bodega Norton Malbec
Bodegas Esmeralda Malbec
Trapiche Malbec
Valentin Bianchi Malbec

Australia
Alice White Cabernet Sauvignon
Banrock Station Chardonnay and Shiraz
Black Opal Cabernet Sauvignon or Shiraz
Bogle Sauvignon Blanc
Jacob's Creek Shiraz/Cabernet
Lindemans Shiraz Bin 50 or Cabernet Sauvignon Bin 45 or Chardonnay Bin 65
Oxford Landing Sauvignon Blanc
Yellow Tail

California
Beaulieu Coastal Merlot or Sauvignon Blanc
Beringer Founders' Estate Cabernet Sauvignon
Buena Vista Sauvignon Blanc
Cline Syrah or Zinfandel
Fetzer Valley Oaks Merlot
Forest Glen Cabernet Sauvignon or Shiraz or Merlot
Forest Ville Cabernet Sauvignon or Chardonnay
Glass Mountain Cabernet Sauvignon
Kendall Jackson Vintner's Reserve Sauvignon Blanc
Kenwood Sauvignon Blanc
McManis Cabernet Sauvignon
Monterey Vineyard Cabernet Sauvignon
Napa Ridge Merlot
Pepperwood Grove Chardonnay
Rutherford Ranch Chardonnay
Smoking Loon Syrah

Chile
Caliterra Cabernet Sauvignon or Merlot
Carmen Carménère
Montes Cabernet Sauvignon
Santa Rita 120 Cabernet Sauvignon
Veramonte Sauvignon Blanc
Walnut Crest Merlot

France
Fortant de France Merlot or Syrah

Guigal Côtes du Rhône

J. Vidal-Fleury Côtes du Rhône

Jaboulet Côtes du Rhône
Parallele "45"

La Vieille Ferme Côtes du Ventoux

Louis Jadot or Georges Duboeuf
Beaujolais-Villages

Louis Latour Ardèche Chardonnay

Mâcon-Villages (most producers)

Michel Lynch

Perrin & Fils Côtes du Rhône

Réserve St-Martin Merlot

Italy
Casal Thaulero Montepulciano Red

Michele Chiarlo Barbera d'Asti

Portugal
Aveleda Vinho Verde

South Africa
Goats do Roam

Jardin Syrah

Washington State
Columbia Crest Sémillon-
Chardonnay

Covey Run Fumé Blanc

Hogue Columbia Valley Chardonnay

Hogue Fumé Blanc

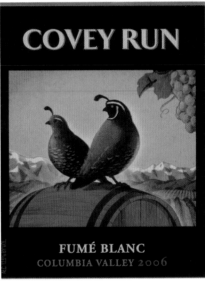

Once-a-Week Wines
($10 to $20)

Argentina
Alamos Chardonnay

Bodegas Catena Zapata

Bodegas Weinert Carrascal

Catena Zapata Cabernet Sauvignon

Clos de los Siete Vista Flores

Domaine Jean Bousquet Malbec

Finca Flichman Gestos Malbec

Kaiken Cabernet Sauvignon Ultra

Navarro Correas Cabernet
Sauvignon "Collection Privada"

Salentein Malbec Gran Reserva

Australia
Greg Norman Estate Shiraz

McWilliams Shiraz

Penfolds Shiraz Bin 28

Peter Lehmann Barossa Shiraz

Rosemount Estate Chardonnay or
Shiraz/Cabernet (Diamond Label)

Rosemount Show Reserve
Chardonnay

Wolf Blass Chardonnay

California
Benziger Chardonnay, Merlot, or
Cabernet Sauvignon

Bogle Zinfandel

Brander Sauvignon Blanc

Calera Central Coast Chardonnay

Carmenet Cabernet Sauvignon

Castle Rock Pinot Noir

Chateau St. Jean Chardonnay or
Sauvignon Blanc

Cline Cellars Zinfandel

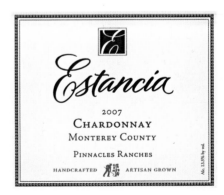

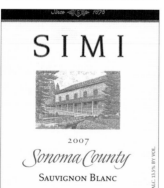

Clos du Bois Chardonnay, Merlot,
or Syrah

Estancia Chardonnay or
Cabernet Sauvignon

Ferrari-Carano Fumé Blanc

Fetzer Valley Oaks Cabernet
Sauvignon, Zinfandel,
or Chardonnay

Francis Ford Coppola Rosso

Frei Brothers Merlot

Frog's Leap Sauvignon Blanc

Gallo of Sonoma Chardonnay,
Cabernet Sauvignon, Pinot Noir,
or Merlot

Geyser Peak Sauvignon Blanc

Girard Sauvignon Blanc

Hawk Crest Chardonnay, Cabernet
Sauvignon, or Merlot

Hess Select Chardonnay or
Cabernet Sauvignon

Honig Sauvignon Blanc

Kendall-Jackson Chardonnay
Vintners Reserve, Syrah, or
Cabernet Sauvignon

Laurel Glen Quintana
Cabernet Sauvignon

Liberty School Cabernet Sauvignon

Markham Merlot or
Sauvignon Blanc

Mason Sauvignon Blanc

Meridian Chardonnay or
Cabernet Sauvignon

Merryvale Starmont Chardonnay

Ridge Sonoma Zinfandel

Robert Mondavi Private Selection

Rutherford Vintners Cabernet
Sauvignon or Merlot

Saintsbury Chardonnay

Sebastiani Chardonnay or
Cabernet Sauvignon

Seghesio Sonoma Zinfandel

Silverado Sauvignon Blanc

Simi Cabernet Sauvignon,
Sauvignon Blanc, or Chardonnay

Souverain Chardonnay or Merlot

St. Francis Merlot or
Old Vines Zinfandel

St. Supery Sauvignon Blanc

Trefethen Eshcol Cabernet
or Chardonnay

Chile
Casa Lapostolle Cabernet Sauvignon
or Merlot Cuvée Alexandre

Concha y Toro Casillero del Diablo
or Puente Alto Cabernet Sauvignon

Cousiño-Macul Antiguas Reserva
Cabernet Sauvignon

Los Vascos Reserve
Cabernet Sauvignon

Montes Merlot

Santa Rita Cabernet Sauvignon
or Casa Real Sauvignon Blanc

Veramonte Primus

France
Château Bonnet Blanc

Château Greysac

Château La Cardonne

Château Larose-Trintaudon

Drouhin Vero Chardonnay
or Pinot Noir

Georges Duboeuf Fleurie

Georges Duboeuf Pouilly-Fuissé

Hugel Gentil

Jaboulet Crozes-Hermitage Les Jalets

Louis Jadot Château de
Bellevue Morgon

Louis Jadot St-Véran

Sauvion Muscadet

Trimbach Riesling

Germany
Strub Niersteiner Oelberg Kabinett

Italy
Allegrini Valpolicella Classico

Anselmi Soave

Antinori Santa Cristina Sangiovese

Bollini Trentino Pinot Grigio

Boscaini Pinot Grigio

Castello Banfi Toscana Centine

Col d'Orcia Rosso di Montalcino

Frescobaldi Chianti Rufina or
Nipozzano Reserva

Lungarotti Rubesco

Marco Felluga Collio Pinot Grigio

Pighin Pinot Grigio

Taurino Salice Salentino

Zenato Valpolicella

New Zealand
Babich Sauvignon Blanc

Brancott Chardonnay or
Sauvignon Blanc

Glazebrook Sauvignon Blanc

Kim Crawford Sauvignon Blanc

Nobilo Sauvignon Blanc

Oyster Bay Sauvignon Blanc

Saint Clair Sauvignon Blanc

Stoneleigh Chardonnay or
Sauvignon Blanc

Oregon
Argyle Chardonnay

A to Z Wineworks Pinot Noir, Pinot
Gris, Chardonnay, or Pinot Blanc

Cooper Mountain Pinot Noir

King Estate Pinot Gris

Willamette Valley Vineyards
Pinot Noir

Spain
Bodegas Montecillo Crianza

Conde de Valdemar Crianza

Washington State
Columbia Crest Chardonnay, Shiraz,
Merlot, or Cabernet Sauvignon

Covey Run Chardonnay and Merlot

Hogue Cabernet Sauvignon, Pinot
Gris, or Merlot

Ports
Fonseca Bin 27

Sandeman Founders Reserve

Sparkling Wines
Bouvet Brut

Codorniu Brut Classico

Cristalino Brut

Domaine Chandon

Freixenet Brut

Gloria Ferrer Brut

Gruet

Korbel

Scharffenberger

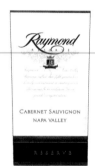

Once-a-Month Wines

($20 to $50; most under $40)

Argentina
Achaval Ferrer Malbec
Alta Vista Malbec Grand Rreserva
Catena Alta Cabernet Sauvignon
Luigi Bosca Malbec Single Vineyard
Mendel Unus
Salentein Malbec

Australia
Penfolds Bin 389

California
Cabernet Sauvignon
Artesa
Beaulieu Rutherford
Beringer Knights Valley
Clos du Val
Geyser Peak Reserve
The Hess Collection
Jordan
Joseph Phelps
Louis Martini
Mondavi
Raymond
Ridge
Turnbull
Whitehall Lane
Chardonnay
Arrowood Grand Archer
Beringer Private Reserve
Chalone
Cuvaison
Ferrari-Carano
Kendall-Jackson Grand Reserve
Mondavi
Sonoma-Cutrer

Merlot
Shafer
Clos du Bois Reserve
Pinot Noir
Acacia
Au Bon Climat
Byron
Calera
Etude
La Crema (Anderson Valley)
Mondavi
Saintsbury (Carneros)
Truchard
Williams Selyem (Sonoma Coast)
Sparkling Wine
Chandon Reserve
Domaine Carneros
Iron Horse
Roederer Estate
Syrah
Fess Parker
Four Vines
Justin
Zinfandel
Ridge Geyserville
Rosenblum (Continente)
Seghesio Old Vine
Champagne
Any non-vintage

Chile
Errazúriz Don Maximiano
Founder's Reserve

France

Château Carbonnieux Blanc

Château de Malle (Sauternes)

Château de Sales

Château Fourcas-Hosten

Château Fuissé (Pouilly-Fuissé)

Château Gloria

Château Lagrezette (Cahors)

Château La Nerthe
Chateauneuf-du-pape

Château Les Ormes de Pez

Château Meyney

Château Olivier Blanc

Château Phélan-Ségur

Château Pontensac

Château Sociando-Mallet

Coudoulet de Beaucastel

Domaine Leroy Bourgogne Rouge

Faiveley Mercurey

Jaboulet Crozes-Hermitage
Domaine de Thalabert

Ladoucette Pouilly-Fumé

Marnier-Lapostolle Château
de Sancerre

Olivier Leflaive Puligny-Montrachet

Pascal Jolivet Pouilly-Fumé

Germany

J.J. Prüm Wehlener Sonnenuhr
Kabinett or Spätlese

Italy

Antinori Badia a Passignano
Chianti Classico

Antinori Tenute Marchese Chianti
Classico Riserva

Badia a Coltibuono Chianti
Classico Riserva

Col d'Orcia Brunello di Montalcino

Mastroberardino Taurasi

Melini Massovecchio Chianti
Classico Riserva

Ruffino Chianti Classico Riserva

New Zealand

Kim Crawford Chardonnay

Oregon

Argyle Pinot Noir

South Africa

Hamilton Russell Pinot Noir

or Chardonnay

Spain

Alvaro Palacios Priorat Les
Terrasses

Bodegas Montecillo Reserva

Bodegas Muga Reserva

Cune Contino Reserva

La Rioja Alta Viña Ardanza
Pesquera

Marqués de Cáceres Crianza

Washington State

Chateau Ste. Michelle Chardonnay
or Cabernet Sauvignon

Chateau Ste.Michelle Eroica
Riesling

L'Ecole No. 41 Cabernet Sauvignon

Once-a-Year Wines
($$$$+)

It's easy to buy these kinds of wines when money is no object! Any wine
retailer would be more than happy to help you spend your money!

Frequently Asked Questions About Wine

What happens when I can't finish the whole bottle of wine?

This is one of the most frequently asked questions in Wine School (although I have never had this problem).

If you still have a portion of the wine left over, whether it be red or white, the bottle should be corked and immediately put into the refrigerator. Don't leave it out on your kitchen counter. Remember, bacteria grow in warm temperatures, and a 70°F+ kitchen will spoil wine very quickly. By refrigerating the wine, most wines will not lose their flavor over a forty-eight-hour period. (Some people swear that the wine even tastes better, although I'm not among them.)

Eventually, the wine will begin to oxidize. This is true of all table wines with an 8 to 14 percent alcohol content. Other wines, such as Ports and Sherries, with a higher alcohol content of 17 to 21 percent, will last longer, but I wouldn't suggest keeping them longer than two weeks.

Another way of preserving wine for an even longer period of time is to buy a small decanter that has a corked top and fill the decanter to the top with the wine. Or go to a hobby or craft store that also carries home winemaking equipment and buy some half bottles and corks.

Remember, the most harmful thing to wine is oxygen, and the less contact with oxygen, the longer the wine will last. That's why some wine collectors also use something called the Vacu-Vin, which pumps air out of the bottle. Other wine collectors spray the bottle with an inert gas such as nitrogen, which is odorless and tasteless, that preserves the wine from oxygen.

Remember, if all else fails, you'll still have a great cooking wine!

Why do I get a headache when I drink wine?

The simple answer may be overconsumption! Seriously though, more than 10 percent of my students are medical doctors, and none of them has been able to give me the definitive answer to this question.

Some people get headaches from white wine, others from red, but when it comes to alcohol consumption, dehydration certainly plays an important role in how you feel the next day. That's why for every glass of wine I consume, I will have two glasses of water to keep my body hydrated.

There are many factors that influence the way alcohol is metabolized in your system. The top three are:

1. health
2. DNA
3. gender

Research is increasingly leaning toward genetics as a reason for chronic headaches.

For those of you who have allergies, different levels of histamines are present in red wines; these can obviously cause discomfort and headaches. I myself am allergic to red wine and I "suffer" every day.

Many doctors have told me that food additives contribute to headaches. There is a natural compound in red wine called tyramine, which is said to dilate blood vessels. Further, many prescription medicines warn about combining with alcohol.

Regarding gender, due to certain stomach enzymes, women absorb more alcohol into their bloodstream than men do. A doctor who advises women that one glass of wine a day is a safe limit is likely to tell men that they can drink two glasses.

Do all wines need corks?

It is a time-honored tradition more than two centuries old to use corks to preserve wine. Most corks come from cork oak trees grown in Portugal and Spain.

The fact is that most wines could be sold without using cork as a stopper. Since 90 percent of all wine is meant to be consumed within one year, a screw cap will work just as well, if not better, than a cork for most wines.

Just think what this would mean to you—no need for a corkscrew, no broken corks and, most important, no more tainted wine caused by contaminated cork.

I do believe that certain wines—those with potential to age for more than five years—are much better off using cork. But also keep in mind, for those real wine collectors, that a cork's life span is approximately twenty-five to thirty years, after which you'd better drink the wine or find somebody to recork it.

Some wineries now use a synthetic cork made from high-grade thermoplastic that is FDA-approved and also recyclable. These corks form a

SCREW-CAP wines represent less than 5% of all bottled wine.

NINEY-THREE PERCENT of New Zealand's bottles have screw-caps, as does seventy-five percent of Australia's.

SOME WINERIES, especially in California, are now using synthetic corks to seal their wine. Since 1993, St. Francis Winery in Sonoma has sealed its wine with a synthetic cork. And the Napa Valley's Plump Jack Winery released their $135/bottle 1997 Reserve Cabernet Sauvignon with a screw cap! Stay tuned for more.

WINES TO BUY NOW AND CELLAR FOR YOUR CHILD'S 21ST BIRTHDAY:

2008 Bordeaux, Napa Cabernet Sauvignon
2007 Sauternes, Rhône (South), Napa Cabernet Sauvignon
2006 Bordeaux (Pomerol), Rhône (North), Barolo, Barbaresco, Brunello di Montalcino, German (Auslese and Sove), Malbec from Argentina
2005 Bordeaux, Sauternes, Burgundy, Southern Rhône, Piedmont, Tuscany, Germany, Rioja, Ribera Del Duero, Southern Australia, Napa Cabernet Sauvignon, Washington Cabernet Sauvignon
2004 Napa Cabernet Sauvignon, Piedmont
2003 Rhône (North and South). Sauternes, Bordeaux, Port
2002 Napa Cabernet Sauvignon, Germany*, Burgundy**, Sauternes
2001 Napa Cabernet Sauvignon, Sauternes, Germany*, Rioja and Ribera del Duero
2000 Bordeaux, Châteauneuf-du-Pape, Piedmont, Amarone, Port
1999 Piedmont, Rhône (North), California Zinfandel, Burgundy**

near-perfect seal, so leakage, evaporation, and off flavors are virtually eliminated. They open with traditional corkscrews and allow wine to be stored upright.

But many wineries around the world use the Stelvin Screw Cap, especially in California (Bonny Doon, Sonoma Cutrer, etc.), Australia, New Zealand, and Austria.

What is a "corked" wine?

This is a very serious problem for wine lovers! There are some estimates that 3 to 5 percent of all wines have been contaminated and spoiled by a faulty cork. The principal cause of corked wine is a compound called TCA, short for 2,4,6-trichloranisole.

When we find such a bottle at the Wine School, we make sure that every student gets a chance to smell a "corked" wine. It's a smell they won't soon forget!

Some of my students describe it as a dank, wet, moldy, cellar smell, and some describe it as a wet cardboard smell. It overpowers the fruit smell in the wine, making the wine undrinkable. It can happen in a ten-dollar bottle of wine or a thousand-dollar bottle of wine.

How do I decant a bottle of wine?

1. Completely remove the capsule from the neck of the bottle. This will enable you to see the wine clearly as it passes through the neck.
2. Light a candle. Most red wines are bottled in very dark green glass, making it difficult to see the wine pass through the neck of the bottle. A candle will give you the extra illumination you need and add a theatrical touch. A flashlight would do, but candles keep things simple.
3. Hold the decanter (a carafe or glass pitcher can also be used for this purpose) firmly in your hand.
4. Hold the wine bottle in your other hand, and gently pour the wine into the decanter while holding both over the candle at such an angle that you can see the wine pass through the neck of the bottle.
5. Continue pouring in one uninterrupted motion until you see the first signs of sediment.
6. Stop decanting once you see sediment. At this point, if there is still wine left, let it stand until the sediment settles. Then continue decanting.

What's that funny-looking stuff attached to the bottom of my cork?

Tartaric acid, or tartrates, is sometimes found on the bottom of a bottle of wine or the cork. Tartaric acid is a harmless crystalline deposit that looks like glass or rock candy. In red wines, the crystals take on a rusty, reddish-brown color from the tannin.

Most tartrates are removed at the winery by lowering the temperature of the wine before it is bottled. Obviously this does not work with all wines, and if you keep your wine at a very cold temperature for a long period of time (for example, in your refrigerator), you can end up with this deposit on your cork.

Cool-climate regions like Germany have a greater chance of producing the crystallization effect.

Does the age of the vine affect the quality of the wine?

You will sometimes see on French wine labels the term *Vieilles Vignes* ("old vines"). In California, I've tasted many Zinfandels that were made from vines that were more than seventy-five years old. Many wine tasters, including myself, believe that these old vines create a different complexity and taste than do younger vines.

In many countries, grapes from vines three years old or younger cannot be made into a winery's top wine. In Bordeaux, France, Château Lafite-Rothschild produces a second wine, called Carruades de Lafite-Rothschild, which is made from the vineyard's youngest vines (less than fifteen years old).

As a vine gets older, especially over thirty years, it starts losing its fruit-production value. In commercial vineyards, vines will slow down their production at about twenty years of age, and most vines are replanted by their fiftieth birthday.

What are the hot areas in wine?

It seems as if most countries are catching the wine craze. Here are some areas where I have seen major growth and improvement in quality, especially with certain grape varieties, over the last twenty years:

New Zealand: Sauvignon Blanc, Chardonnay, and Pinot Noir
Chile: Cabernet Sauvignon
Argentina: Malbec
Hungary: Tokaji (one of the greatest dessert wines in the world)

1998 Bordeaux (St-Émilion/Pomerol), Rhône (South), Piedmont (Barolo, Barbaresco)
1997 Napa Cabernet Sauvignon, Tuscany (Chianti, Brunello), Piedmont, Amarone, Port, Australian Shiraz
1996 Burgundy, Piedmont, Bordeaux (Médoc), Burgundy**, Germany*, vintage Champagne
1995 Bordeaux, Rhône, Rioja, Napa Cabernet Sauvignon, vintage Champagne
1994 Port, Napa Cabernet Sauvignon and Zinfandel, Rioja
1993 Napa Cabernet Sauvignon and Zinfandel
1992 Port, Napa Cabernet Sauvignon and Zinfandel
1991 Rhône (North), Port, Napa Cabernet Sauvignon
1990 Bordeaux, Napa Cabernet Sauvignon, Rhône, Burgundy**, Tuscany (Brunello), Piedmont, Amarone, Sauternes, Champagne, Germany*
1989 Bordeaux, Rhône, Piedmont, Rioja
1988 Sauternes, Rhône (North), Piedmont
1987 Napa Cabernet Sauvignon and Zinfandel
1986 Bordeaux, Sauternes, Napa Cabernet Sauvignon
1985 Bordeaux, Port, Rhône (North), Champagne, Piedmont, Amarone

*Auslese and above **Grand Cru

Austria: Grüner Veltliner
Portugal: Not just Port anymore! Try Bacca Velha and you'll see what I mean.
South Africa: Sauvignon Blanc, Pinot Noir, and Syrah

And what will you be writing about in the year 2025?

Argentina, the United States, Australia, Chile, and China.

What are the most important books for your wine library?

Thank you for buying my wine book, which I hope you have found useful for a general understanding of wine. As with any hobby, there is always a thirst for more knowledge.

I hope that you noticed that at the end of each chapter, I recommended specific wine books for the different wine regions.

The following is a list of general books I consider required reading if you want to delve further into this fascinating subject:

The Essential Wine Book, Oz Clarke
Oz Clarke's New Encyclopedia of Wine
Oz Clarke's Wine Atlas
Great Wine Made Simple, Andrea Robinson
Hugh Johnson's Modern Encyclopedia of Wine
World Atlas of Wine, Hugh Johnson
The Wine Bible, Karen MacNeil
Wine for Dummies, Ed McCarthy and Mary Ewing Mulligan
Keys to the Cellar by Peter D. Meltzer
Oxford Companion to Wine, Jancis Robinson
The New Sotheby's Wine Encyclopedia, Tom Stevenson
The Wine Report, Tom Stevenson
Parker's Wine Buyers Guide, Robert M. Parker Jr.

Since the above volumes are sometimes encyclopedic in nature, I always carry with me two pocket guides to wine:

Hugh Johnson's Pocket Encyclopedia of Wine
Oz Clarke's Pocket Wine Guide

Where can I get the best wine service in the United States?

The James Beard Awards have recognized the following restaurants with the Outstanding Wine Service Award:

1993	Charlie Trotter's, Chicago	2001	French Laundry, Yountville, California
1994	Valentino, Santa Monica		
1995	Montrachet, New York	2002	Gramercy Tavern, New York
1996	Chanterelle, New York	2003	Daniel, New York
1997	The Four Seasons, New York	2004	Babbo, New York
		2005	Veritas, New York
1998	The Inn at Little Washington, Washington, Virginia	2006	Aureole, Las Vegas
		2007	Citronelle, Washington, D.C.
		2008	Eleven Madison Park, New York
1999	Union Square Café, New York	2009	Le Bernardin, New York City
2000	Rubicon, San Francisco		

The past winners for Wine and Spirits Professional of the Year Award are:

1991	Robert Mondavi, Robert Mondavi Winery
1992	Andre Tchelistcheff, Beaulieu Winery
1993	Kevin Zraly, Windows on the World, New York
1994	Randall Grahm, Bonny Doon Vineyard, Santa Cruz
1995	Marvin Shanken, *Wine Spectator*
1996	Jack and Jaimie Davies, Schramsberg Vineyards
1997	Zelma Long, Simi Winery
1998	Robert M. Parker Jr., *The Wine Advocate*
1999	Frank Prial, *The New York Times*
2000	Kermit Lynch, Berkeley
2001	Gerald Asher, *Gourmet*
2002	Andrea Immer, French Culinary Institute
2003	Fritz Maytag, Anchor Brewing Co.
2004	Karen MacNeil, Culinary Institute of America
2005	Joseph Bastianich, Italian Wine Merchants, New York
2006	Daniel Johnnes, The Dinex Group, New York
2007	Paul Draper, Ridge Vineyards
2008	Terry Theise, Terry Theise Estate Selection
2009	Dale DeGroff, Dale DeGroff Co., Inc.

What's the difference between California and French wines, and who makes the better wines?

You really think I'm going to answer that? California and France both make great wines, but the French make the best French wines!

From production strategy to weather, each region's profile is distinct. California wines and French wines share many similarities. The greatest similarity is that both France and California grow most of the same grape varieties. They also have many differences. The biggest differences are soil, climate, and tradition.

The French regard their soil with reverence and believe that the best wines only come from the greatest soil. When grapes were originally planted in California, the soil was not one of the major factors in determining which grapes were planted where. Over recent decades, this has become a much more important aspect for the vineyard owners in California, and it's not unheard of for a winemaker to say that his or her best Cabernet Sauvignon comes from a specific area.

As far as weather goes, the temperatures in Napa and Sonoma are different from those in Burgundy and Bordeaux. The fact is, that while European vintners get gray hair over pesky problems like cold snaps and rainstorms in the growing season, Californians can virtually count on abundant sunshine and warm temperatures.

Tradition is the biggest difference between the two, and I'm not just talking about winemaking. For example, vineyard and winery practices in Europe have remained virtually unchanged for generations; and these age-old techniques—some of which were written into law—define each region's own style. But in California, where few traditions exist, vintners are free to experiment with modern technology and create new products based on consumer demand. If you've ever had a wine called Two Buck Chuck, you know what I mean.

It is sometimes very difficult for me to sit in a tasting and compare a California Chardonnay and a French white Burgundy, since they have been making wines in Burgundy for the last 1,600 years and the renaissance of California wines is not yet 50 years old.

I buy both French and California wines for my personal cellar, and sometimes my choice has to do totally with how I feel that day or what food I'm having: Do I want to end up in Bordeaux or the Napa Valley?

How long should I age my wine?

The Wall Street Journal recently came out with an article stating that most people have one or two wines that they've been saving for years for a special occasion. This is probably not a good idea!

More than 90 percent of all wine—red, white, and rosé—should be consumed within a year. With that in mind, the following is a guideline to aging wine from the best producers in the best years:

WHITE

California Chardonnay	3–8+ years
French White Burgundy	2–10+ years
German Riesling (Auslese, Beerenauslese, and Trockenbeerenauslese)	3–30+ years
French Sauternes	3–30+ years

RED

Bordeaux Châteaux	5–30+ years
California Cabernet Sauvignon	3–15+ years
Argentine Malbec	3–15+ years
Barolo and Barbaresco	5–25+ years
Brunello di Montalcino	3–15+ years
Chianti Classico Riservas	3–10+ years
Spanish Riojas (Gran Reservas)	5–20+ years
Hermitage/Shiraz	5–25+ years
California Zinfandel	5–15+ years
California Merlot	2–10+ years
California/Oregon Pinot Noirs	2–5+ years
French Red Burgundy	3–8+ years
Vintage Ports	10–40+ years

SOME WINES THAT ARE READY TO DRINK IMMEDIATELY:

Riesling (dry)
Sauvignon Blanc
Pinot Grigio
Beaujolais

THE OLDEST bottle of wine still aging in Bordeaux is a 1797 Lafite-Rothschild.

There are always exceptions to the rules when it comes to generalizing about the aging of wine (especially considering the variations in vintages), hence the plus signs in the table above. I have had Bordeaux wines more than a hundred years old that were still going strong. It is also not unlikely to find a great Sauternes or Port that still needs time to age after its fiftieth birthday. But the above age spans represent more than 95 percent of the wines in their categories.

Windows on the World:
A Personal History

BY KEVIN ZRALY

"One evening in 1975, my father, Joe, came home late for a family dinner. After another marathon day of creating and planning, he was full of excitement and teeming with enthusiasm. 'What do you think if we called the place Windows on the World?' he asked. In my infinite wisdom I thought, Not bad, but will people remember the name?"

—CHARLES BAUM

"The building wasn't finished when we first went up to the 107th floor. We stepped out of the elevator into a cavernous, undifferentiated space; onto a million sheets of plywood, ducking under scaffolds, the winds blowing, inching closer and closer to the edge to take in the view. I was petrified, and then I saw it: the shocking beauty of the city my father loved."

—HILARY BAUM

Joe Baum on top of Two World Trade Center, overlooking One World Trade Center and Windows on the World

WINDOWS ON THE WORLD OPENED its elevator doors for the first time on April 12, 1976, as a private luncheon club. The press had been writing about its opening for months, speculating on whether the whole project—both the restaurant and the World Trade Center complex that housed it—could be pulled off. After all, never before had a project this large been attempted. The World Trade Center was not only designed to include the tallest building in the world, it was going to be one of the largest urban centers ever built, with more than 40,000 World Trade Center office workers and 150,000 commuters passing through the complex every day.

All eyes were on Joe Baum, the man in charge of food services for the World Trade Center complex and mastermind behind the Windows on the World Restaurant. Joe had created some of New York's most successful landmark restaurants, including the Four Seasons, La Fonda del Sol, and the Forum of the Twelve Caesars.

He was known in the industry as a maverick, a restaurant genius, and a pit bull, and was often called all these names at the same time. In 1970, Joe Baum had signed a contract with the Port Authority of New York and New Jersey to design and manage all the restaurant and food-service areas of the World Trade Center. Joe and his associates, Michael Whiteman and Dennis Sweeney, conceived and organized twenty-two restaurants that were to be located throughout the complex.

Joe had grandiose ideas for the restaurant on top of the World Trade Center—ideas that would cost a lot of money.

In the early seventies, New York City was in the midst of a severe fiscal crisis, and many New Yorkers were against building the World Trade Center to begin with. So Joe called his former classmate from Cornell, Curt Strand, president of Hilton International, to partner with the Port Authority, and together they formed a company called Inhilco.

Hilton International named Joe Baum president of Inhilco. With the backing of the Port Authority, more than $17 million was spent developing Windows on the World. Their main focus was the 107th floor of One World Trade Center, which they divided into five parts: the restaurant (which seated nearly three hundred guests); the City Lights Bar; Hors D'Oeuvrerie, which served everything except the main course; the Cellar in the Sky, a glass-enclosed working wine cellar that seated just thirty-six guests and served a seven-course, five-wine, one-seating dinner; and six private banquet rooms capable of accommodating more than three hundred people. All together, Windows on the World spanned one acre, 107 stories up in the sky.

Joe Baum was a master contractor. He hired the best culinary talent available. He asked James Beard and Jacques Pépin to help develop the menus, Warren Platner to design the restaurant, Milton Glaser to design all the graphics, and Barbara Kafka to select everything from glassware to table settings. Joe also hired top restaurant managers, including Alan Lewis, his partner in other great New York restaurants, and a staff that would do anything Baum requested.

Joe was looking for a young American to run his wine department. I was lucky enough to be hired as the first cellarmaster at Windows on the World. I took the job after consulting with friends, many of whom warned me about leaving my job as a wine salesman to work at Windows. They gave me three reasons not to take the job:

1. In 1976, no one went downtown after 6 p.m.
2. Rooftop restaurants weren't considered quality operations.
3. Joe Baum had the reputation of being difficult to work with.

On all three counts, I learned it just wasn't so. In fact, I knew it was going to be a great restaurant and job when I asked Joe about creating the wine list. He said: "It's very simple. I want you to create the biggest and the best wine

The Cellar in the Sky Restaurant

"As one of the first to join the 'Baum Squad,' I caught Joe's contagious fervor about Windows on the World right away and always knew it would be a smash success. And having the opportunity to work with Joe's 'kitchen cabinet'—James Beard, Craig Claiborne, Albert Stockli, Pierre Franey, Jacques Pépin, and Albert Kumin—was an education in itself. But nothing in my life will ever compare to opening day in April of 1976, a day of such excitement and wonder over this uber-restaurant."

—DENNIS SWEENEY

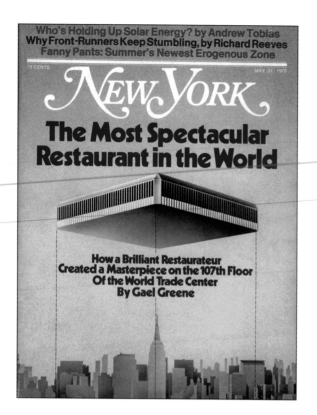

New York magazine cover, May 1976

"On July 4, 1976, Windows on the World was filled with celebrities for the bicentennial fireworks display. I was given the very pleasant task of escorting Princess Grace of Monaco. As we watched the extravaganza over the Statue of Liberty, Princess Grace held my hand very tightly because the fireworks made her somewhat nervous. I asked if the moment reminded her of To Catch a Thief and her very famous, very passionate scene with Cary Grant, set to the backdrop of fireworks. She was astounded I knew the film and the scene. So I told her that if she wanted to watch the film again, she could that night, because it was being shown at 11:30, on Channel 2."

—MELVIN FREEMAN, Page, 1976–93 and 1996–2001

list that New York has ever seen—and don't worry about how much it costs!" There I was, a twenty-five-year-old kid in a candy store—only it sold wine!

In May of 1976, before Windows on the World's official opening, the cover of *New York* magazine read: THE MOST SPECTACULAR RESTAURANT IN THE WORLD—HOW A BRILLIANT RESTAURATEUR CREATED A MASTERPIECE ON THE 107TH FLOOR OF THE WORLD TRADE CENTER. The article was written by the illustrious Gael Greene. Some of the superlatives from that article included: "a miracle," "a masterpiece," "a dream," "a triumph," and "almost unreal." It went on, "No other sky-high restaurant quite prepares you for the astonishment of the horizon."

The World Trade Center and Windows on the World also became symbols for the financial turnaround of New York City and their completion played a key role in the revitalization of lower Manhattan. This was underscored the year Windows on the World opened, 1976, which was also America's bicentennial year. Imagine an unobstructed view from the 107th floor of the spectacularly refurbished Statue of Liberty and the entire New York Harbor with its flotilla of tall ships. What a sight it was! Seeing the bicentennial fireworks from Windows became the hottest ticket in the world.

On that memorable July Fourth evening, I went alone to the top of One World Trade Center (the broadcast antennae and barriers had not yet been erected) and watched all the fireworks displays within a sixty-mile radius. I knew I'd made the right decision to work at Windows on the World; I remember thinking that life didn't get much better than this. I was serving wine to kings, queens, presidents, sports heroes, and movie stars. During the next five years, I met every celebrity I had ever heard of or read about.

Windows on the World was an instant success and was booked months in advance.

The Windows on the World Wine School has operated continuously for the last thirty years, since the opening of the restaurant in 1976, even during times of uncertainty. The Wine School started with a small group of ten lunch club members in 1976. Club members started inviting their friends, who then invited their friends. Soon the friends of club members outnumbered the club members. Still, the class list kept growing. In 1980, we opened the Wine School to the public. Since then, more than nineteen thousand students have attended classes.

So what made Windows on the World so great? Was it the sixty-second elevator ride? Was it the menu concept? Was it the youthful, energetic staff? Was it the extensive and outrageously low-priced wine list? Or was it the most spectacular view in the world?

For me, it was all of the above.

I continued as cellarmaster and, over the next four years, Windows on the World sold more wine than any other restaurant in the United States—and probably the world. The first five years of Windows on the World had been nonstop.

In 1980, I was named wine director for Windows on the World and Hilton International, and in 1981, I cofounded the New York Wine Experience, which is a celebration of the best wines from all over the world. The New York Wine Experience was held for the first three years at Windows on the World. Events like this, combined with our superb, well-priced wine list, helped establish Windows on the World as a true destination for wine lovers. We drew amateur wine enthusiasts as well as professionals; we attracted students and teachers alike; anyone seriously interested in wine stopped up for a bottle or two and a meal, including many who wanted to work in our wine cellar.

In 1985, my book *Windows on the World Complete Wine Course* made its debut, putting the Wine School in print for the first time. Over the next eight years, Windows continued to be one of the most successful restaurants in the world, the Wine School enrollment continued to grow, and the book became the best-selling wine book in the United States.

By the time Windows' fifteenth anniversary rolled around in 1991, both the restaurant and lower Manhattan had experienced their share of ups and downs. In 1987, Wall Street suffered a steep drop in stock market prices, which affected the restaurant business for several years. That same year, Ladbroke, a hotel and gaming company, bought out Hilton International and became the owner of Windows. As the stock market recovered, so did the businesses in lower Manhattan. By then, however, the notion of opening a fine restaurant near the financial district was no longer a novelty, and business at Windows faced quite a bit of competition from the proliferation of restaurants in its neighborhood.

"Windows on the World was a miracle to conceive and open. In the early seventies, rooftop restaurants were failing—it seemed like an impossible dream. But with the genius of Joe Baum, and the determination of many individuals, including myself, to have a restaurant on top of the World Trade Center, the dream became a reality."
—GUY TOZZOLI, Director, World Trade Center Association, 1970 to present

"Even more than high school and college, my 'education' at Windows on the World University has stood me well in tackling the challenges of the world at large."
—MICHAEL SKURNIK, Assistant Cellarmaster, 1977–78

"It has been the greatest privilege for me to be part of Windows on the World and its wonderful team members, from the inception of the one-acre restaurant complex back in 1974 and during its first 12 years of operation. Windows on the World wore a smile of confidence from the day it opened. Overnight, the restaurants and banquet rooms gained worldwide recognition. Its attention to detail, its definite philosophy about wine and food, and its innovative approach to wine merchandising and education were Windows' greatest assets. Windows became a 'premier' destination—a place to celebrate, host a party, or entertain in style for business or romance."
—TONI AIGNER, President, Inhilco, 1978–90

"I moved to New York in June 1990 and worked in the wine department of Windows during 1991 and 1992. . . . My greatest memories are the nights when the view north over the city captured all the excitement and energy of New York." —BRUCE SANDERSON, Assistant Cellarmaster, 1991–92

FRIDAY, FEBRUARY 26, 1993—THE BOMBING AT THE WTC

The first terrorist attack on the World Trade Center took place on February 26, 1993, at 12:18 p.m. Six people were killed, including one of our employees who worked in the receiving department in the World Trade Center basement. Food and wine author Andrea Robinson, cellarmaster at the time, escorted all our patrons down 107 flights of stairs to safety.

Windows on the World shut down after the bombing, leaving more than four hundred food-service people without jobs. Within six months I was the last Windows on the World employee on the payroll. Windows on the World lay dormant from February 26, 1993, until June 1996. My Wine School coordinator and I were the only people allowed to enter Windows on the World after the 1993 bombing. It was a very lonely time.

Although the restaurant was closed from 1993 until 1996, with the help of Andrea; Johannes Tromp, the director of Windows on the World; and Jules Roinnel, the director of the World Trade Center Club, the Wine School kept going. After the 1993 bombing, American Express gave us a temporary office across the street from the World Trade Center. Our view was of One World Trade Center and we would often stand at the windows watching tow trucks remove car after car—all destroyed—from the underground World Trade Center garages.

"I remember the first terrorist attack in 1993. We walked down the stairs with our lunch guests. I returned to work with Kevin when we reopened in 1996. I will never forget the extraordinary joy of seeing and touching those wines again, and welcoming our wine students back, and just being 'home,' where everything sparkled, most of all, the people."
—ANDREA ROBINSON, Cellarmaster, 1992–93

"Windows on the World was brilliantly conceived and truly unique. Being a Dutch immigrant managing the complex of restaurants and private dining rooms, with its 440 culinary and hospitality professionals high above Manhattan, was an unforgettable experience. I feel honored to have been a temporary guardian of this magnificent New York City institution."
—JOHANNES TROMP, Director, 1989–93

"Windows was silent when I ran the Wine School, but I relished its solitude. I roamed its floors, inspected its rooms, absorbed all that was left frozen in time. Like Jack Nicholson in The Shining, I could sense the energy it embodied, feel its buzz, envision its diners, find myself immersed in the dream. But unlike Jack's, my visions embodied warmth and peace. The space lived and breathed even when empty and will continue to do so in our hearts."
—REBECCA CHAPPA, Wine School Coordinator, 1994–95

"When I reflect on the 22 years I spent at Windows, no singular event immediately comes to mind but rather a series of images: the faces of children pressed up against the windows, the sun setting over the Statue of Liberty, and the laughter and joy of thousands of guests who created a lifetime of cherished memories."
—JULES ROINNEL, Director, The World Trade Center Club, 1979–2001

World Trade Center, view from New Jersey

During the spring semester of 1993, Andrea and I moved the school to the top of Seven World Trade Center. It remained there for the rest of 1993 and all of 1994. From 1994 to mid-1995, we held classes in the oval room on the forty-fourth floor of One World Trade Center, and from mid-1995 until the restaurant reopened in 1996, we operated from the newly reopened Vista Hotel (Marriott). I'm proud the Wine School remained open during those difficult years. It kept the memory of Windows alive and became a symbol to everyone that Windows would come back.

Following the 1993 bombing, the Port Authority concluded that both the 106th and 107th floors needed structural repairs, and meanwhile they would begin a search for a new operator for the restaurants. Again, requests for proposals went out, and this time more than thirty restaurant operators expressed interest in taking over Windows on the World. A review committee was formed by the Port Authority to examine each proposal and make recommendations. They narrowed it down to three entries: Alan Stillman of the Smith & Wollensky Restaurant Group, owners of Smith & Wollensky, the Post House, The Manhattan Ocean Club, Park Avenue Café, Cité, and Maloney & Porcelli; Warner LeRoy, of Tavern on the Green, Maxwell's Plum, and later, the Russian Tea Room; and Joe Baum, the original creator of Windows on the World, who was then operating the Rainbow Room.

The Port Authority awarded the contract to Joe Baum, and the renaissance of Windows on the World began. Both Andrea and I were brought back: Andrea to develop the wine list and beverage program, and I to continue with the Wine School. In all, the new staff totaled more than four hundred employees and represented some twenty-five nationalities.

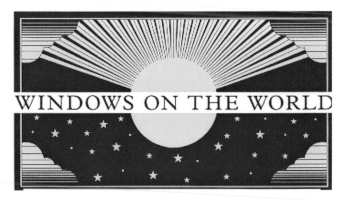

Both the Windows logo designed for the reopening in 1996 and the original logo on page 318 were created by Milton Glaser.

"Windows was the kind of place that let you come as you are, or wanted to be. You could be formal or relaxed, fancy or plain, intimate or gregarious. . . . Tourists, workers, lovers, families, dancers, and partygoers: Windows welcomed the world to the Trade Center."
—TIM SHEEHAN, Port Authority of NY/NJ

"Despite its ultimate destruction, my recollections of Windows are those of triumph. We opened it in 1976 during the depths of New York's recession, and its astounding success symbolized the city's commercial and social recovery. We re-created it after the 1993 terrorist attack on the World Trade Center and established a triumphant return as the country's largest-grossing restaurant. Windows triumphed by proving that a rooftop restaurant wasn't by definition a tourist trap. It triumphed by providing interior excitement that was better than the view. It triumphed by proving that quality beats gimmickry and that great design outlasts ephemeral themes. Most of all, it triumphed because its employees loved the place as much as its customers."
—MICHAEL WHITEMAN

"At Windows, Joe Baum led us to the promised land, an adventure in imagination, the pursuit of the unexpected and enormous scale. There has never been anything else like it." —MILTON GLASER, Designer

"What I remember most about Windows on the World is the employee cafeteria. It was in that room that friends congregated to eat, talk, and enjoy the view of the three bridges below us. It was here where laughter and happiness prevailed. Windows was my family in New York, my world that I loved so dearly."
—INEZ RIBUSTELLO,
Beverage Manager, 1999–2001

"There I saw the world from one and all other Windows of opportunity. . . . There my future began, from educating myself to educating my kids. There I learned the art of hospitality and traveled to teach others, those in the industry who remain and those who will be remembered."
—CARLOS A. GARCIA, Chief Executive Steward, 1976–86 and 1996–2001

"Windows on the World was an opportunity for Joe Baum, me, and everyone who worked with us to explore their dreams and pursue their ambitions in a spectacular environment."
—DAVID EMIL, Owner, 1995–2001

"Directing what was perhaps the most famous restaurant operation in the world challenged my intellectual and emotional being every day. The greatest of these challenges was, by the single element of location, that we would have the privilege of serving the most diverse clientele of any restaurant in the world and, in turn, employing the most diverse workforce of any restaurant in the world. The social interaction and collaboration of so many unique human beings, on both sides of the equation, was the Windows on the World experience. To have had the opportunity to be an integral part of the success of that collaboration made it an incredibly rewarding experience. In this respect, we truly were the Windows on the World." —GLENN VOGT, General Manager, 1997–2001

"Windows on the World was an inviting and hospitable place. . . . At Windows, everything seemed possible: fine wine, great food, and conviviality. There, floating high above the Earth, we never forgot we were citizens of the World. We welcomed one and all to dine, drink, and enjoy the sweetness of life."
—MICHAEL LOMONACO, Executive Chef/Director, 1997–2001

The reopening of Windows on the World in June of 1996—twenty years almost to the month after its first opening—was accomplished with Joe Baum's usual kinetic energy, *joie de vivre*, and theatrical hoopla. Joe and his partners, the Emil family, reconceived the restaurant to make it the ultimate American-style food and wine experience. They took a big risk by committing to American cooking, but it paid off. Their willingness to do so made Windows the best it ever was. Windows on the World received two stars from *The New York Times*, three stars from *Crain's*, a 22 in the *Zagat* restaurant guide, and ranked in the top listings in *Wine Spectator* for overall dining.

Sadly, as Windows resumed its place on top of the world—having achieved high marks for both quality and service—Joe Baum died. That was in October 1998.

Over the next three years, Windows on the World remained a premier destination for wine, dining, and special events. One important change for me was the closing of the Cellar in the Sky, that intimate, romantically lit dining room lined with wine bottles. The Cellar in the Sky had been an integral part of the old Windows on the World, but by 1996 restaurants around the country were also doing food and wine pairings. It was time to replace the Cellar with something new. That something new was a restaurant called Wild Blue. Wild Blue was a

Executive Chef/Director Michael Lomonaco and Chef Michael Ammirati in the Windows on the World kitchen

restaurant within a restaurant—a place for chef Michael Lomonaco and his staff to show off their culinary skills. Wild Blue received four stars from *Crain's*, a 25 in *Zagat*, a spot in the top-ten list of New York restaurants in *Wine Spectator*, and a rating as one of New York's best by *Esquire*.

Windows was the best it could be on September 10, 2001. It was generating more than $37 million in revenues and was the number-one dollar-volume restaurant in the United States. Of that $37 million, upwards of $6 million came from the sale of wines from among our 1,400 different selections. We were enthusiastic about our future and were excitedly preparing for our twenty-fifth anniversary celebration in October 2001.

On September 11, 2001, the world changed. What began as a beautiful, pristine September morning ended in a dark nightmare of death and destruction. Seventy-two coworkers, one security officer, and six construction workers, who were building the new wine cellar at Windows on the World, died in the worst terrorist attack in American history.

For me, the day is still incomprehensible. The loss of my friends and coworkers remains heavy in my heart. The World Trade Center complex was my New York City. It was my neighborhood. I shopped there. I stayed at the Marriott Hotel with my family. I lost my home and community of twenty-five years, a community I watched being built.

Windows on the World no longer exists, but the reflections of those windows will remain with me forever.

Overlooking the Brooklyn Bridge

"On Monday, September 10, I was hosting my class called 'Spirits in the Skybox,' a name that has haunting implications. When we finished, my cohost and I invited a few friends and some members of the press to join us for a quick drink in the bar. I usually have cocktails, but this time we ordered Champagne. There was no particular celebration; the group just seemed to click, so we had several more bottles of Champagne and food. A woman DJ began spinning records. Someone in our group knew her, so we stayed and ended the evening dancing. I awoke Tuesday morning to the horror of the terrorist attack that finished off that medium-sized city called the World Trade Center. I will cherish the gift I was given of that last spontaneous celebration in Joe Baum's majestic Windows on the World. We were unknowingly lifting our glasses that night in farewell to all those friends and colleagues we would lose the following day."
—DALE DeGROFF, Master Mixologist

Afterword: Looking Back, with Gratitude

WILL ALWAYS REMEMBER:

- working with and learning from John Novi at the Depuy Canal House, 1970–76
- my first visit to a winery, in 1970
- my first wine classes, in 1971 (one where I was a student and the other where I was the teacher)
- hitchhiking to California to visit the wine country, in 1972
- teaching a two-credit course as a junior in college (open only to seniors), in 1973
- Father Sam Matarazzo, my early spiritual leader
- living and studying wine in Europe, 1974–75
- planting my own vineyard (three-time failure), 1974, 1981, 1992; making my own wine, in 1984 (so-so)—trying again (2006)
- the excitement of opening Windows on the World, in 1976
- the support and friendship of Jules Roinnel, going back to our earliest days together at Windows
- wine tastings with Alexis Bespaloff
- Mohonk Mountain House in New Paltz, New York, where ideas come easy
- Curt Strand and Toni Aigner of Hilton International
- evening, late-night, and early morning wine discussions with Alexis Lichine in Bordeaux
- the adviser and great listener Peter Sichel, whose generosity of spirit inspired the way I teach and share my wine knowledge
- sharing great old vintages with Peter Bienstock
- Jules Epstein, for his advice and sharing his wine collection
- touring the world with wine expert Robin Kelley O'Connor
- those who are no longer here to share a glass of wine: Craig Claiborne, Joseph Baum, Alan Lewis, Raymond Wellington, and my father, Charles
- creating and directing the New York Wine Experience, 1981–91
- witnessing the success of Michael Skurnik, who worked with me at Windows in the late 1970s and quickly rose to fame as a great importer of wines
- watching my former student Andrea Robinson turn into a superstar wine-and-food personality and author
- the Food Network's *Wines A to Z* with Alan Richman

- reading and enjoying the observations of the great wine writers and tasters (listed throughout the book)
- having the opportunity to meet all the passionate winemakers, vineyardists, and owners of the great wineries of the world
- the wine events, wine dinners, and tastings around the country that I have had the privilege of attending
- all the groups that have invited me to entertain and educate them about wine
- writing the first chapter of this book with Kathleen Talbert in 1983
- the original Sterling Publishing team of Burton Hobson, Lincoln Boehm, and Charles Nurnberg
- Marcus Leaver, CEO of Sterling Publishing, for his tremendous support on the twenty-fifth edition
- the Sterling Publishing team of Jason Prince, Carlo DeVito, Leigh Ann Ambrosi, Caroline Brown, Tara Cuskley, and Kate Rados
- Steve Magnuson, who has a special talent for taking my ideas and helping me put them into words
- all my editors over the last two decades, especially Felicia Sherbert, Stephen Topping, Hannah Reich, Becky Maines, and Mary Hern
- the Sterling team assembled for the twentieth anniversary edition—Laurie Kahn, Rena Kornbluh, Julie Schroeder, Jeff Ward, Becky Maines, Mike Hollitscher, Pip Tannenbaum, and Sara Cheney—and the more recent additions of Chrissy Kwasnik, Nancy Field, Melanie Gold, Amy Lapides, Matt Mullin, Josh Karpf, Fritz Metsch, and Celia Fuller
- Karen Nelson for twenty-five years of beautiful cover designs
- Mary Hern, for her diligent work on the twenty-fifth anniversary edition
- Jim Anderson, who designed the original edition; and Richard Oriolo for capturing my spirit in subsequent editions
- Barnes & Noble, for always supporting my book
- Carmen Bissell, Raymond DePaul, and Faye Friedman for their help with the Wine School
- all my pourers at the school over the last thirty years
- having a great relationship with my New York City wine-school peers, especially Harriet Lembeck (Beverage Program); Mary Ewing-Mulligan (International Wine Center); and Robert Millman and Howard Kaplan (Executive Wine Seminars)
- the nineteen thousand students who have attended the Windows on the World Wine School, which celebrates its thirty-fourth anniversary in 2010
- the Baum-Emil team, who re-created Windows on the World in 1996
- conducting the Sherry-Lehmann/Kevin Zraly Master Wine Class with Michael Aaron, Michael Yurch, Chris Adams, and Shyda Gilmer

- Michael Stengel and Kathleen Duffy at the Marriott Marquis Hotel NYC, and a special thank you to Carlos Vegerano
- Jennifer Redmond, who assisted with the Wine School both in New Paltz and in New York City
- John and Linda Bono of Headington Wines & Liquors in New York City
- Alan Stillman, founder, chairman, and CEO of the Smith & Wollensky Restaurant Group
- the changing role of women in the wine industry (thank God!)
- being honored for "loving wine" by the James Beard Foundation
- teaching wine at Cornell University and the Culinary Institute of America
- being a member of the Culinary Institute's Board of Trustees
- Frank Prial and Florence Fabricant of *The New York Times* for their continual support
- Robert M. Parker Jr., who so generously donated his time and talents to aid the families of September 11th
- all the "special" wine friends who have "helped" me deplete my wine cellar over the years
- those who have tried to keep me organized in my business life: Ellen Kerr, Claire Josephs, Lois Arrighi, Sara Hutton, Andrea Immer, Dawn Lamendola, Catherine Fallis, Rebecca Chapa, Gina D'Angelo-Mullen, and Michelle Woodruff
- Herb Schutte, my distributor analyst
- my wife of 19 years, Ana Fabiano (a former student who needed extra help after class!), thanks for all of your support on the twenty-fifth edition!
- my four best vintages: Anthony (1991), Nicolas (1993), Harrison (1997), and Adriana (1999)
- my mom, Kathleen
- my sisters, Sharon and Kathy
- everyone who worked at Windows on the World, especially my colleagues in the wine department
- my continuing grief at the loss of those friends and coworkers who lost their lives on September 11th

A Final Note

If this were an award-acceptance speech, I probably would have gotten the hook after the first three bullet points. Still, I'm sure I've forgotten to name at least one or two folks—an occupational hazard of consuming so much wine! So, to everyone I've ever known, from grammar school on: *May all your vintages be great!*

Selected Glossary

Acid: One of the *components* of wine. It is sometimes described as sour or tart and can be found on the sides of the tongue and mouth.

Acidification: The process of adding acid, usually tartaric or citric, to grape *must* before fermentation in order to boost low levels of acidity creating a more balanced wine.

Aftertaste: The sensation in the mouth that persists after the wine has been swallowed.

Alcohol: The result of *fermentation* whereby yeast converts the natural sugar in grapes to alcohol.

AOC: Abbreviation for Appellation d'Origine Contrôlée; the French government agency that controls wine production.

Aroma: The smell of the grapes in a wine.

Astringent: The *mouthfeel* created by tannins in wine.

AVA: Abbreviation for American Viticultural Area. AVAs are designated wine-producing areas in the United States.

Balance: The integration of the various components of wine such as acid, alcohol, fruit, and tannin. To be balanced, no one component should dominate the wine's taste.

Barrel-fermented: Describes wine that has been fermented in small oak barrels rather than stainless steel. The oak from a barrel will add complexity to a wine's flavor and texture.

Biodynamics: A type of holistic farming created by Rudolph Steiner in the 1920s based on similar principles of organic farming. Compost and manure are used instead of chemical fertilizers or pesticides.

Bitter: One of the four tastes of wine, found at the back of the tongue and throat.

Blend: A combination of two or more wines or grapes, to enhance flavor, balance, and complexity.

Body: The sensation of weight of a wine in the mouth. A wine high in alcohol feels heavier than a wine with low alcohol.

Botrytis cinerea (bo-TRY-tis sin-AIR-e-a): Also called "noble rot," *botrytis cinerea* is a special mold that punctures the skin of a grape allowing the water to dissipate, leaving a higher than normal concentration of sugar and acid. *Botrytis cinerea* is necessary in making Sauternes and the rich German wines *Beerenauslese* and *Trockenbeerenauslese*.

Bouquet: The smell of a wine, influenced by winemaking processes and barrel aging.

Brix (bricks): A scale that measures the sugar level of the unfermented grape juice.

Brut: A French term used for the driest style of Champagne and/or sparkling wine.

Chaptalization: The addition of sugar to the must before fermentation to increase the alcohol level of the finished wine.

Character: Refers to the aspects of the wine typical of its grape varieties, or the overall characteristics of the wine.

Classified châteaux: The châteaux in the Bordeaux region of France that are known to produce the best wine.

Colheita (coal-AY-ta): Means "vintage" in Portuguese.

Components: The components of a wine make up its character, style, and taste. Some components are: acidity, alcohol, fruit, tannin, and residual sugar.

Cru: Certain vineyards in France are designated *grand cru* and *premier cru*, the classification indicating level of quality.

HERE IS A LIST OF RED GRAPE
VARIETALS, AND SOME OF THE
REGIONS WHERE THEY CAN BE
FOUND:

Agiorgitiko (Greece)
Barbera (Italy, California)
Blaufränkisch (Austria)
Cabernet Franc (Bordeaux, Canada,
  Loire Valley)
Cabernet Sauvignon (Argentina, Australia,
  Bordeaux, California, Canada, Chile,
  Hungary, South Africa, Spain,
  Washington)
Cariñena (Spain)
Carménère (Chile)
Cinsault (Rhône Valley)
Concord (United States)
Gamay (Burgundy)
Garnacha/Grenache (Spain/France)
Kadarka (Hungary)
Kékfrankos (Hungary)
Malbec (Argentina)
Merlot (Argentina, Bordeaux, California,
  Canada, Chile, Hungary, Spain,
  Washington)
Monastrell (Spain)
Nebbiolo (Piedmont)
Petite Syrah (California)
Pinot Meunier (Champagne)
Pinot Noir (Austria, Burgundy, California,
  Canada, Hungary, New Zealand, Oregon)
Portugieser (Hungary)
Sangiovese (Tuscany)
St. Laurent (Austria)
Syrah/Shiraz (Argentina, California,
  Canada, Chile, Rhone Valley, South Africa,
  Spain, Washington/Australia)
Tempranillo (Spain, Argentina)
Xinomavro (Greece)
Zinfandel (California)

Cuvée: From the French *cuve* (vat); may refer to a particular blend of grapes or, in Champagne, to the select portion of the juice from the pressing of the grapes.

Decanting: The process of pouring wine from its bottle into a carafe to separate the sediment from the wine.

Dégorgement (day-gorzh-MOWN): One step of the Champagne method (*méthode champenoise*) used to expel the sediment from the bottle.

Demi-sec (deh-mee SECK): A Champagne containing a higher level of residual sugar than a brut.

DOC: Abbreviation for Denominazione di Origine Controllata, the Italian government agency that controls wine production. Spain also uses this abbreviation for Denominación de Origen Condado.

DOCG: Abbreviation for Denominazione di Origine Controllata e Garantita; the Italian government allows this marking to appear only on the finest Italian wines. The G stands for "guaranteed."

Dosage (doh-SAHZH): The addition of sugar, often mixed with wine or brandy, in the final step in the production of Champagne or sparkling wine.

Drip irrigation: System for watering vines that applies water directly to the roots through a network of emitters or microsprayers; drip irrigation conserves water and nutrients and minimizes erosion.

Dry: Wine containing very little residual sugar. It is the opposite of sweet, in wine terms.

Estate-bottled: Wine that is made, produced, and bottled on the estate where the grapes were grown.

Extra dry: Less dry than *brut* Champagne.

Fermentation: The process of transforming sugar into alcohol in the presence of yeast, turning grape juice into wine.

Filtration: Removal of yeasts and other solids from a wine before bottling to clarify and stabilize the wine.

Fino (FEE-noh): A type of Sherry.

Finish: The taste and feel that wine leaves in the mouth after swallowing. Some wines disappear immediately while others can linger for some time.

First growth: The five highest-quality Bordeaux châteaux wines from the Médoc Classification of 1855.

Flor: A type of yeast that develops in some Sherry production.

Fortified wine: A wine such as Port or Sherry that has additional grape spirits (brandy, for example) added to raise the alcohol content.

Fruit: One of the components of wine that derives from the grape itself.

Grand Cru (grawn crew): The highest classification for wines in Burgundy.

Grand Cru Classé (grawn crew clas-SAY): The highest level of the Bordeaux classification.

Gran Reserva: A Spanish wine that has had extra aging.

Hectare: A metric measure of area that equals 2.471 acres.

Hectoliter: A metric measure of volume that equals 26.42 U.S. gallons.

Halbtrocken: The German term meaning "semidry."

Kabinett (kah-bee-NETT): A light, semi-dry German wine.

Maceration: The chemical process by which tannin, color, and flavor are extracted from the grape skins into the wine. Temperature and alcohol content influence the speed at which maceration occurs.

Malolactic fermentation: A secondary fermentation process wherein malic acid is converted into lactic acid and carbon dioxide. This process reduces the wine's acidity and adds complexity.

Mechanical harvester: A machine used on flat vineyards. It shakes the vines to harvest the grapes.

Meritage: Trademark designation for specific high-quality American wines containing the same blend of varieties that are used in the making of Bordeaux wines in France.

Méthode Champenoise (may-TUD shahm-pen-WAHZ): The method by which Champagne is made. This method is also used in other parts of the world to produce sparkling wines.

Mouthfeel: Sensation of texture in the mouth when tasting wine, e.g., smooth, or tannic.

Must: Unfermented grape juice extracted during the crushing process.

"Noble Rot": See *Botrytis cinerea*.

Nose: The term used to describe the bouquet and aroma of wine.

Phenolics: Chemical compounds derived especially but not only from the skins, stems, and seeds of grapes that affect the color and flavor of wine. Tannin is one example. *Maceration* can increase their presence in wines.

Oenology: The science and scientific study of winemaking.

Phylloxera (fill-LOCK-she-rah): A root louse that kills grape vines.

Prädikatswein (pray-dee-KAHTS-vine): The highest level of quality in German wines.

Premier Cru: A wine that has special characteristics that comes from a specific designated vineyard in Burgundy, France, or is blended from several such vineyards.

Proprietary wine: A wine that's given a brand name like any other product and is marketed as such, e.g., Riunite, Mouton-Cadet.

Qualitätswein (kval-ee-TATES-vine): A German term meaning "quality wine."

Residual sugar: Any unfermented sugar that remains in a finished wine. Residual sugar determines how dry or sweet a wine is.

Riddling: One step of the Champagne-making process in which the bottles are turned gradually each day for weeks until they are upside down, so that the sediment rests in the neck of the bottle.

Sediment: Particulate matter that accumulates in wine as it ages.

Sommelier (so-mel-YAY): The French term for cellarmaster, or wine steward.

Sulfur dioxide: A substance used in winemaking and grape growing as a preservative, an antioxidant, and also as a sterilizing agent.

Tannin: One of the components of wine, tannin is a natural compound and preservative that comes from the skins, stems, and pits of the grapes and also from the wood barrel in which wine is aged.

Terroir: A French term for all of the elements that contribute to the distinctive characteristics of a particular vineyard site that include its soil, subsoil, slope, drainage, elevation, and climate including exposure to the sun, temperature and precipitation.

Varietal wine: A wine that is labeled with the predominant grape used to produce the wine. For example, a wine made from Chardonnay grapes would be labeled "Chardonnay."

Vintage: The year the grapes are harvested.

Vinification: Winemaking.

Vitis labrusca (VEE-tiss la-BREW-skah): A native grape species in America.

Vitis vinifera (VEE-tiss vih-NIFF-er-ah): The grape species that is used in most countries in the world for winemaking.

HERE IS A LIST OF WHITE GRAPE VARIETALS, AND SOME OF THE REGIONS WHERE THEY CAN BE FOUND:

Albariño (Spain)

Assyrtiko (Greece)

Chardonnay (Argentina, Australia, Austria, Burgundy, Canada, Chile, Hungary, New Zealand, South Africa, Spain, United States)

Chenin Blanc (California, Loire Valley, South Africa)

Furmint (Hungary)

Gewürztraminer (Alsace, Germany)

Grüner Veltliner (Austria)

Hárslevelı (Hungary)

Macabeo (Spain)

Moschofilero (Greece)

Olaszrizling (Hungary)

Pinot Blanc (Alsace)

Pinot Grigio/Pinot Gris (Italy/Canada, France, Hungary, United States)

Riesling (Alsace, Austria, Canada, United States)

Roditis (Greece)

Sauvignon Blanc (California, Chile, Graves, Loire Valley, New Zealand, Sauternes, South Africa)

Sémillon (Australia, Graves, Sauternes)

Szürkebarát (Hungary)

Torrontés Riojano (Argentina)

Trebbiano (Italy)

Verdejo (Spain)

Vidal (Canada)

Viognier (California, Rhône Valley)

Index

P. PHILIPPE

Sofia Perpera

David Strada

Christine Brichard

Fiona Donald

Rory Callaha

Jana Kravitz

David Slingsby Smith

S K Pidgeon

Blair Watt

Louisa Rose

J Atwood

Chris Burdin

Dirk Richter

Rute Monteiro